Jennifer Chapman is the author of *The Last Bastion: the case for and against women priests*, and of *Barnardo's Today*, also published by Virgin. Marriage as an institution has always fascinated her, and has been the subject of the four novels she has had published to date. She is a partner in Multi Media, an industrial public relations company, and lives in Royston, Hertfordshire with her husband and three of their five children.

Also by Jennifer Chapman from Virgin

Barnardo's Today

Made in Heaven
Talking about marriage

Jennifer Chapman

First published in Great Britain in 1993 by
Virgin Books
an imprint of Virgin Publishing Ltd
332 Ladbroke Grove
London W10 5AH

A catalogue record for this book is available from the British Library

ISBN 0 86369 770 4

Typeset by TW Typesetting, Plymouth, Devon
Printed and bound in Great Britain by
Cox & Wyman Ltd, Reading, Berkshire

Thanks to David Barkla of Relate

To my husband

Contents

Introduction

Edwina Currie told me that she was still learning after nineteen years of marriage. Elizabeth Taylor said she was too busy to talk about it. Shirley Conran said she tried not to annoy her first two husbands, and that the third was not worth mentioning.

All I can say is that it was nice of them to reply to my letter, which also went to many other people who did agree to tell me the intimate stories of their married lives, and with the sort of candour reserved for a stranger. Such vivid confessions can be too potent, too close to the soul of truth to make to a partner, to a friend, and for this reason, many of the people talking in this book have been given different names – to protect the innocent, as they say, if there can be such a party within marriage.

Their stories, some going back to the early years of this century, provide a vivid impression of the way marriage has altered but endured during the period of greatest social change in history.

There are couples in their nineties, among them a pair of newlyweds; there are people who have loved and lost, a woman who has married ten times, others who have been together a lifetime but whose relationships are not recognised in law, and those who have overcome huge barriers to love and somehow made their marriages work. I have asked people why they have married, now that it no longer seems to matter. I've talked to clergy, solicitors and private detectives, and I have done my own detective work among the dusty archives housed in Rugby at the headquarters of Relate, which used to be known as the National Marriage Guidance Council. Its records go back 50 years, and have provided me with a rich seam of facts and figures and anecdotal material that, together with the personal stories, reveal how attitudes towards and within marriage have shifted in unexpected ways. Yet, what comes through most clearly is how the changes, such as they are, have been orchestrated by women. Marriage is a partnership, but as the twentieth century has progressed, wives have become the managing partners while their husbands have slept. Three times as many wives compared with husbands petition for divorce, and, with their single status regained, it is the women alone who live happily ever after. Surveys today show that the happiest and most healthy people are single women and married men, so it is no wonder that women have become the driving force for change in marriage, and the only surprise is that so many of us – more than 90 per cent – still choose to marry at all.

Morally, socially and economically women no longer need to marry, and the balance of power has shifted in favour of wives. Dependency has done an about turn and it seems that women hold all the trump cards, particularly when it comes to children. As short a time ago as the 1920s a husband still retained the autocratic control of the patriarch, *owning* all those who bore his name, while today, it is rare for a father to gain custody of his children unless his wife has agreed.

How have these changes come about? Surely it is through the greater power of women rather than the acquiescence of men, leaving people like the doctor in Chapter Thirteen aghast at the way the tables have been turned on them; the way not just his children, but a man's home and the major part of his income can be wrested from him on the whim of his wife. Ah, such power! Have women misused it, or have they not yet even begun to get their own back for the centuries when it was otherwise?

The book begins with a trailblazer, a woman who 60 years ago started something of a crusade to change the way we are married, the way we live together and accommodate, or otherwise, lovers and mistresses. In her nineties, Naomi Mitchison recalls, with the detailed clarity peculiar to the very old, what it was like to be a teenage bride at the beginning of the century, how the First World War ripped up hearts and hopes and sowed the seeds of cynicism for love and romance. By the end of the Second World War this cynicism was such that David Lean's now classic film *Brief Encounter* was greeted by cinema-goers with ribaldry and tears of mirth rather than the weepy sentimentality it engenders today. The characters played by Trevor Howard and Celia Johnson were viewed as pathetically hidebound by a morality that seemed to belong to a forgotten age. Marriage was set to become a victim of consumerism as well as cynicism, yet it can be argued that a couple of generations on we now take marriage more seriously than has ever been the case – why else should there be so much divorce?

Apart from the power base, the greatest change in marriage this century has been the shift from *institutional* marriage to *companionship* marriage. In the former, stability was what mattered. Property, religion and respectability were the key considerations, and it was almost vulgar to mention personal fulfilment. Today, nothing matters more. Yet, Western Christian marriage, as devised during the last centuries of the Roman Empire in an attempt to sort out disorderly family relationships in pagan society, is the model we still work to.

Of course, there has been a lot of meddling over the centuries; what started out as a fairly sensible arrangement, maintained through a general psychological atmosphere of distance, manipulation and deference, with husband and wife enjoying equal benefits at a level of basic survival, began to change by the seventeenth century – an earlier era of post-feminism. 'If ever thou purpose to be a good wife and live comfortably, set down this with thyself; mine husband is mine superior, my better; he hath authority and rule over me; nature hath given it to him. . . . God hath given it to him,' was the advice given to women.

By the eighteenth century things had changed again with the idea of an affectionate relationship being possible between husband and wife, and the radical notion that conjugal rights could actually be enjoyed – that is, the husband could take pleasure in his wife rather than be expected to find it elsewhere. Pleasure, it seems, did not become the province of women until our time. It is only in recent years that women have been allowed to be dissatisfied with their sex lives and in doing something about it have not incurred 'stoning', sorrow and shame.

As everyone knows, it has been modern birth control that has emancipated women, and this did not become widely available until the 1930s. Undoubtedly it is birth control that has enabled women to chip away at the authority of men in marriage. It has brought the possibility, now the reality, of economic independence, which has to be the key to equality. But it has brought other, less talked-about benefits as well: 'Pill-takers,' I discovered in the more recent Relate archives, 'enjoy a decrease in ear wax.'

By the 1950s, before any of us could have heard of the Pill, the freedom to work was already the pressing issue. The marriage experts agonised over the question: 'Should a wife work?' Many had during the war, and found it hard to go back to the draining board. Most of the wives who appear in the early chapters of this book did not have jobs outside the home, and if they tried to get them, circumstances, rather than disapproval from their husbands, thwarted their attempts. If they were not looking after children, there were elderly relatives to care for. Women who put their children into day nurseries were said to be endangering family life, and were also seen as more likely to be morally lax.

My storytellers in these early chapters compare their own marriages with those of their parents and grandparents, who seem to have had a much greater influence than has been the case for newlyweds in more recent decades. Yet the husbands and wives who are now grandparents cast a forward glance at their children and grandchildren that is more often admiring and envious than censorious, and in an age fat with divorce, cohabitation and illegitimacy – all words that have lost their bitter meaning and shrivelled to insignificance in the trail of new-wave tolerance.

As skirts got shorter in the 1960s, so did marriage, although the simpering advice handed out to sixties girls looking for a husband assumed the coquetry of a much earlier age when little more than ankles were on show. 'Cut out the melon slice grin,' they were told, 'in favour of little smiles and a sweet curving of the lips, little wide-eyed glances followed by a modest downcasting of the gaze – more attractive than a bold, unwavering stare . . .' (I tried it on the greengrocer and quite clearly he thought I had some sort of affliction.)

Whether or not the short skirts were to blame, the sweet smiles began to disappear in the seventies and only the lawyers were grinning as we began the huge heritage of heartache we have been loading up for our children ever since. I don't want to sound precious about this – after all, I've been through the divorce court myself, which is, perhaps, why I know that much of the tidal wave of divorce that began in the 1970s was largely unnecessary. We convinced ourselves otherwise at the time, we had to in order to wreak such havoc. The divorce chapter is sad – how could it not be? – but what surprised me was the continuing roaring trade in matrimonial work enjoyed by private detectives. They may no longer be leaping from wardrobes or maintaining all-night vigils outside tacky hotel rooms, but they are still very much on the job – and a dangerous one it is, too.

It is true that Britain has one of the highest divorce rates in Europe, but there is more than one way of looking at the statistics, which also show that two-thirds of marriages remain intact, and two-thirds of these endure 40 years or more. Statistics also have it that married people live longer, although the quick riposte to this is that it merely seems longer. With longevity already under their belts, one couple I have talked to went for extra time and married in their nineties. A passion as thrilling and as intense as anything experienced in youth blazed between them when they met at the old people's home where they made their new home together – and it's a setting and lifestyle that has made for complete equality.

I did not ask any of my storytellers to talk about their sex lives (although most have), least of all the nonagenarians; yet I don't really understand why we tend to be reticent and surprised when old people want to talk about sex. I remember being horrified when my grandfather told me about his wedding night and blood on the sheet, and neither he nor Grandma knowing from whom it had come or why it had appeared. The point he was making was more to do with innocence and chastity than anything else I didn't want to hear about, although as one's own flesh gets older the subconscious sense of taboo gives way to the sort of tolerance hoped for from one's own children.

Val and Don had been fortunate in this respect. Their

children didn't mind a bit when, on occasion, Dad became Doris. But transvestism tests the wife's tolerance more than the children's: 'He had got everything as a man, career success, the whole lot, and there he was, wanting to be a woman as well,' says Val. The story of her marriage to Don is touching, funny and extraordinary, although at the same time they are a very ordinary couple in every respect other than Doris; and, continuing my hypothesis that women are now the managing partners in marriage and the driving force for change, it is Val who has become the campaigner, who appears on television championing tolerance and understanding.

Emancipation, however it is dressed, has been the province of women and wives this century, while their husbands have embraced the give and take of equality with somewhat restrained vigour. The attractions of staying at home and looking after the children have not sold well to men, and society, however radical it thinks itself, still views the house-husband as a creature out of place. Men who have tried it find the only way they can live with themselves (and the neighbours) is to make out that being at home is merely an expedient towards a greater endeavour – studying for some sort of exam, planning a new business, building a boat. Arguably the most important job of all, bringing up children, is never sufficient in itself. It's not really the fault of the men, after all; the task has fallen to them, more often than not, because their wives have found something better to do.

In the old days, the roles within marriage were clearly defined, the lack of choice obviating a great deal of angst. So-called modern marriages may start out with ideals of shared opportunity, but biology usually wins the day, delivering a particularly cruel defeat to those who believed the propaganda of an impossible equality. Marriage does seem to be more to do with women than with men, and women may have driven all the changes to date, but the truth about equality lies in the increasing number of women who choose to remain single. I have four daughters, and I'm not sure I'd advise any of them to marry. Let each be their own person, because staying single is the safest way of avoiding slavery and prostitution, or a state of being that can still be very much like it.

Setting aside the safe option (because this book is not

against marriage, merely a commentary on how it is), just about all of the people telling their stories in the following chapters married for love, which is how most of us in this country like to think we have been motivated to marry. That said, as short a time ago as 1986 a survey among newlyweds revealed that most placed the significance of their married status above that of the quality of their marriage. Half a decade on, the idea of such superficiality is knocked on the head by John Patterson, the founder of Dateline, Britain's leading marriage bureau. He says we are more serious and heartfelt about love and marriage than ever before, or, to be more precise, we are prepared to admit our seriousness. Patterson says that, 25 years ago, when Dateline started, everyone treated computer dating as a bit of a laugh, although, secretly, many hoped to find the partner of their dreams. Incidentally, women who read about dream lovers in the pages of Mills & Boon and the like are said to make love 74 per cent more often than readers of the Booker shortlist. (If you are reading this I am not sure where you figure.)

In recent years there have been various attempts to interfere with marriage, for better or for worse. There has been talk of a Ministry for Marriage, and, borrowing an idea from America, marriage contracts that dictate not only the number of times per week for sex, but a limit on weight-gain. Another very recent suggestion has been automatic expiry of the marriage contract after five years, which leads us into the realms of 'serial monogamy' becoming the *status quo*. For a growing minority on their third or fourth marriages, this is already a reality, but not so new – 150 to 200 years ago, many men, if not women, married several times.

Ideas that would bring about a fundamental change in marriage tend to emanate from the cynical and the disappointed, while the majority of us just get on with things as they are, enjoying the happy mediocrity that is a satisfactory marriage. Anything else is just too exhausting to maintain for the long haul. As Bob Geldof said to a passion-seeking interviewer: 'To live your life in fervour would be disenabling. You equate passion with sex. If that were the case, 98 per cent of marriages in this country would not last.'

So, what makes for a successful marriage in the 1990s? The

same as always, I would say, and am joined in saying by just about every golden and diamond wedding anniversary couple you see featured in the local press. 'Give and take,' they say. Give and take what? Space for individual fulfilment but rooted in a place where both want to be. Loving and liking help, but there is that other something that is different but the same for every successful marriage, the little piece of chemistry that keeps the whole thing together. As a friend said to me: 'I dislike nine out of ten of the things about Terry, but it's that one thing that makes me want to stay with him.'

My own, enduring idealised image of the British marriage brings me back to *Brief Encounter*, not Celia Johnson and Trevor Howard enacting a different ending, but Celia and the pipe-and-slippers husband to whom she returns; and who calls her 'Old Thing' (I'm sure he does) and says he's glad she's home again even though she never really left, and certainly hasn't told him she might have, and everyone knows they will get on with their marriage and make the best of things and live long in comfort and companionship and with the wisp of longing for what might have been but never was.

1 Married in black and green and gumboots

ONE SUNDAY MORNING when my husband and I were taking a late bath, the *Desert Island Discs* signature tune faded on the radio and Sue Lawley introduced her guest of the week, the eminent nonagenarian writer Naomi Mitchison. When I set out to write this book I hadn't expected to find anyone who had married more than 70 years ago. Naomi Mitchison was not only married as long ago as 1916, but also had what is termed an 'open' marriage. I wrote to her, and a fortnight later was invited to lunch at her London flat.

I was rather in awe of her, having heard that she'd been known to hit those who annoyed her; but the little old lady who greeted me seemed to have the substance of a candle flame, the hitting power of gossamer. I spent the first ten minutes in her flat chasing a queen wasp she was unable to swat herself.

After hearing her *Desert Island Discs*, I had read about her life in the biography by Jill Benton, and in her own autobiographical books. She grew up in Oxford and her teenage friends included people like Aldous and Gervas Huxley, and Lewis and John Gielgud. Her father was a distinguished physiologist, J. S. Haldane; her uncle a Liberal Lord Chancellor, and her husband, old Etonian Dick Mitchison, was to become a prominent Labour politician. Naomi became engaged to him when she was sixteen, he 22, and they married two years later. Neither knew the first thing about marriage, and they were not in love, although they thought they were. Aldous Huxley came to stay with the Haldanes after the engagement and asked Naomi what being in love was like, 'but I, not being "in love", did not answer satisfactorily'.

The driving emotion was more to do with the war than romantic love, trying to make something permanent in the overwhelming cyclone of uncertainty. 'The dawn of 1916 finds us still deep in the tremendous conflict which we have been waging for seventeen anxious months,' it was reported in *The Times*. 'It has brought to scores of millions amongst the belligerents calamities of a magnitude unapproached in the story of civilised mankind. Tens of thousands have given their young lives for England on the battlefields of Flanders, of France, and of the Dardanelles. There is scarce a home in the country, from the highest to the poorest, which does not grieve over its wounded or mourn its dead.'

Naomi was no exception; childhood friends were dying in France, family friends losing not just one son but three. Dick was considered lucky because he sustained a wound bad enough to keep him from the Front, and Naomi, still a teenager, went out to France to nurse him. Yet, three years after her marriage, Naomi was still living with her parents in Oxford, still being chaperoned, still having her hair brushed for her. She had control of neither her social life nor her income, and, until Dick returned from his wartime staff job in Italy, her life seemed little changed by marriage, even though she had a baby.

Sexually, the Mitchisons got off to a bad start, but they were not alone; the legacy of Victorian decades placed women on pedestals of virtue beyond the reach of lust. The English gentleman had been brought up to think of his women as chaste and pure and largely sexless, his wife, a dependent creature to be cherished and protected. Yet the first 'new women' were emerging, educated women who took jobs during the war, and those who worked in the munitions factories; also people like Dr Marie Stopes, although in 1916 she was still struggling to find a publisher for her eventual bestseller *Married Love*, the first explicit non-fiction account of sex and marriage. Publisher after publisher rejected the book because it not only knocked the pedestal, but threatened to remove it altogether. During this time, the best publishing offer for *Married Love* was an initial print-run in French, based on the premise that this would prevent the book being read by the working class, who ought to be kept ignorant regarding sex. Those who wanted to know about married life and how to make a success of it were more likely to be directed towards *Mrs Beeton's Household Management.*

'We made an awful mess of the physical side,' Naomi, herself far from working class, told me. 'We both knew singularly little about it – far less than anyone does now. My mother, at the last moment, tried to tell me a little, but I really couldn't make head nor tail of it. I knew scientifically what it was all about, and I knew a lot about guinea pigs and their feelings – how, if they were friends they would suckle one another's babies, but if they were not they would bite them. I got more idea from guinea pigs than anywhere else.' She also knew about genetic inheritance through studying rats, and during the three years after her marriage had continued as a home student at Oxford. She knew much about the mechanics, but little else.

'I thought it was all very exciting to be married, but messier than I had expected. My husband knew just as little, but this was not uncommon. He was twenty-four and very few of his friends had any idea either – they didn't, on the whole, as they would have done in France, get introduced to some lady who might give them some idea of what it was all about. It was very secret still, but we all thought we knew.'

Finding out for Naomi was a miserable let-down. 'I thought, "Oh, dear, this is going to go on the whole of my life, and it's so boring," but you don't want to hurt someone you are fond of. I should think it was pretty boring for him, too.'

By good fortune, a regular visitor to the Haldane house in Oxford at that time was Marie Stopes, and although sex was never discussed, Naomi managed to come by a copy of *Married Love* soon after its publication in 1918. She read it and sent a copy to Dick in Italy. 'It was mainly about going slowly. We tried various things and it really worked quite well. Sex became something to look forward to, although I was never really mad about it.'

The Mitchisons' marriage was always based more on friendship than sex, and although they were to have seven children and live happily together until Dick died in his seventies, both had lovers, and from 1925 they agreed to an 'open' marriage. 'Both Dick and I found ourselves much attracted to other people who were friends and interested in the same things. My chap was an historian for the period in which I was setting my books at the time, and Dick's person was in politics. We all got on and we all knew. It all just seemed to happen, and it seemed to work all right. We had a lot of shared holidays and we always tried to organise it so that the two other people involved were arriving more or less at the same time so we could both go out for long walks – it seemed a very happy time.

'The children were pretty young and not aware of what was going on. By the time my eldest son realised, he was having his first love affairs and he was very sympathetic.'

'It was all a very long time ago,' Naomi says, screwing up her eyes as if trying to focus on such distant memories and see not just how it was, but why. 'The killing in that war – oh, God. I am sure this had something to do with the way I conducted my marriage. We got tighter and tighter in one way; being young was stopped and we were suffering together from the same thing – we had lost so many friends. We were happy when either of us got something else. We had to make up for a lot and we were deeply fond of one another.

'It was immoral – against the custom, what we did. My parents didn't know – they would have felt they had to speak to me if they had – but I wouldn't have taken any notice.' Her parents may not have known, but an aunt did, and in a letter defending her new way of marriage, Naomi wrote: 'I don't believe you realise how much the war has upset our generation – mine and the one immediately after it. The first wave of disturbance was the one at the time, and now we're in for the second, after the period of calm and exhaustion immediately following the thing. I think this is much what happened after the Peloponnesian and the Napoleonic Wars. Ours was worse than either. You have still a balance in your life: all that incredible pre-war period when things seemed in the main settled, just moving solidly and calmly like a glacier towards all sorts of progress. But we have had the bottom of things knocked out completely; we have been sent reeling into chaos and it seems to us that none of your standards are either fixed or necessarily good because in the end they resulted in the smash-up. We have to try and make a world for ourselves, basing it as far as possible on love and awareness, mental and bodily, because it seems to us that all the repressions and formulae, all the cutting off of part of our experience, which perhaps looked sensible and even right in those calm years, have not worked. Much has been taken from us, but we will stick like fury to what is left, and lay hold on life, as it comes to us.'

'My chap disappeared from my life after the relationship had been going on for ten years,' Naomi told me. 'He got married and it became quite clear that it wouldn't work. Dick still had his person – I remember, when he was dying, I called her and said "Do come along. It will be sad for you, but I think he could just manage to like it." Afterwards, he said to me, "she always had better hats than you" – we made jokes about one another right up to the end.

'You try to keep hold of any sort of affection between people. It is so vulnerable: I think wherever one sees it one should feed it – with a cake. We love one another or we die – it's quite simple.'

Was the marriage happy? 'Yes. We'd got the children and so much in common. We did a lot together and there was a great deal of fun. My marriage was not like my parents', but I very much doubt that they got much pleasure out of it. I think marriage is enhanced by affairs, they can make the whole thing shining again; but there are difficulties and there were bad patches for us, but not terribly bad. We would threaten one another with things, "talking to lawyers", but we didn't really mean it – you have no idea how getting through that war knitted people together, even if it was with a rope of pain.

'We always shared a bedroom, although, I must say, it was a good-sized bed – big enough to get away from one another. I think from the beginning Dick knew I was never going to be "possessable", that I had a bit of a "fairy" edge.'

'No, I won't be your ballast, if it's to prevent the balloon going up. I only ballast in order to put the balloon on its mettle and make it go higher . . . Nou, I do love you so,' Dick wrote home to her in 1930 when he was working in South Africa.

Naomi, as well as being 'unpossessable' was also, perhaps abnormally, unpossessive. Dick had other lovers and they were always welcome visitors to the family home for the rest of their lives. And if there were husbands, they too were included in the circle of friends and lovers. Of course, such a 'have your cake and eat it' way of life was not without its casualties, and some of the marriages did not survive; but Naomi and Dick, perhaps because they had never been in love, but always enjoyed that more lasting emotion fondness, kept together.

The Mitchisons were able to live the way they did because they had money, knew about birth control, and didn't care what the neighbours thought. Naomi wore black and green for her Oxford registry office wedding in 1916, yet she was not entirely without concern for appearances and paid someone five shillings to sweep out the registry office staircase because she couldn't bear it being dirty. There was a wartime sugarless cake cut with Dick's cavalry sabre, and the expectation that one kind of life was over and a new, magically transformed grown-up one about to begin.

A decade later, a quite different kind of wedding and marriage was being planned in the Cambridgeshire Fenland between a young couple with no expectations other than getting through life together without incurring debt or family displeasure.

The room is narrow and small but full of light. From the window, where Fred has his chair, you can see all the comings and goings of the cul-de-sac with its mix of new housing for the young, the middling and the old. Fred and his wife, Nellie, spend most of their day in the room; there's not a lot in it, one or two upright chairs for visitors, a small display case with ornaments that are precious only by association – presents from seaside holidays, plaster of Paris animals bought with pocket money. There are colour snaps of grandchildren and great-grandchildren, black and white pictures of brides and grooms, but Fred and Nellie don't have any photos of their own wedding.

They married on Boxing Day 1927 and had woken that morning to find the ground thick with snow. They'd hired a car to collect the wedding party but it had skidded off the road and tipped into a Fenland dyke, taking the photographer and all his cumbersome gear with it. Nellie, her silver wedding shoes tucked under her arm, had trudged to the village church in her pale cream crêpe-de-chine and wellington boots, keeping them on throughout the service and the making of vows. 'We were half an hour late getting there, and because you couldn't get married after three o'clock the vicar said there was no time to change. He met us at the door and started marrying us as we went up the aisle. That vicar, he married us all – and buried most of us, too.'

The crêpe-de-chine wedding dress, complete with silver panels, had been bought to last, and was to have served on outings and special occasions for years to come. Nellie bought a hat to replace the veil – 'you always had to have a hat' – and wore the outfit while picnicking at the local agricultural show a couple of years after the wedding. 'There was this horse nearby and it was frisking about. Suddenly it jumped over the rope and trod on the back of my dress, ripping it right up to the waist. That was the end of that wedding dress.'

Nellie was born in the village and brought up there in her grandparents' home. Her father had returned from the Great War too sick and tired to work again and at the age of 33 had dropped dead at his wife's feet. A month later Nellie's only brother was born, and a war later he too died. Nellie's mother had lost both her men to her country but remained too poor to keep a home of her own or to give her three daughters any sort of start in life. When Nellie left school she went to work in the nearby shirt factory, but the wages were too low for her keep, and her mother had to put her into service at the local hotel, where she remained until she married Fred.

He came from the neighbouring parish, a child of the land, one of eight children brought up in an old farmhouse with too few beds; he shared with three brothers, 'two one end and two the other'.

Fred got his first job when he was nine, pushing a wheelbarrow, delivering the early morning milk, and left school at the age of eleven to go on the land. The flat and fruitful unemphatic fields bordering the Fens may have produced a rich harvest for some, but Fred and his brothers spent their nights bird-catching, trawling the hedgerows with a 'clap' net. On one side of the hedge a brother would clap while on the other side the net was held ready to catch startled blackbirds and sparrows. 'We'd get forty or fifty a night and Mother would make pies and stews.'

'I thought too much of birds to let him carry on with it after we were married.' Nellie and Fred, like most of their newly-married contemporaries in the neighbourhood, took rooms in someone else's house after their wedding. Before the Second World War housing was not seen as a problem; there were twelve and a half million separate dwellings, and this matched the number of families nationwide, even if, in many areas, there were empty houses while two or more families shared single homes. 'People didn't think anything of it. They just struggled along through life.'

Fred and Nellie viewed marriage as a practical step in their own struggle. Their expectations were as unambitious as those of their parents and grandparents. Getting through life was the thing; being together, having children, making ends meet. Their courting days had consisted of two or three years of going for walks together and occasional visits to the local cinema where someone played the fiddle to dramatise silent films about cowboys and Indians, 'but we liked the serials best and could relate them to our own lives'.

Nellie had liked one other boy before she met Fred, but nothing had come of it. 'He was very pious and interested in the Church.' Fred had known other girls, too, but at 86 he's still not telling. He met Nellie one balmy evening while he was parking his bicycle – his pride and joy, a sturdy machine strong enough to take his mother on the crossbar for shopping trips into town. Nellie didn't need a bike, never has; her life has always been within walking distance. Fred doesn't remember asking her to marry him, how it was done, only that it would have had to be him that did the asking. ' "Are we going to get married, then?" that's what you said.'

The protocol was always there, unchanging over generations: he did the asking and she had to make up her mind whether life would be easier or more difficult with this man. 'We couldn't afford to get married until we did, and not really then. We had ages on 29s 3d a week. I still worked after we were married – we shouldn't have lived if I hadn't.' Counting the pennies was Nellie's territory, and Fred gave her all that he earned, including the half-crown she would give him back for pocket money. More than half a century later she remembers with bitter precision that they had to pay ninepence insurance, and there was a week when she couldn't afford tuppence for a reel of mending yarn. 'Being married wasn't romantic even if we thought it was. When we were single we didn't worry about anything.

'Being married was all work; you can't say play because there wasn't any. We worked from seven till five every day, including Saturdays, and we literally rolled out of bed in the morning because we were too tired to stand up.' As far as bed was concerned, the most enticing advantage in being married was not having to share it with more than one other person.

Nellie gave birth to a son a year after the wedding and by this time the family had a council house to themselves. It was to be their home for the next 50 years and a place where they were as happy as they might ever have expected to be. 'We've always been equal partners and we've never really quarrelled, only about money, but there again, that wasn't anything to quarrel about because we didn't have any. I remember when our little girl was born – you had to be in bed for a fortnight then – and he'd gone "brushing", beating out the pheasants for the shoot. Well, the farmer gave him ten shillings and when he brought it home to me and laid it on the bed we thought we had got the world. I shall never forget that.

'People had to share in those days to survive, but things got better during the war. There was more work and more money.'

Fred, in a 'reserved' occupation, keeping the Fens drained, had a good war, yet there was never enough money for the third and fourth babies Nellie would have liked. 'Having the children, those were the highlights of my life; I was as happy as all the birds in the air when I had them.'

I met Fred and Nellie one spring afternoon in the council flat they moved into after Nellie's stroke. Just around the corner is the church where they married and where their ancestors are buried. The son and daughter, grandchildren and great-grand-children don't live far away. Fred, in his chair by the window, has Nellie next to him, and beside her is Joey the budgie, who wants to know if I've had my breakfast and whether I'll kiss the little mark. Nellie's eyesight and hearing are poor. Voices have to be raised, and everyone's talking together, shouting through the deafness, Joey, feathers puffed out, loudest of all – 'Kiss the little mark' 'Have you had your breakfast?' On Saturday, one of the grandsons is marrying for the second time: 'He had a lovely wife but he told us they just couldn't agree, so they divorced. I think if they'd had a family the marriage would have stayed together. Ours has been happy because of the children.'

Fred and Nellie never even thought of divorcing – running away, but not divorce. 'Sometimes I did feel like running away, but there was nowhere to go,' Nellie recalls, and she means it. Fred would too, if he was the type to say that sort of thing, because parting was never an option, there was nowhere else for either of them to go. 'You knew what you were letting yourself in for and you just went through life,' Nellie says, making it sound like the Channel Tunnel of love, long and dark, narrow and unromantic. 'Too much money causes divorce. These days I never dare ask people how their husband or their wife is in case they've parted. We had just enough money to live on, and to stay together.' All in all, the 64 years have been happy ones, but the happiest, Fred and Nellie say, are now.

In their own ways, both Fred and Nellie and the Mitchisons have been among the lucky ones, although perhaps they made their own luck. Many a marriage might have been made in heaven but the experience turned out to be hell. Most pre-war marriages, good or bad, were for life, and whichever direction was taken afterwards, death was the only release. Yet, 'till death us do part' came to mean a lifetime with one partner only in relatively recent times, at least as far as many men were concerned. During the nineteenth century a man could expect to marry and wear out three wives, and it has been only in this century that golden and diamond wedding anniversaries have become reasonable expectations. The point is that not until this century has marriage had to withstand such an endurance test.

Of course, the two world wars took their toll, but both also led to much marital misery for the men who came back and their wives. One in six British soldiers returning from abroad in the 1940s brought home venereal disease, an insidious aftermath of victory that was to bring unforeseen despair to thousands of wives and their unborn children. The issue was so grave and concerning that it was discussed in the House of Commons, and the country began to cast about for something to be done. But the same problem had already been identified from the First World War by those who had worked among the troops and their families, and a small group of benevolently minded intellectuals had already begun to tackle matters. Their leader was the Revd Dr Herbert Gray, and his group was to become known as the Marriage Guidance Council.

The Council came into being in the late 1930s with the idea of educating the populace about marriage. It sounds horribly patronising and fearfully unromantic, but Gray was neither of these things. A handsome cleric, and blissfully married himself, it is clear from his writings that his motivations sprang from a desire that others should have the chance to find the same sort of marital harmony that he enjoyed. 'It is not by accident that men in love are found trying to write poetry (though it may be a bad accident if other people have to try and read it),' he wrote. 'Of course we laugh at this naive habit, because poetry seems a thing incongruous with the ordinary prosaic man, with his baggy trousers and clumsy ways. But for my part, I rather incline to thank God that such an impulse should ever disturb the average man. What could be better than that at one stage of his life at least he should try to reach the stars?'

Gray wrote many books, but *Men, Women & God*, published in 1923, was his blueprint for happy married life, and eventually it was to become the catalyst for the formation of the MGC – but not before it had caused a sensation. Published by the Student Christian Movement, it was said to be the first book to tackle frankly the problems of sex and marriage from a Christian point of view. It became an immediate bestseller, not least because it was banned initially in the United States, and by 1951 it had run to nineteen editions and had been translated into fourteen languages. Yet among its many thousands of readers there must have been considerable frustration and disappointment for those seeking the hard facts of life. Under the heading 'The Art of Being Married', Gray wrote: 'It is extraordinary what a jolly business housework can be when two people go at it together and get all the possible fun out of it.'

His comments on sex were restricted to dark warnings, not so much about the act itself, but as to how young people might find out about it. 'The worst possible way in which to get it [knowledge of sex] is to pick it up bit by bit in connection with evil stories, the reports of divorce cases, and the hints of vice which lurk in life's shadowy corners.' Gray believed that 90 per cent of boys had the subject of sex spoiled for them in this way before adolescence. His advice was to find out from an older man or woman 'with a clean mind and a large heart'.

As to masturbation, this was not only a wasteful pastime, but could lead, in both boys and girls, to pitifully acute mental sufferings. He was opposed to it only because he believed it harmed its practitioners by making them feel that sex was impure, and as a result could prevent a man from loving his wife.

For all this theory as opposed to specifics, Gray's book was considered too outspoken even though he prefaces the first chapter 'Knowing the Facts' with the following: 'I would quite gladly attempt to put them down here could I only be assured that my words would only be read by men and women when alone and in a reverent mood. That being impossible I can only begin by insisting that they ought to be known . . . The most interesting thing about the world for many of each sex is that the other sex is in it also.' The book is a gem and ought to go into its twentieth edition.

Gray had been an army chaplain during the First World War and had become aware of the problems in store for soldiers and their families. *Men, Women & God* was perhaps too late to rescue many pre-war families from the 'sins of the fathers', and in his preface to the book he said he deliberately omitted reference to disease, but not because 'I am unimpressed by the terrible penalties with which nature visits certain sins, but because I do not believe in the power of fear to deliver us. Though there were no such things as venereal disease, immorality would still be a way of death, and morality would still be the way of life and joy. Till we perceive that we are not on the path of progress.'

'The book brought so many people to consult him that he couldn't cope alone,' his daughter, Margaret, told me, explaining how the MGC came into being. A retired headteacher, the youngest and only surviving child of the founder of the MGC lives in an attic in Kew and has never married. Her rich voice sounds like Scottish aristocracy spiced with tobacco; it's the family voice, known to millions via her niece, the journalist and broadcaster Katharine Whitehorn, and it must have contributed to the considerable charisma of Herbert, prematurely white-haired, pipe-smoking, and undoubtedly Britain's mid-twentieth-century marriage guru.

His endearing comment about sharing housework, far from being a cop-out in discussing the art of being married, showed him to be an early feminist, and he said he couldn't understand why it had taken women so many centuries to shatter the conception that they had no place in society except as wife or mother.

It's hardly surprising that women liked Gray, some of them a little too much, although his daughter hesitates to suggest this as there was never any challenge to her mother.

Arthur Herbert Gray was born in 1868 in Edinburgh, the third son of Alexander Gray, ironmonger and locksmith. He was educated at various schools but finally at The Leys in Cambridge. He took an arts degree at Edinburgh and stayed on to study theology. He married Mary Dods, daughter of the principal of New College, and until the outbreak of war ministered to some of the poorest slum congregations in Scotland. After the war he worked on the Archbishop of Canterbury's 'Purity Campaign' among demobilised soldiers, and in the 1920s became travelling secretary of the Student Christian Movement, a job that took him to Europe and America for a number of lecture tours.

Mary, whose father, Marcus Dods, was famously acquitted in Scotland's last heresy trial when he was accused of bringing scholarship to bear on the Bible, had money – sufficient to ensure a comfortable family life for the Grays and their children. Margaret, who was born when her parents were in their forties (her mother spent the entire pregnancy in bed), remembers her mother as the down-to-earth one and her father as the more romantic and impulsive partner. 'He had a great tendency to give everything away – all his clothes to old lags just out of prison.

'His sympathies were with the working class. He was unpopular at times, but he was always ahead in his thinking. His ideal was chastity before marriage and fidelity within it, but he never turned anyone away and he always felt the divorce laws were uncivilised, having to prove adultery, etc. He felt that some marriages were mendable, but some were not and a clean break was the only hope. He never took the stern Anglican view. He died in 1956, a very young eighty-six. I think he would have been a bit sad about the sixties and seventies – he would have felt that the easy ways of those decades belittled the most important relationship in life.'

The Gray family moved down to London in the 1920s, and as well as ministering to the Presbyterian congregation of Crouch Hill, Herbert wrote his books, and founded one of the earliest housing associations and the Peace Pledge Union. But the same pragmatism that allowed him to accept divorce eventually forced him from the Union when Hitler and the Nazis presented a worse-than-war scenario.

He was in his seventies when he became the first chairman of the MGC, some fifteen years after pronouncing to people who eschewed the opposite sex that 'a certain mysterious loneliness will overtake you in your thirties, and life will lose its flavour'. He also challenged the notion that love burned itself out in the forties; and although he thought lust was one of the commonest causes of failed marriages, it was no more so than 'a mistaken spiritual view'. Indeed, the waiting-rooms of specialists in nervous diseases were crowded with men and women suffering from nerve trouble brought on through failure to attain harmonious sexual relations in married life. Gray maintained that in many interesting (but never specific) ways, sex was beneficial to a woman's physical system, and that it brought to men a general balance and repose of being which was of enormous (though again, not specific) value.

It was also his firm belief that idle men made unhappy husbands and that the same, but to a lesser degree, was true of wives. He deplored inherited wealth for this reason, saying that love alone was never enough in marriage and that husbands and wives needed the hard toil of daily labour in order to be happy. Inherited wealth not only took its toll on the marriages of those who had it, but also on those of the poor people who sustained it, and with these two extremes in mind, Gray found the laws of inheritance quite indefensible.

He accepted that married life on any terms, for the great majority, would have monotonous and trying periods; but as a romantic he was convinced that by some mysterious and kindly providence, couples attracted to one another physically were usually suited mentally and spiritually as well. Like all of us who are or who have been married, he couldn't help but base his theories and beliefs on his own experience, and in his case this seems to have been pretty close to the ideal. He had a loving and tolerant wife, and children who adored him. Margaret Gray's memories of her childhood include her parents reading Browning to one another, and walking hand-in-hand during holidays in the Highlands.

'My father was immensely humane, kind, generous and liberal in outlook. I think he was a great man – he wasn't dismissed as just a do-gooder.'

Nevertheless, this is what he and his various friends in medicine and the Church were about when they got together to form the council. Marriage in Britain needed help, as evidenced by the immediate and overwhelming demand for guidance, but in 1938 everything was about to change, and hostilities within the battleground of marriage were soon to be superseded by the more straightforward conflict of a world again at war.

2 Supperless for three months to buy a ring

ARY RANG ME after I'd made an appeal through the local radio station for couples who'd been married a very long time. She wanted to help with the book, but maybe she wasn't what I was looking for. She said she'd had a wonderfully happy marriage but now she was alone.

I went to see Mary expecting to find a sad old lady, sustained only by her memories; but the woman I met was neither old nor lonely and seemed like the sort of person one might expect to be involved with meals-on-wheels in the mornings and the juvenile bench in the afternoons – a Home Counties good sort produced from generations of the comfortable middle class. But Mary had been brought up by her grandparents after her parents split up in the London of the twenties.

An only child, she was a bright girl, especially good at maths, and the plan was for her to go to university; but at fifteen she met Frank at a school hockey match and that was it. 'I made a point of finding out who he was and I didn't really look back after that. For me it was love at first sight. I made excuses not to go to university, left school and got a job in the City with a firm of insurance brokers. I married Frank when I was nineteen and he was twenty-one.'

Frank, the eldest of four boys, came from generations of army people and had spent much of his childhood in India. His family was Catholic and Mary converted to marry him. She had visited his home and loved the idea of becoming part of a big family, so different from her own solitary upbringing. Frank was waiting to join the RAF when they met at the hockey game, and by the time they were married he was through training and ready for posting. It was 1941, and the innocence of their courtship had survived the first traumatic years of the war. Frank had gone supperless for three months to save fifteen pounds for the solitaire engagement ring he'd given Mary at Christmas 1939, the first time he had taken her to meet his family.

'The first couple of years I hadn't taken him home and he certainly didn't take me home. A lot of deception went on – my grandparents did not approve of boys. What's so nice today is that everyone brings everyone home. In my day taking someone to your house for tea had to be arranged a fortnight in advance and then only for a special occasion.'

Mary had known she was to have a ring that Christmas. 'We'd been out walking, which was all we usually did. There was a bit of snogging I suppose, and he said he hoped one day we might get married, and I murmured "yes". I was sixteen then. We met really so rarely, but we wrote every day, long, long letters. I haven't kept them; they went with the war. I think my grandmother must have thrown them out.

'I never had any doubts at all. He asked me if I had – the day before the wedding. Perhaps he had some himself, but I hadn't and he must have made up his mind. It was all fairy-tale as far as I was concerned, and I didn't really think about it; I felt it was going to be happy ever after, that we'd have two or three children. I was quite happy for him to take the lead in our life together, and he did. He had to do as he was told, go where he was sent, so there wasn't a lot of room for manoeuvre all the time he was in the RAF, but he was very considerate towards me.'

As soon as they were married Frank was posted to Northern Ireland. He found rooms, for one pound a week rent, sharing with another family. 'We were Catholics and they were Protestants, but we were so innocent that it never occurred to us there could be trouble. The family we were staying with were amazed.'

Mary, of course, had given up her job to be with Frank in Ireland, and she saw her future as housewife and mother. She had no thought of working, even though she had enjoyed her clerical job in London, and both her mother and grandmother had worked most of their lives, if more through necessity than choice. 'Right up to the war, women were not expected to have jobs after marriage. Teachers, civil servants, all left their jobs when they married, but the war changed all that.'

The Irish idyll lasted just six months, although this was a lot longer than many newlyweds had together during the war. Frank was posted to Burma, and Mary didn't see him again for three years. 'It was grim. I wrote to him five times a week and he wrote back when he could, but there was a lot of censorship. I had to do something with my time and I talked about joining one of the services, but their reputation wasn't good and Frank wouldn't let me, so I took a residential job looking after children. I didn't argue about it.'

When the war ended and Mary was able to accompany Frank to his various postings, the absence of children began to be a worry. 'My husband was a strict Catholic – full of ideas of sin and guilt, so there had never been any question of using birth control. We hadn't had sex before marriage, although I was always the one to back off at the last minute for fear of getting pregnant. We enjoyed our sex life. It took a while to get proper satisfaction and I was quite shattered the first time I had an orgasm. I knew only the basic facts of life before I married; I had no real idea, only what I'd learned at school in science lessons.'

By the sixth year of their marriage Mary and Frank were looking into the possibility of adoption. They had been posted to Germany and had seen the desolation of war orphans living in the displaced persons' camps. There were also the many illegitimate children of British servicemen. Then, in 1947, Mary had a daughter. But the longed-for child was almost an intrusion: 'Frank and I went on being very much in love for a long time and certainly our first child suffered because we were more interested in each other than in her. A friend once said to me: "We all love our husbands, but you and yours are just wrapped up in one another." ' For the little girl looking on, the loving arms seemed out of reach, reserved for the two adults to wrap around each other. She had a recurring dream in which her mother and father walked hand-in-hand into the distance while she ran and ran to try to keep up, but could never reach them. Mary's eyes water when she thinks back and sees the unintentional neglect neither she nor Frank noticed at the time. Might it have been different had the baby been a boy? Mary pauses; perhaps, she can't be sure.

There were to be more children: an adopted daughter, then three more babies, the last when Mary was in her forties. Frank stayed on in the RAF until 1960. Most of his postings were far away, sometimes Mary went with him, but for long periods she stayed at home, alone with the children. Letters remained the long-distance fuel for a passion that lasted longer than most, but the reality of day-to-day life bringing up a family eventually gave rise to an unexpected bitterness and resentment in Mary. When Frank was with her there tended to be some more pressing and immediate demand on his time. He was a keen games player and regularly found himself picked for the hockey team. Mary, initially delighted to have her husband home, began to realise that he was hardly ever there.

'I would weep and then I would sulk. I bitterly resented being left alone on Saturdays when it seemed that everybody else had their husbands with them. I didn't have a chance to develop my own interests. He would say that he had to play because he had been picked and that was that. He couldn't let the team down. His sport was the main reason we fell out, and then there was the stopping for drinks on the way home, and me worrying – and I got so bored!'

Remembering my own first marriage and the jealous frustration brought on by the sight of hockey kit being loaded into the back of the car every weekend, I sighed and said I knew how she felt (although I doubted whether she too had hurled the offending stick into the compost heap, leaving it there like a huge admonishing finger, but that's another story). It is so often the nice, good men who go out to play, otherwise why would we want them home?

'Frank was good. He loved babies and wasn't afraid to bath them and look after them. He was very undemanding. He didn't expect his meal to be on the table as soon as he got in, and he never complained if the place was untidy.' But he took major decisions without consulting her – leaving the RAF, buying a house. 'I was very doubtful about him coming out of the services. I thought he was too much of an innocent to cope with civilian life; in the RAF he didn't have to worry about anything, not the smallest thing. If a window was broken someone would come and fix it for him.' Frank bought the house, which was to be the family home for the next 25 years, without Mary having even seen it. He didn't make it seem like an autocratic move, he was always a mild-mannered man, but he went ahead all the same. 'He was always very honest, but he made decisions without telling me. He shared his money very readily and I knew how much he earned. I still meet friends today who were never allowed to handle money or know what their husbands earned. In that way Frank was very enlightened.'

The job he found after the RAF was again to take him out of the country for weeks and months at a time. 'He had travelled all his life, but he never said to me that he couldn't stand not travelling; he would tell me he was being "sent". Later I found out he had always volunteered. He liked to go to the really remote places, where there was no sanitation and little civilisation. He revelled in it, but it took me a long time to realise that. Eventually, I developed a village life for myself and became chairman of everything, so we both had our own lives.'

Mary had come to terms with her life, and despite the hockey and the long absences, she views the greater part of her marriage as exceptionally happy and good. However, there was a really sour patch which she blames on herself. 'The menopause came late, when I was in my early fifties. My father-in-law was living with us and my mother had moved to the village. There was a lot of strain. I became irritable and cool towards Frank; he took the brunt of it. I can hear myself, nag, nag, nagging him. Once, I thought he was going to hit me, but he didn't. I remember feeling very ill with high blood pressure, and Frank's father, and awful night sweats that would keep me awake for hours. Frank could get away, but I couldn't. I talked about being glad to die; life was too hard. I was not a very nice person to live with. Frank would do all he could to help, yet in the end I found it easier when he wasn't there. I could feel him getting restless and then he'd tell me he was going off somewhere. I had stopped writing to him when he was away.

'I think all this time we still appeared to be the perfect couple, and all marriages go through bad patches, especially during the menopause. Then suddenly one day I looked at myself and decided I wasn't very good as either a wife or a mother. I had got into a habit of denigrating Frank, making him feel small.' Mary says the realisation was a bit like a religious experience, but was more likely due to hormone replacement treatment. 'After about a year he said I had changed, and I had. I'd curbed my tongue and stopped being petty about things. I felt better.'

There were to be happy years ahead, and a rediscovery of the closeness that had seemed to mark out the marriage as special, but the remaining time together was short. The youngest child had left home, and retirement was looming for Frank. 'Looming' was the right word, because the end of his career meant no more sojourns overseas, and walking holidays with Mary didn't have quite the same allure. 'But we went to Northumberland for a fortnight; we could hear the curlews calling, and it felt as if we had started a new life together.'

Frank retired at 65 and within a year had developed cancer. 'He had worried about being thrown on the scrap heap, but I loved having him home. He had started an Italian course and we did a lot of walking. Our youngest daughter had married soon after he retired, so the first few weeks were busy with all the wedding arrangements. He had been shattered at the prospect of us being on our own, but then he said it was quite nice being alone together – I was surprised he had thought it might be otherwise.

'I had a hysterectomy, and I was back home recovering. It was New Year's Day and we decided I was fit enough for a walk. We went to the pub and I suddenly realised that he couldn't drink properly. He thought he had chronic catarrh, but when the doctor made a hospital appointment for him so quickly, I knew he had cancer. I knew he wasn't going to get better. He didn't understand why I wanted to go with him to the hospital, but it was the day they told him, and he asked them how long he had got. They said months, but not a year. He died three weeks later. The last little patch was painful and miserable, but he was still totally undemanding and we were so close. It was great. We came right back to the very beginning. He died at home, which was what he wanted. In one sense it was a happy ending. My first feeling was one of relief. I didn't really think about myself. I never felt I wanted him back. I felt complete about it. At the funeral a friend said, "Poor Frank, he never had much luck", but I couldn't understand what she meant.'

Today, Mary lives alone and likes it that way. 'I don't want to marry again and give up my independence. I would say I had a good marriage – I don't know anyone who has had a better one – but I wish we had talked more. I do envy these people who talk all the time – I bottled up my resentments. He would say "Let's talk about it", but we never really talked about feelings. He wasn't very perceptive and he didn't know what was making me difficult. Silly, really.

'He never tried to hold me back. I got a job once, clerical. I loved it, but two weeks after I'd started, my father-in-law became ill and needed looking after. Part of my trouble was that I didn't know what I wanted to do.

'The last year or so was the happiest time we had together, that and the early years after the war – but I did resent his rotten hockey.'

The success of Mary's marriage relied to a large extent on satisfactory sex. Maybe it is too simplistic, too much of a truism to say that good sex is the basis for a good marriage, but if this is the case there must have been many miserable couples in the 1940s. It was reported in the MGC Journal in 1948 that a review had been carried out, revealing that 50 per cent or more wives were sexually frustrated and 'ready to clutch with pathetic eagerness at any straw held out to them'. Mary was one of the lucky ones. She didn't know much about sex, but it worked between her and Frank, and continued to do so throughout most of the marriage. For Ria it was different, and if Mary's marriage worked because of sex, both of Ria's failed because of it.

Ria wrote to me about her first husband, the father of her five children, and described him as a male chauvinist pig because he wouldn't help her lay the table when they were on holiday. She also said she had been a guest on Central Television's *The Time – The Place* when the subject was 'Cheating Wives'. Between the ruled lines of Ria's letter there seemed to be a story of clutched straws.

Like Mary, Ria lives in a village where people know about their neighbours. Ria's stone cottage is a few doors along from the house where her first husband lives, and across the street is the post office and stores that used to be run by her lover. It is all so cosy and close and absurd; and in my memory of our conversation there I feel sure we must have whispered.

After Ria's lover died she married her second husband, but when he went to his solicitor to make his last will and testament, he couldn't remember her name. 'Well, he'd always called me "Duck".' Ria's experience of marriage has not been good.

Her abiding memory of meeting her first husband is that it was at the place where Mary Queen of Scots had her head chopped off, although, to be more precise, they met at the church in Fotheringhay. 'He was in the choir and I was a regular churchgoer – that's where people met before the war. I was in service and we didn't get much time off; Sundays once a fortnight and half a day in the week, but we always had to be in by nine o'clock, and if you were five minutes late woe betide you. The butler would make you feel very small and undignified. So going to church was my only fun. There were dances, but I had to be in too early to go to them.' Ria had left school at fourteen to go into service. One of two children, as a girl she was denied the college education afforded her brother. 'Education was considered wasted on girls in those days.

'I started at the bottom and worked up to lady's maid. It was a good life really, especially when I went to work in the Bishop's Palace at Peterborough. It was great, working for the old Bish. Then I moved to Fotheringhay, and met my husband. He used to rush to get his surplice off after the service, and then he'd tear round the church to walk me home. He was six or seven years older than me and he worked on a farm. We got engaged when I was seventeen; it was on my birthday, he asked me what I would like and suggested an engagement ring. He was my young man and pretty good-looking, so I said "yes".

'The war had started when we planned our wedding, but I had a white wedding and four bridesmaids, and my mother made a cake. The vicar told me I was a very lucky girl because mine was the last wedding to have the church bells. There was a clamp-down after that and they were only rung to herald an air raid.

'My wedding dress cost ten shillings. It was white satin, slim-fitting, long. The shoes cost half-a-crown, the veil the same, the gloves, sixpence. My father made the bouquet. I had sixty people at the reception.

'Because I was a virgin I was very frightened about what was going to happen on the wedding night. I knew the facts of life, my husband had told me while we were engaged, but he was a virgin as well, and he didn't know what he was doing. So the wedding night was a nightmare and I was very disappointed. It gradually improved and I used to read up about it in books. I was pregnant within two months, and delighted.

'I was sort of happy, but he was so untidy and I used to throw things at him – the clock, that sort of thing. We would make up, but he used to drink. We lived in an old cottage, and there was a tin bath and no hot water supply, but that didn't make us different – most of the people we knew lived in the same way. Until the baby came I had two evacuees, two boys from London, their heads alive with nits.

'My husband was in a reserved occupation, being on the land, and he used to work really hard. He was a better husband than I was a wife, but he used to play hard too, that was his problem. He would go to work at 5.00 a.m. and I'd have made him sandwiches, then I'd be busy all day doing the housework; there were no "mod cons" and it all took ages. We were equal in decision-making, but I always handled the money.

'Within two months of my son's birth I was pregnant again and after that I had a four-year break. It made my husband irritable, but we never had separate bedrooms and although we didn't have intercourse, we had foreplay. More often than not, though, he was too tired. After the break I fell pregnant straight away, and then again. I suppose I was able to cope because I was young, but soon I started getting ill and having operations. There was another break – this time it was seven years before we started making love again. I thought it would be all right, after so long, but I was pregnant yet again straight away.

'There were real problems then and I had to have a hysterectomy when I was thirty-nine. I felt marvellous afterwards, very sexual and loving, knowing I wouldn't have a baby; but it had the opposite effect on my husband. He said to me "You're not a woman anymore" and we had an amazing row and he threw me down the stairs. I couldn't eat for three weeks as the fall partially cut my throat. The doctor said I could take him to court, but I didn't want to.

'I'd taken a part-time job, bar work, and I absolutely enjoyed it. My marriage was really on the rocks and I was dating other people behind my husband's back. I had sexual freedom, knowing I wasn't going to get pregnant. I was still sleeping with my husband, but he didn't want it very often. He sought other interests, flower-arranging, darts' – flower-arranging! 'Yes, he was really good at it and used to win all the prizes – he'd do anything that didn't include me.'

Ria eventually left her husband. One day she packed her things, her husband kissed her goodbye on the doorstep, and that was the end of 30 years together. 'I'd met a young man. He was twenty-four and I was forty-eight, but I was attractive – oh, I know it sounds boastful, but I was slim and dark. We'd had a bit of a fling and he wanted to marry me, but he wasn't the one. I'd had lots of affairs. I was looking for the right chap, but they were all exciting at first, then boring. Then I met Sam, the love of my life. He'd never married, but he'd had several live-in relationships in his life, and children. His family accepted me and we had eleven years together. We didn't bother about marrying, although his brother told me at the funeral that Sam had planned for us to marry that Easter.'

The young man who had wanted to marry Ria had agreed to be cited as co-respondent when she divorced. He knew it was over between them when she met Sam, but arrangements were made for her to leave the village for six months and work in a hotel until Sam was ready for her to move in with him at the village shop. He didn't want to be cited himself because he felt he was too well known in the village and the shop might suffer. So, like a character from Thomas Hardy, Ria went away to a strange town to sit it out alone until she was sent for by her lover. 'I never looked at another man in the years I knew him. I fell in love for the first time.'

Sam gave up the shop soon after he and Ria were reunited, and for the next seven years they both worked at night and slept together during the day. 'Lack of a good sex life was the main problem with my husband. Until I lived with my lover I never had an orgasm, and you couldn't talk to anyone about it then, not even your husband, who probably wouldn't know what you were talking about if you did. Orgasm could have kept the marriage together. It was ecstasy with my lover, and I felt so pleased to be able to give him such pleasure, too. He knew how to please a woman and he taught me how to please a man.'

Ria says she's been alone for the ten years since Sam died, subconsciously omitting the six months she spent with her second husband, the one who couldn't remember her name. She married him on the rebound. Sam had died of cancer and she had got it herself. She met her new husband while he too was convalescing in the cancer ward. 'He was impotent. The whole relationship was useless. He put his friends before me. We were married for two years, but split after six months. It's a period of my life I'd rather forget. He was very hostile. We never made love.'

Ria's heart belongs to Sam, but her memories are of the 30 years in which she had her five children and struggled to be the wife she thinks she never was. 'A wife should always be there for her husband, and be neat and in a clean frock and make-up when he comes home. She should never be too tired for him and she should listen and share the hours of the day they have been distant from one another.' It sounds like a code of conduct memorised like the Brownie Promise.

'My first husband married again through an agency, but his new wife walked out after a few months, or maybe he told her to go. I don't think he was very pleased with her. We're good friends now, we get on much better now than we did when we were married. He was a bit of a pig, always keeping me in my place. He was Victorian in his attitude – he insisted on keeping the oil lamps when we could have had electricity. He was very religious, much more than me – he was almost over-religious – and he'd quote the Bible at me.

'I'm not sure whether I regret marrying him. There was someone else, but my parents wanted me to marry my husband. They had to accept it when we got divorced. They must have felt guilty about pushing me into it. I felt like an Asian girl – I felt as if I was acting in a play the day of the wedding. It seemed artificial: I was all dressed up, looking beautiful, and I felt I wasn't in control anymore, just fumbling along. I talked to my own children very openly and made sure they were better prepared than I was. I think they look upon me as a friend.'

Ria, alone in her sixties, looks back and says that she was happiest with Sam, but no happier than she is now, 'with no one to have to ask whether I can put on the telly. I find I'm selfish and I don't want to marry again. I have a friend, but he's married anyway. I joined a lonely hearts club and met him. His wife disappeared years ago. I'm not lonely by myself, but it's nice to have somebody special to pal up with now and again.'

Ria was never in love with either of her husbands, so she didn't even have the 'Greek sickness' (as an American friend calls being in love) as an excuse for getting it wrong twice. Of course, young people didn't have as much choice 50 years ago, before the days of increased mobility, and even after the war, those who did get about were considered 'fast'. 'How to Find a Wife', an article published in the Marriage Guidance Council's Journal in 1947, talked about 'the tragedy facing shy types in the modern world – they have all the gifts and all the longings of the true home-maker, but nowadays all the opportunities go to the gadabouts who like dances and cocktail parties, and who often make the least suitable marriage partners, while the home-loving types, who hate crowds and mass-produced entertainment, eat out their hearts in loneliness and despair'.

The answer was said to be arranged marriages, through the *Matrimonial Times* and *Matrimonial Post*, monthly journals devoted to advertisements for marriage partners. Another avenue was marriage bureaux, and the MGC recommended a new one, The Marriage Society, located at 1 Green Street, London W1 (today the office of the Ice Cream Federation) and run by a Captain Whitehouse with the assistance of a psychiatrist. But there was a serious practical difficulty facing the

Captain and his clientele: 'The bureau has on its books a disturbing preponderance of members of the female sex. Many of them are women of culture and refinement, capable of making splendid wives; but the men who might gain these attractive prizes are not coming forward as they should.' Yet there were close on 400,000 marriages each year in the immediate post-war period, the same number as today and 50,000 a year more than in pre-war totals.

For those who had managed to find a partner in the post-war years there was still plenty to worry about. Questions posed to marriage counsellors of the day included: 'Is it wise to have friends of the opposite sex after marriage?' 'Would it be a good thing for husbands and wives to take holidays apart?' 'Should a wife work?' and 'Is chastity outmoded?' But the really difficult one was 'How are you to know, when you are engaged, that the partner you've chosen is the right one?' In practical, if not emotional, terms, it was more important to make the right choice first go in the 1940s, because another serious question under debate was 'If a man with children finds his wife has been unfaithful, is he setting a higher example of morality by refusing to let her remain in the house, or by forgiving her?' Either way, the wife was in a dependent position, which, in itself, might seem immoral. But attitudes were changing, and it was suggested that Punch and Judy set a bad example of married life to children because it encouraged the idea of wife-beating. A husband's God-given rights were beginning to be questioned.

3 Back to the battleground

MEG DIDN'T MARRY until after the war and she was glad she'd waited. War had removed her from a cosy, insular existence in the heart of London, where everyone she knew lived in the same street or just around the corner, and falling in love was something to do on a Saturday night. A goodnight kiss that brought out the stars was enough to start planning a wedding because you already knew the boy and his family, and the delicious discovery of him as a man was heightened by having been nasty to him at school. But the war, particularly for families living in blitzed Blackfriars, was to bring unimaginable change. Meg's fiancé, John, was posted to India and ended up a six-stone prisoner of war in Europe; she was to join a bomber squadron in Yorkshire and fall in love with a Canadian fighter pilot.

Life before the war for Meg was uneventful but happy. She was a pretty girl and boys liked her, but she was never 'that sort' of girl, not like her friend Elly, who 'couldn't help herself' and had a baby at fifteen. 'The family had to leave the neighbourhood.' Meg's parents – her father was a tailor – were, like their neighbours, Victorian in their ways and outlook. In the block of flats where they lived people were expected to be respectable, although Meg remembers there was a couple living there as man and wife, but not married. Everyone knew, but nothing was said, and because they didn't appear any different to anyone else, they sort of mixed in. Meg's parents were happily married and had five children, but they had a great and abiding sadness which is almost too horrible to relate. Their first child, a boy, died at eighteen months after pulling down a pan of scalding water on to himself. 'My mum would never let my children go near the stove. What had happened never left her.'

Meg met the man she was to marry when she was fifteen, although she'd seen him often enough in the playground at school and remembered him as a scruffy, mucky boy, her friend's big brother. But 'meeting' was nothing to do with already knowing. 'I liked him, but he showed how much he liked me, so I wasn't very keen. He bought a pair of trousers specially to take me out. I never dreamed then that I would ever marry him. I didn't expect to get married until I really fell in love, but I didn't mind dating and kissing goodnight – any girl who went further was looked down on.'

The first outing with John, in his new trousers, didn't go well and was not repeated until three years later when they met by accident and she asked him to see her home. 'Things always happened to me with a bang. I said "Aren't you going to kiss me goodnight?" and he did. That was it. I fell in love during that kiss and I felt I wanted his children; but he didn't feel he could trust me because I had been nasty to him in the past and told him I didn't want him but his friend. He was going to marry someone else, but as soon as the war broke out and the first air raid warning came he was round like a shot to be with me.

'He was one of the first to get his call-up papers, and that last fortnight before he went to war he was with me all the time. We knew we were in love, but there was no time to buy a ring and he never asked me to marry him, we just took it for granted. We had our last Christmas together and when we said goodbye it took a long time – until about three in the morning. I remember thinking "I might never see him again" and I felt quite ill over it. We didn't know what was going to happen, how long the war was going to last. We thought possibly two years.'

John, whose experience of things foreign extended no further than the Turkish baths at the Elephant and Castle where he'd been training as a masseur, left for India a few hours after the long goodbye with Meg. 'He went for two years and we corresponded. When Vera Lynn's song *Yours* came out I jotted down the words because they exactly fitted us . . . "Yours, to the end of life's story . . ." It was our song. I sent the words to India, but meanwhile he had been moved to the Western Desert with the Desert Rats, and I got a letter from Basra. He said he had received my letter and that he and the other soldiers had sat round in the tent and sung the song.'

Back home in London, Meg had left her office job and was working in munitions where she had met another boy, but John's parting words of two years earlier – 'If you ever marry anybody else I shall still find you' – seemed as potent as the lyrics sung from the desert. 'He was the one-man, one-woman type.' Besides, Meg was about to pack in the munitions job and leave London.

'I got a job with Plessey in Ilford, but I hated it and went on the dole. I'm surprised they didn't catch up with me, because if you weren't married and didn't have children to look after, you had to work. After about three months, I joined up with the RAF; I was fed up with sitting at home looking at our settee where John and I used to snoggle.' It was December 1942, the same month the telegram came reporting John missing.

Was it better or worse, the uncertainty? One moment there would be hope, but the next, you'd hear about someone else reported killed and it seemed as likely that that was what had happened to the one you loved. The war had already lasted longer than anyone had expected and there was no end in sight, no vision of how the future might be. People grabbed at happiness as if it was rationed, taking what they could while it was on offer, because next day the supply might disappear. 'Better to have loved and to have lost than never to have loved at all' reached new heights of poignancy and shattered the notion of British reserve.

'There were twenty WAAFS to a thousand airmen where I was stationed and we had dates galore. I had cried and cried when the telegram came about John, but I felt I was in a different world when I was on that bomber squadron. That's why war breaks up marriages. I always felt how terrible it must be for men abroad whose wives wrote and told them they were leaving. I'm really glad I wasn't married.'

Whether or not she might have written one of those letters Meg can't be sure. She met a Canadian airman, and although she now knew that John was a prisoner in Italy, she was living for the moment. 'I never told him about John, and I think I would have married him, but he was killed on his last "op". Your emotions got very mixed up in the war. I still loved John the deepest, but where I was seemed so divorced from my real life. I didn't see John from 1939 till 1945. He nearly starved to death as a prisoner, but when Italy gave in and the Germans took over he was all right.'

John could have got back to Britain when the Italians capitulated, but he chose to stay with a sick friend and missed the chance of escape. On 26 January 1944 he wrote to Meg. 'My Own Darling, I hope by now you have received my other letters posted from a transit camp. It is nearly seven months since I last heard from you and really, darling, it seems like years, for I miss you terribly and long for our reunion, that which for over four years we have longed and patiently waited for. Darling, we will be happy after this war, for we will certainly make up for all we have lost.'

Her airman dead, Meg applied for posting, but there were always more boyfriends, though none serious, and John's letters kept coming, either full of gratitude and endearment for letters received, or dismay over those not: 'Darling, I have had no mail from you, and with no letter to reply to it really is hard for me to think of anything to write about' (12 September 1944). 'Darling, Only Sweetheart, I have had no mail from you for three weeks' (19 September). Five letters arrived in November, but on 28 November, John wrote: 'My Own Darling, have just received another letter, and I was really surprised at the shortness of it – surely your letters are not limited to that extent? However, I must consider myself lucky for what I have had, and I hope you are receiving mine. I miss you and live only for our reunion.'

'When the war was ending I arranged to go to John's mother's on leave. She had moved out of London and taken a cottage in Somerset. I don't know why, but I just had this feeling that John would be there, and when I arrived, the first thing I said was, "Where is he?" ' Neither woman knew that John was back in England and searching for Meg in London. 'The second week I was there I woke one morning to the sound of heavy boots coming along the lane. I got up, but the heavy boots were already on the stairs. It was John. He just grabbed me, threw me on the bed, and it was wonderful, seventh heaven.' They were married by special licence ten days later. It cost 17s 6d instead of 7s 6d and Meg had a chromium wedding ring, which necessity had made fashionable. She bought her wedding outfit on the black market, shell pink and grey, with blue accessories.

'We had three weeks' honeymoon in Devon and I felt we were one when we made love, although I was a bit disappointed on our wedding night. We didn't want any children at first and as John hadn't got any condoms we couldn't make love. He'd been too shy to buy any, but a friend gave him some the next day.

'Sexually, we were perfectly matched and very happy. John was very unselfish. After all that time apart we just wanted to be on our own, to be able to make love when we liked – I've never understood what all the fuss was over making love – it's always just come naturally to me.'

In the context of 40 years together, the six years apart still seem set aside from reality. John and Meg slipped back into togetherness with all their pre-war expectations of married life still intact, and for 40 years they felt that what they had was special, but not quite special enough. 'After we were married I always felt something was missing, the spiritual side.' This was the cue for the unexpected. I felt I had been hearing the sort of story made of Sunday afternoon black and white films in the minds of those of us born after the war, except that in the movies the hero and heroine don't end up as Jehovah's Witnesses. John and Meg might have been married longer if he had been able to have a blood transfusion, but that's another story, and with Armageddon just around the corner Meg is confident that she and John will soon be reunited for a second time.

I left Meg's terraced house with a disingenuously accepted *Watchtower* and a joyful promise of doom. I also had an uncomfortable feeling of having been caught in my own trap; I had receded down Meg's narrow hallway aware of the sniff of a conversation snapping at my heels. But is it surprising that couples like John and Meg found they needed a rigidly structured faith after their war experiences? In 1947 the MGC listed the four main causes of marriage troubles as lack of adequate preparation, housing and in-law problems, sexual maladjustments, and, over and above all the rest, the absence of any kind of spiritual background – 'these people are virtually rudderless'.

The year before, the Lord Chancellor had accurately predicted 50,000 divorces (thought to be a peak, but barely a third of today's figure) in England and Wales in 1947, with one marriage failing for every four new ones. 'The battle of the family is on with a vengeance', the MGC told the country, reaffirming its aim, to foster sound family life on the basis of sound marriage, which, in those days, was still supposed to be a three-party union between husband, wife and Creator.

Church remained the most popular place for weddings after the war, but it was suggested that religious marriage should be refused to those who did not appear to be sufficiently prepared, on the basis that quality was ten times more important than quantity. Professor Emile Cammaerts, who wrote about the foundations of marriage in the 1940s in *For Better, for Worse*, said the Christian view was the same as that of G. K. Chesterton – 'Man and woman are always incompatible' – and attempts to achieve 'oneness' were fatal to married love. Harmony could be achieved, but not in unison, was the bleak prognosis, and the only way marriage could be sustained was through belief in God and a sense of duty.

Appropriately, it was left to the War Office to take the lead in practical preparation for marriage, and the Army found itself overwhelmed with volunteers to take part in pioneering four-day courses on 'Successful Marriage and Family Life'. But the same year, 1947, revealed almost unbelievable cynicism in post-war attitudes towards marriage – cinemagoers up and down the country were laughing at *Brief Encounter*.

The MGC had cited the David Lean film as a shining example of facing up to moral responsibility and doing the right thing – even if the cinema in general was being blamed for setting a bad example to married people. 'Those who have wide experience in marriage guidance work know only too well how widespread amongst men and women today are the loose and low standards which the wrong type of film has implanted and encouraged. *Brief Encounter*, on the other hand, blazes a new trail and deserves the encouragement and support of all who care about the morals of the multitude.' Yet, the multitudinous cinemagoers of the late forties were reported to be treating the film with ribaldry, their handkerchiefs wet with tears of mirth, not sentiment. The characters played by Trevor Howard and Celia Johnson were seen as pathetically hidebound by a pre-war and out-of-date morality.

Hard to believe, isn't it, that people could have been cynical about that film? It's still my favourite and I wasn't born until three years after its first showing. I still think of the archetypal British marriage as that between the Celia Johnson character, a lipstick but not mascara woman, and her pipe-smoking, beslippered husband – a sort of extension into adulthood of *Janet and John*. At the risk of spoiling the film for anyone who has not yet seen it, the Celia Johnson character falls in love with a doctor, the Trevor Howard character, but as both are decent, married people, they end their affair before it has begun.

The poignancy of the story lies in the decency of the characters. 'Marriage, as we still understand it in the West,' wrote Professor Cammaerts, 'is the result of the transformation of two natural instincts – sex and procreation – by a supernatural belief – permanent monogamy. It is on the preservation of these three foundations, natural and supernatural, and on their relationship with one another, that the preservation of marriage itself depends. There is no harm in idealising sex and calling it "love", but there is great harm in considering romantic love in the same light as married love. A passionate attraction cannot alone lead to the foundation of a sound family. In fact, it leads in the opposite direction – [to] adultery. It is by nature temporary, it courts the excitement of danger, it thrives when faced with opposition. It is part of the philosophy of revolt spread for so long by poets and novelists. It provides good dramatic situations.' Too right, and *Brief Encounter* was the best.

Inadequate preparation, both practical and spiritual, and godlessness were, no doubt, cause for much marital grief, but the more prosaic difficulties in the late forties and early fifties were to do with housing, or the lack of it. Nearly half a million homes were wrecked during the war, but the housing shortage had more to do with the baby boom after the First World War. Those born in 1919 and 1920 reached marriageable age in the 1940s and there weren't enough houses for them. Added to this, the very low rate of unemployment in the late forties, less than 2 per cent, meant that more couples were able to afford to rent houses of their own instead of sharing rooms; but as the housing stock had not kept pace, this simply meant some people were getting more of the housing 'cake' while others didn't have any.

Newlyweds had to live with parents and in-laws, sometimes for years. They had no independence and no privacy, and most had to put off having children. Even if they did manage to get rooms away from the family, many landladies would not take couples with children. It's hardly surprising that the Royal Commission on Population reported great national worry over lack of babies, with the number of births falling below replacement level.

Post-war housing was not expensive by today's standards – rent represented, on average, between six and seven per cent of income – there just wasn't enough of it. (My own parents, who did manage to buy their first home at about this time, remembered that the nearby street of shops was occupied not by butchers and bakers, but by squatters.) There was criticism that too much of the limited supply of building materials was being used for new offices; it seemed that 'every clerk who pushes a pen over an insurance form must do so in a citadel' while, at home, his wife and children spent their day in a squalid shared home. After the war, 795,000 new homes had been built by 1950, but a third of the population was still living in slums.

The further cause of marital disharmony cited by the MGC after the war, sexual maladjustment, must have been exacerbated by the housing problem, but there was also a clash of attitudes. The post-war woman was still not expected to enjoy sex in the same way as her husband, according to Esther Adams in an article entitled 'Eros and Agape' published in the MGC Journal. 'It is certainly desirable that men should learn to consider their wives' needs in intercourse, but modern books, in stressing the need for women to achieve a satisfaction and climax comparable with that reached by men, may encourage a selfish attitude in a woman which defeats its own ends. My own view is that, in a woman, the sex impulse is not naturally an urge for a brief self-gratification, which must be controlled in the interests of society, but a generous self-giving to a man she loves or to the future of the race, and that her own happiness is perhaps most likely to be found in it when it is least sought.'

This 'lie back and think of England' approach was actually a drain on the country, and was recognised as such by both marriage counsellors and the doctors whose waiting-rooms were awash with the niggling misery of psychosomatic disorders suffered by sexually frustrated wives. But hadn't women been expected to 'lie back' etc. from time immemorial? Why, in 1949 and 1950 was it suddenly a problem? The simplistic answer is books. Everyone was writing 'how to' books about marriage, the sort of books that in a previous age would never have been published, even between plain brown covers. Bliss was ignorance, because what you'd never had you didn't miss; but knowing about it and not getting it gave rise to the age of acute neurotic doubt and confusion. 'It's hard to believe that there can have been any great lovers, or any successful marriages, before the twentieth century,' wrote one reviewer of a 'how to' book.

4 And back to the draining board

As if laughing at *Brief Encounter* wasn't shocking enough to the romantic soul, there was worse to come in the immediate post-war years. For at least a century, there had been more women of marriageable age in Britain than there were men. Apart from the losses during the two world wars, there had also been many men lost through emigration, and the number of surplus women was put at around two million. What was to be done with all these poor, pathetic spinsters? The answer was polygamy.

It seems hard to believe that as short a time ago as the late 1940s serious consideration was given to such a plan. Herbert Gray had said in the twenties that he understood the East had allowed polygamy to solve the problem of excess women as a result of war through the ages, but I doubt his Christian principles could have stretched beyond tolerating the practice overseas. Needless to say, the concern, even in this country, was not wholly about the 'surplus' women themselves, but probably more to do with worries over the declining birth-rate.

Statistics though, were as always a movable feast. The MGC had other figures and said that the two million was a gross exaggeration: the situation had changed as a result of female emigration far exceeding that of males. What they were talking about was the huge number of British girls who had married foreign soldiers during and after the Second World War. In addition, there was another, longer-term consideration. Throughout time there have always been more boys born than girls – 105 to 100 – although until the twentieth century fewer boys survived, the male having always been more susceptible to accident and disease. But with the greatly improved modern standards of child care, the race had become more even.

Polygamy may have been under consideration after the war, but polyandry appears to be what was actually happening if the statistics for 1948 are to be explained. The number of married men in the country was given as 10,920,000, but the number of married women 120,000 fewer. It had been a feature of each previous census that the number of married women exceeded the men, and this was ascribed to the temporary absence of husbands abroad; but no logical explanation was ever offered for the reverse situation.

That there could have been many women, post-war, with the energy for more than one husband seems unlikely. British wives of the 1950s were still a long way behind their American counterparts in the discovery of labour-saving machinery in the home. Domestic drudgery lived on, and Herbert Gray's visionary advice about husbands and wives having a jolly time together sharing the housework was not going to be heeded without the powerful fascination of new gadgetry. In 1950, society certainly didn't expect husbands to help their wives in the home, and a man could still sue for damages over the loss of his wife's services.

It would be a mistake, as in nearly all feminist issues both then and now, to see the domestic arrangements of 1950 as imposed on women by men. There were plenty of wives who still felt that their place was in the home, and who resented the word 'drudgery' being associated with household work; and if labour-saving devices were to be used, then let this be to the greater good of home-making rather than as a means of allowing women to have a career.

Yet being 'confined to pram-pushing distances' as one 1950s wife and mother put it, was too much of a deprivation for the career women who had come into their own during the war years by stepping into the jobs vacated by servicemen, and stressful and exhausting as it was to combine home and career, for some there was no other course. These women were in the era of guilt over going out to work, but they were better off than their daughters, who were to suffer the seventies syndrome of two-way guilt when staying at home was as culpable as having a career.

The 1950s husband was thought, generally, to prefer a wife who stayed at home, but who nevertheless exhibited an intelligent interest in outside affairs. If she did have a job, then it should not be more interesting or important than her husband's, and should never pay more. As well as the husband's emotional reaction to his wife working, there was also the question of motive. How many 1950s wives went out to work for their own satisfaction rather than as a contribution to society? A survey of the day revealed mixed motivation, with a gratuitous comment from one career-minded contributor that she still got 'a real Victorian kick out of a well-arranged linen cupboard'.

Maintaining order and harmony in the home was the major consideration for the 1950s working wife who, it seems, was neither expected nor ready to accept the concept of shared domestic responsibility. That she could go out to work at all during her child-bearing years was as a result of increasingly efficient and more widespread birth control.

Among women who married before 1910, only 15 per cent used contraceptive measures, but of those married in 1940 to 1942, 35 per cent did so immediately, and a further 28 per cent in the first five years. For those who did become pregnant in the 1950s there was a breakthrough in early diagnosis. Hitherto, pregnancy could not be confirmed until nearly three months, but by injecting samples of urine into a toad, a result became possible within the first six weeks.

This amazing advance in pregnancy testing encouraged women from throughout the country to post samples to the Family Planning Association's pregnancy diagnosis laboratory in London, where 1,000 toads were kept ready and waiting. The test was read by looking at the toads 24 hours after injection, and recording whether or not eggs had been laid. It was said to be an ideal method because the creatures were easy to keep, cheap to feed, and as they were unharmed could be used repeatedly, given a short rest in between. Accuracy was put at over 95 per cent, and if anyone doubted the likelihood of the whole enterprise, visitors were welcome to the laboratory to see the toads swimming in their tanks. I did check to see if this story might have been published on 1 April, but no; and the creeping realisation came to me that this must have been how my own arrival in the world was first heralded.

Martha and Cyril, born two decades earlier, were falling in love in the early 1950s and thinking about getting married. I met Cyril in London a few weeks before his retirement. He's a man who has seen the world, has had sustained truck with the rich and powerful, and joined those ranks himself, if more as a 'man in a grey suit' than as a visible leader. Retirement was a state of being he approached with mixed feelings, but on the plus side he relished the prospect of spending more time with his wife, who, for more than a decade, he had seen only during weekends and holidays. Martha had remained at their home in Yorkshire while Cyril spent his working week in London, living at his club.

Martha was not brought up to expect marriage to a man who would have the facilities of a London club at his disposal. She was born in Lancashire, where her mother worked in a sweet shop in the 1930s after Martha's father, an engineer, was reduced to a two-day working week at a time when many had no work at all. 'I didn't like it much, my mother working, but I was proud of her, and none of the other children at school had a mother who worked. My grandmother lived with us and she looked after me, and Mother working meant we had extras like going to the theatre and holidays.

'Most girls of my generation were brought up to get married and work just for a few years beforehand. None of my friends went to university, just to secretarial college. I wish now that I had gone to art school, but my parents never thought about education for girls. I was their only child.'

Martha is a small, neat woman with a demeanour that suggests energy and enthusiasm for life, whatever it has to offer. At sixteen she went to work at a wines and spirits store and never thought about finding another job, she so enjoyed the one she had. 'If my parents had people round, it was for tea; but the people I worked for had cocktail parties. It was a case of seeing how the other half lived, and it was wonderful.'

Martha's employers treated her like a child of their own, and included her in their parties and gave her extras like tickets to a ball. This was how she met Cyril, himself an only child, but from an 'old' family which might have been justified in placing itself in a drawer or two above that of Martha's.

'There was a crowd of us, and I dated one or two boys – it was quite different in those days, you never jumped into bed with them; if you kissed them you were being adventurous. There was no such thing as the Pill, and if I'd got pregnant my mother would have been horrified. It would have hurt her bitterly, and I wouldn't have done that for anything.

'Cyril and I started to go out together. It was two years, off and on. We went to dances, mostly with the crowd; they were 'old boys' dances and the Conservatives. We had a great time, it was a very happy period.'

Not so happy, though, was Cyril's mother. Martha was not good enough, but it's doubtful any girl could have been for the son of this matriarchal paragon, who envisaged nothing short of starvation for those who emigrated beyond her culinary clutches. Accordingly, the first few years of married life for Martha were punctuated by regular visits from her mother-in-law, if not laden with food parcels, then well equipped with apron, oven-gloves, and a wooden spoon.

Yet Cyril's parents knew what it was to be in love, a state of grace they were to sustain themselves for more than half a century, and if there were any misgivings about their son's choice of bride, there was no doubting his happiness.

Martha doesn't remember Cyril asking her to marry him. 'You don't just suddenly say, "Let's get engaged"; you just start talking about when you are married – it sort of creeps into the conversation, into your life, and one Christmas Eve Cyril turned up with a ring.'

Cyril remembers it differently. He says he not only asked her to marry him, but asked her father's permission, too. Nearly forty years later he tells her she's rotten for not remembering and declares that he's always been the romantic one. It seems quaint to them now that Martha's father's permission was sought, and that Cyril was nervous about asking, but the tradition lives on, and ten years ago their daughter's future husband addressed the same question to Cyril.

For Martha and Cyril in 1953, the Christmas Eve engagement was celebrated with hot-pot and champagne at the wines and spirits store and a drive home in the Morgan sports car his parents had bought him when he was seventeen. 'We were engaged for nearly two years but I really don't know why we waited – we could have got married straight away. We had more disagreements while we were engaged than we ever have since. We were probably frustrated; we didn't sleep together before we were married.' Martha says she can't remember what the quarrels were about, only that it wasn't politics, which is the most fertile ground for the arguments they have now, although both are blue as blue.

What did Martha expect from marriage during the quarrelsome engagement? 'Obviously I wanted a nice home. I wanted a family, more than one child. One would not have been enough – there's too much pressure on an only child to keep the parents happy. I wanted a better life than my parents had.'

Martha said she couldn't think why she and Cyril had waited to marry, but he can: 'Banks didn't lend then as they do now. You saved, you didn't borrow. My mother would not have had a credit card to save her life.' But the newly married couple did borrow £1,295 from a building society to buy their first home, a two-bedroomed semi near Cyril's work in the neighbouring county. 'I was a bit worried; I remember being told "Never take an English girl to live abroad", and I felt I was doing that, moving Martha from Lancashire to Yorkshire.'

While the house was being built, Martha carried on living with her parents, and Cyril, who was a gas engineer, spent the week abroad in Yorkshire, coming home only at weekends, which he and Martha spent with his parents. By the time they moved into their own home, Martha was expecting their first child, and there was no thought of her finding a new job.

'We hadn't bothered to take precautions. Our son was born nine months, two weeks and two days after the wedding. When we told our parents about the baby they were so worried about the possibility of it being born prematurely and people thinking we'd had to get married.

'I was twenty-six when our son was born and I wouldn't have liked to have waited any longer. It was wonderful, the whole thing. I loved being in control of my own home. I could cook, go out, get up, when I liked. We would stay up late at night just because there was no one to tell us to go to bed. We had no money, but a lovely home with beautiful furniture, even a television, although there was nothing much on in those days. We played bridge and saw our friends, and they were all having babies, too. It was all wonderful.' Almost. There was still Cyril's mother.

'I was immature and quite naive,' Cyril says. 'I had no clear idea about married life, but I loved Martha and I'd wanted to leave home. I did feel I was dominated by my mother.'

'When we were first married, your mother insisted on furnishing our first house,' Martha recalls. 'She was an interfering old . . . ,' Cyril murmurs.

'She was a good cook and she was always coming over with cakes and things. She used to drive me mad. She really did come over with alarming regularity, and she'd take over my kitchen. I would think "Here I am, setting the table, and she's in my kitchen, cooking the meal". Cyril would tell me to tell her I didn't like it, but I wouldn't. I felt mean, and, anyway, life's too short to get het up about these things, and as she got older she mellowed, and I think she realised her son was not going to starve to death. In later years, when she came to live with us, she thought I was the best thing since sliced bread.'

You let her come and live with you! The landmarks in Cyril and Martha's marriage have been such. The birth of children, the buying and selling of houses, Cyril's changes of job, caring for parents, and illness – both Cyril and Martha have had serious illnesses. Otherwise, nothing extraordinary has happened, and nothing of the kind was ever looked for, except the time during the first years when they won the football pools and threw a big party to celebrate. The next day they discovered they were sharing the win with a thousand others and their part didn't even cover the cost of the party.

Cyril left the gas industry years ago and began climbing a long career ladder that for the past decade or so has brought the marriage full circle, keeping them apart during the week. 'We love our home. The trick is to live in the sticks on a London salary,' Cyril says, as we sit in the drawing-room of his 300-year-old stone house overlooking the *Last of the Summer*

Wine valley. There is a courtyard with a loose box full of black puppies – the Golden Retriever has been 'a naughty girl', I am told. There is a barn that has been converted into a 'granny flat', and served as one until Cyril's parents died. Fourteen years they had lived there, and it was all right, once they'd sorted out the house rules which included not having to report all comings and goings. 'I had to tell them how it was going to be, that we were too old to have to tell them what time we were coming in at night.'

The gardens dip and roll towards the valley view, manicured lawns and flower beds bordered by hedges and shrubs curtailed into topiary. The house is an exquisite culmination of a labour of love, a showpiece of elegance and homeliness combined. It has the feel of a mini stately home, antiques set beside plump new sofas, polished wood floors with densely-piled pastel rugs for the dog to lie on. The detail is painstaking; nothing jars. 'This is chauvinist, but when I come home after being all over the world, I want everything nice, things organised, a haven of peace. If I'd had to come home and start washing my socks and cooking, I would have been pissed off. Actually, I'm not really chauvinist, but I do like to come into an oasis of calm, and wonderful food. I would not have stopped Martha working, but if I am brutally honest I would have resented it spoiling my lovely home life.'

'We have put the weekends on one side and made more of them than we would otherwise have done. We have missed one another during the week; it could be very lonely for me, but I took up more bridge, and my daughter is in the next village. Cyril suffered more; he doesn't like being on his own. He doesn't like me going to bed before him, and if he wants to go early, he wants me to as well.

'In the winter I used to get great feelings of being unfulfilled, but they would go away by the spring, with the garden to do. I am more assertive and self-assured than I was when younger, but I take the huff and I sulk more, too. It takes a long time for me to get annoyed, but I can't just switch it off afterwards, and then I feel full of remorse.'

Do they still feel passionate about one another? 'I do,' answers Cyril, immediately, while Martha is already saying: 'I don't really.' But sex has always been good between them, and still is. 'We wonder how long it can go on, into our seventies, eighties?' Cyril muses. 'But it's not the core. Sex is essential, but love is the core, having someone who will forgive you anything, because after your parents have gone, who else will do that?'

'I did throw a tin of paint at him once,' Martha says.

'We do argue like Joe Buggery. We are always arguing,' Cyril says, as Martha begins to relate the story of a friend whose husband has just left her after 30 years, '. . . and they never argued.' 'But most married friends of our antiquity are still together,' Cyril adds.

'Nothing has ever threatened our marriage, yet we are both Leos.'

'We've been married for thirty-five years and we've enjoyed every minute of it, although I, for one, couldn't tell you why.' Obvious delight in one another and each knowing their place according to a workable pattern circa 1955 would be my guess.

Cyril has always 'brought home the bacon', and Martha has always cooked it, but the big marriage issue of the fifties appears to have been the blurring of these roles, although it was, as it is today, more a case of the wife doing two jobs while the husband continued with only one. The debate gathered force in the pages of the MGC Journal, and in April 1955 an entire issue was devoted to the subject – the first time any issue had been given over to just one topic. 'This is a question on which at present there is much controversy,' the editor, John Crowlesmith, wrote. ' "Should I keep on my job after marriage?" is a question we often hear on the lips of young women who are getting married. It is always difficult to give a definite answer as, in this matter, circumstances so much alter cases. Indeed no standard reply is possible.'

In her contribution to the debate, Mrs Jean Mann, then the MP for Coatbridge and Airdrie, talked about the background to the controversy, the thirties, unemployment, and what she called 'downright jealousy' if married women were working and men were not. 'War brought a radical change. The services of women were in such demand that nurseries were opened for the children of the mothers engaged in war work. Near my house there was a large nursery. I saw in the cold, miserable winter mornings young mothers arriving with their children at seven, and again at 6.00 p.m. taking them home. I hated the sight of it. It could not but be bad for the poor, tired mothers and their children. I thought, "When the fathers come home it will be different. Mum will stay at home, and Dad will go out to work." But it has not turned out that way.' Declaring herself firmly against married mothers working, she said that in her own experience 'all that I gained on the roundabouts, I lost on the swings. Extravagance inside my home that I would never have incurred had I been there all day. My boys getting into mischief. The only time the police ever called at my home was during that period. And they called twice. Torn clothing. Shoes kicked out. Pots of jam supped up in two days: tinned milk too – alas, what profit had I? The clattering tongues of neighbours. "Her children are running wild." "They are neglected." My mother was angry. She said, "It is the mother who is neglected. In every case where the mother has to go out to work, she neglects herself." '

War had produced exceptional circumstances, and husbands were not around to lend a hand in the home, but 'What of today?' wrote Mrs Mann in 1955. 'We now accept the situation of Mother going to work, but I am still resolutely opposed to it. I think she needs all her time for her home and children.'

But psychiatric social worker Mrs Lois Hieger referred to a recent survey of the social life of young mothers in a new suburb and the revelation of how barren and depressing it could be. 'When a girl leaves a sociable factory job because she is expecting a baby, she has no idea what a tremendous change she has to face; it may mean solitude, fatigue and anxiety, such as she has never known before.' And it was just as bad for the new, post-war professional woman finding herself suddenly washed up on to the dread shores of domesticity. 'Interest and achievement at work may transform her from a harassed to a cheerful person, because fulfilment in her career has removed the sense of frustration that is so prevalent among those who find domestic life too limiting. If the children gain a less irritable mother, and the husband is glad that his wife has regained her vitality and drive, because she is back at work with wider interests, then she is justified in taking a job, provided the family does not suffer in other respects.' As long as the working wife and mother still had enough energy to fetch her husband's pipe and slippers with grace and enthusiasm there was nothing much to worry about, and to this end, Mrs Hieger concluded that a part-time job was the answer if there had to be one at all.

But if the British wife felt hard done by in the fifties, Robert Morley, writing in *Picture Post*, thought he could offer comfort by comparing her lot to that of the Arab wife 'living in the harem and allowed nothing to do all day other than listen to the radio and play canasta'. Morley thought the British wife ought to be grateful 'to have been given a position of authority and freedom unequalled in any other country in the world, except America. The British woman marries when she wants to (and not before) – not the man she is in love with, but the man who is in love with her – she knows life will be easier for her played that way.

'In her early married life she is not so much ungenerous as over-cautious. More suited by temperament to be the guard than the driver, in the rare instances when she takes over the controls she is liable to emulate her American sister and kill her man in about thirty years. As a guard she effectively slows her man down, but usually contrives not to run him off the rails.

'Early in his married life she will discipline her husband, until he realises he is only half the fellow he thought he was. He will learn to change his ways quite a bit, and give up most of his old friends and hobbies. He will sample his wife's cooking gingerly, and find, to his relief, that it is much the same as his mother's. Unless he goes abroad he will proceed from his cradle to his grave happily unaware that in other parts of the world women take an interest in food. His wife's attitude to sex will largely depend on his own. Naturally, she will tend to concentrate chiefly on what is known to viewers of *What's My Line* as the "end product", and any day now, if he is lucky, he will be given children. The doctor takes the credit for these on the first evening, if they turn out all right, and his wife ever afterwards.

'While the children are growing up, his wife will be getting old, but he won't notice. He will be worrying about himself. No one else will have time to. He will cease to be a husband to his wife and became just another (although the least satisfactory) of the kids. Perhaps half a dozen times a year he will feel supremely happy for about five minutes. He will be filled with a sense of achievement, even of immortality. There will be no reason for this – it is merely a device of Mother Nature's to keep the nest warm and provided for until the young birds are ready to fly. When the children have flown he will suddenly realise that he is a middle-aged man married to a middle-aged stranger. Now is the time when he will really be able to get to know his wife, if she wants him to do so. Usually this is the moment (when it's far too late) when his wife will begin to worry about her appearance, and, if he's unlucky, about his, too.

'Once she settles for old age . . . nothing suits a British wife better. Indeed, it suits her a good deal better than all other ages. Old British wives look nicer, smell nicer – and are nicer – than old Arab wives, or old Chinese wives, or even old French wives. When they push their husbands about, they do it in bathchairs, and when they bury them it is usually with genuine sorrow. That is because she has at last learned to love him. Given sixty years, a British man can make any woman love him, even a British wife.'

Anyone still interested in embarking on such a course in the fifties was advised to make sure the partner of their choice was 'fit for the purpose', and there was even talk of requiring couples by law to exchange medical certificates. Colonel Malcolm Stoddart-Scott, Conservative MP for Ripon, proposed a Private Member's Bill entitled 'Marriage (Certificates of Medical Examination) Bill', under which couples would have to exchange certificates within six weeks of their wedding, or postpone the marriage until this was done. The curious thing about this idea was that neither party had to tell the other what their examination might have revealed, but simply had to hand over the piece of paper that confirmed they had been given the once-over – rather like having an MOT test that nevertheless couldn't stop you endangering others' lives and limbs with a clapped-out old banger.

The proposed Bill does not appear to have got far enough

to warrant much thought by the British Medical Association, who were more interested in what was going on in the bedrooms of those who were already married. At an early fifties BMA conference in Glasgow it was suggested that wives might find it easier to tolerate their husbands' snoring if they were told it was a throw-back to caveman behaviour when the male made a noise at night to frighten off marauders. 'This rather attractive theory should be explained to the wife,' Dr A. H. Douthwaite told the conference, 'and she might be encouraged to regard it as a sign of deep affection. If not, it is wise to insist on separate rooms.'

Another, newer disturbance to married life was television, described as 'one more terror added to the timetable of life', and by the 1950s, no longer the status symbol it had been a decade or so earlier when people had been known to put up dummy aerials to impress the neighbours. By 1950, seven out of every ten viewers had left school by fourteen or fifteen, and socio-economically, it was the 'have nots' who were indulging in Britain's 'most expensive form of professional entertainment'. Television cut down time spent in the pub, but the experts didn't reckon this was necessarily a bonus for home life and marriage; it could easily be just another source of irritation and disagreement, and any positive influence it might have in the home had to be measured against practical points such as 'the effect of Mother's viewing on the darning of the family's socks'. But for better or for worse, it did bring another chance to see *Brief Encounter*.

5 Chastity under fire

JUST AS I WAS about to start writing this chapter I saw a programme on television saying that it was the 1960s when women started having sex before marriage. Post-Pill, pre-AIDS, the 1960s were the beginning of two sexy decades. But according to marriage guidance experts, the whole thing had started a decade earlier and it was the 1950s when chastity came under fire.

There's nothing in my Longman's dictionary to suggest that chastity is, or ever was, exclusively the province of women, but nobody seems to have talked about it as an equal opportunities issue since the Revd Dr Herbert Gray in his 1920s classic, *Men, Women & God*. The MGC's Professor David Mace, writing in *Housewife* magazine in the 1950s, said: 'In the Western world today, just beneath the surface, a furious controversy is brewing up. The subject under dispute is premarital sexual intercourse. We must put it quite plainly in order to be specific. "Sex relations" is too vague. There are forms of mutual stimulation short of intercourse which are also the subject of controversy. But the real controversy is concerned with actual intercourse between people who are not married; and the heart of the controversy concerns the behaviour of the unmarried girl.'

As the century reached middle age, luminaries such as the writer and broadcaster Marghanita Laski were saying that it was now accepted as all right for a girl to sleep with her boyfriend if marriage was in mind – as evidenced by her estimate of the number of girls marrying because they were pregnant. She put the figure at nearly 40 per cent of brides under twenty. The MGC cast the figure nearer 30 per cent, but this did not indicate acceptance of such a state of affairs.

'The right basis for personal and social life is that sexual intercourse should take place only within marriage,' they declared, citing the American Kinsey report *Sexual Behaviour in the Human Female*, which made it clear that women who had sex before marriage were twice as likely to be unfaithful after marriage.

Professor Mace told *Housewife* readers it was all the fault of the Victorians. He pointed out that, historically, our Western tradition followed the great Eastern civilisations in so valuing chastity among women as opposed to men because the integrity of the child-bearer appeared to matter more than that of the mere progenitor. But all the sensible reasons for chastity were lost during Victorian times when ignorance and fear became the lost key to the chastity belt, and the whole subject was so utterly unspeakable that it was impossible to discuss the logic behind the tradition.

Mace himself, writing in the fifties, sounds like a kindly old gentleman, apologetic about raising so improper a subject for public discussion. But his argument was 'needs must' because in dark corners all over the country, girls were surrendering to boys in the belief that this was the fifties' route to the altar and happy-ever-afterness; while anyone with the slightest understanding of male human nature might see the altar, but little in the way of bliss beyond. Forced marriage ended up with the girl feeling cheated, the boy trapped, and the baby resented. According to Mace, the girl had played her last card when she gave up her virginity. Pregnancy appeared to be inevitable, and the alternatives to marriage – abortion or an illegitimate birth – too dangerous or degrading to be worth the risk. The only answer was to reaffirm the value of chastity in the minds of young people by appealing to their better natures, telling them to forget about sex and concentrate on 'the creative tasks and obligations which should be love's fundamental expression'.

At the heart of the chastity debate was much more than concern for girls with unwanted babies and miserable marriages; there was the fear that here was the beginning of a decaying society. In Roman times civilisation had gone downhill with the brakes off when marriage began to lose its sanctity and became little more than licensed promiscuity. The Roman citizens, who tolerated a society where people married as many as twenty times, were party to their own doom for standing by and failing to lambast those who treated marriage like last season's toga. With the Romans in mind, 1950s Britain had to make a stand before it was too late, and Mrs Jean Mann MP made a start by suggesting that society should make fun of famous people who hopped in and out of marriage. Film stars and the like who, by Roman standards, married a modest four or five times, should be criticised and derided, she said, for casting off husbands as they would an old hat, and in so doing, setting a shocking example to the country's young people.

The business of upholding the sanctity of marriage was a tricky one for the third party in twentieth-century Britain, just as it had been for the onlooker in fifth-century Rome. The current debate extended to what should be done by a hostess who suspected goings on in her house between unmarried or adulterous guests. Should she go and make a scene in the middle of the night; not intrude at the time, but deliver a lecture in the morning; or pretend it was merely the plumbing system that caused all that creaking? The morally correct 1950s answer appears to have hovered somewhere between the midnight scene and the lecture, or courteous interruptus.

While chastity was an easy point of focus for the nation's concern over the future of a society which had always relied on marriage and the family as its bedrock there was, of course, consideration of other factors thought to influence the success or failure of marriage. In what was termed 'The English Kinsey', Dr Eustace Chesser's *The Sexual, Marital and Family Relationships of the English Woman*, marriage was shown to have a better chance of being happy if the English woman had not seen her parents having intercourse, did not expect her husband to change his habits or behaviour after marriage, stayed at home instead of going to work, and had a belief that sex could be pleasant. She was also more likely to be happy if she had only recently married.

Her husband, according to Shaw Desmond, the author of a book entitled *Adam and Eve*, was most likely to be happy if his wife had no more than a modicum of intelligence – just enough to give spice to their sex life.

Mr Desmond, who also wrote an advice column under the pseudonym 'A mother of five', declared marriage to be the greatest failure of all human institutions, and advocated what has become commonplace three and four decades on: trial marriage and trial love. 'I believe that sexual experience of one kind or another for girls of any age, with of course exceptions, is vital to their spiritual as well as mental development,' he said, while still insisting that men hated intelligence in their women. On the basis that those who want it both ways tend to end up with nothing, it's probably not surprising that Desmond had such a jaded view of marriage. He also predicted free divorce by declaration, but we'll have to wait and see about that one.

Whatever the state of marriage in the 1950s, those for and against it seem to have been united in placing the responsibility for its success on women. 'I am just an ordinary businessman,' began E. J. Schatz in an article called 'An ordinary man's solution to many divorce problems' in which he said that enough sex, intelligent or otherwise, would keep any man happy. He was, and is, probably correct, but maybe went a bit far in suggesting that the wife of a particular sex offender should have stood beside her husband in the dock 'since this unsavoury business started from the time when she refused him marital relations'. Wives who began to find sex distasteful had only to make a little extra effort and Schatz was convinced that the sum total of human happiness would be considerably increased.

Letters came in thick and fast in response to this universal panacea for the world's ills. One correspondent suggested that breakfast in bed on Sundays could be a good start, but others doubted the aphrodisiac powers of toast and marmalade. Fishing and bowls were put forward as alternatives to sex, but when it came to finding new interests outside the home, another letter-writer thought it was simply a matter of deciding between blonde and brunette.

Husbands who soldiered on through all the frustration and breakfast debris had, not surprisingly, a sour view of how a wife spent her day. 'Just look at my wife,' a *Times* reader said. 'What does she do? Messes about in the house for an hour or so after I've gone in the morning, goes out to coffee with her cronies, puts her feet up in the afternoon, goes out to tea with more cronies, gossips or worse still plays bridge, suddenly realises the old man is due home in half an hour, rushes home, opens a few tins and is always absolutely worn out by the time I get in.' Notice there is no mention of children, but this was an area where marriage in Britain was undergoing a huge change.

It was in the fifties that husbands began to be with their wives during childbirth. Some of the pioneering husbands fainted, some of the wives worried about not looking their best, even if a doctor of the day said their husbands were being given the opportunity of seeing 'indescribable radiance, such as only a Botticelli or Raphael can portray', but the shared experience was generally seen as strengthening and enriching and the beginning of shared child care as we know it today. And with one bride in six pregnant at the time of her wedding, according to statistics for 1957, plenty of couples had the opportunity for strength and enrichment from the outset.

The most common age for marriage at this time was 23 for men and 21 for women, but in 1957 two men under 30 married wives over 70, and two girls under 25 married men over 70. These four couples were unlikely to have taken part in one of the controversies of the day, the postponement of children, with those against delay arguing that young couples had become too concerned with material wealth, and that society would benefit from a return to big families on small budgets. There was a feeling that the country was becoming both childless and childish, that postponement of children was not just down to materialism, but immaturity among urban society. In the good old rural days, huge families meant children had to grow up quickly and find their own way in the world; but the children of small urban families were often still in full-time education in their twenties, and still being treated like children by parents, teachers and society in general. These 'children' were the sort of people who, when they did eventually marry, were too concerned with what was in the marriage for them, and when romantic passion waned, as inevitably it always did, they would divorce and start again. Marriage was becoming too selfish with all this misguided quest for romance, and couples were not doing themselves any good by thinking only of themselves. The experts of the day warned gloomily of lonesome old age, because only the level-headed large families knew about care and understanding from generation to generation where there was barely a gap between childhood and child-bearing.

Among the array of selfish reasons for postponing children was, of course, the higher education of women, which brings us back to the debate about working wives. Some of these women were not only failing to get on with having babies, but were also denying men sufficient opportunity to go to university. Those unfamiliar with the postponement of children debate argued that women shouldn't be educated to such a level because it was all a waste of time and money seeing as how they'd be off having babies within a couple of years of getting their degrees. Give all the university places to men if national resources were to be used wisely; and, for that matter, save the grammar schools for them, too. 'Home, the joys of motherhood and, as life wears on, the rich fulfilment of hope in grandchildren, remain always the central things in a woman's life,' said MP Mrs Mann, talking about marriage versus career. 'Without these things, a career, however brilliant, remains an empty shell.'

Nevertheless, Mrs Mann thought it a good idea for women over forty to find some sort of employment outside the home, if only to stop them interfering in the lives of their newly married sons and daughters. Mrs Mann had, perhaps, also read an article in the *Manchester Guardian* headed 'Just a Kept Woman', which detailed a conversation between a middle-aged wife and a newly married one. 'Will you take a job when you're settled in London?' 'Of course. What else would I be likely to do?' 'Well, you seem to take it for granted, but women who married before the war, like me, didn't go on working.' 'And do you mean to tell me that you expected your poor husbands to provide you with everything?' The older woman confided to the reader, 'The condemnation in her voice was like a slap in the face. I felt a worm . . . a parasite . . . a kept woman.'

The same writer went on to say, 'I won't pretend that I disliked the knowledge that I hadn't to turn out in the morning; that I could arrange the day's programme to suit myself. There was opportunity to do things I'd never had time for before – as long as they didn't cost too much. I joined a class at the School of Art, I helped with a newly established baby clinic, and I extended my work in the Girl Guide movement. There was no lack of interesting work, and play too, available to a woman with free afternoons.' Chastity had, perhaps, been under fire for quite a long time.

Anna is a woman in her late sixties, who still has splendid legs, a pretty face, and unchaste memories from the 1950s. She doesn't seem like the type to have been 'the other woman' – if type there is – not with her seedlings and cuttings sprouting gamely in the conservatory. What's more, she reminded me of Joyce Grenfell. But Anna had been 'the other woman' for nearly a decade, from her mid-twenties, carrying on an illicit affair with a married man nearly old enough to be her father. It was an affair that, when it did end, brought the most terrible tragedy and then mental anguish that was to last for years.

Anna's parents' marriage had ended in divorce when she was in her teens. Her mother came from a West Country family, well-to-do people in banking who might have been horrified, but weren't, when a young mining engineer turned up in Falmouth and was brought home to tea. 'My father was lovely and I adored him, but he was wild and Irish, and I think my grandparents were foolish to let my mother marry him so quickly.'

The marriage was itinerant from the start; they never stayed anywhere for long, not even in the disasters they fell into. Irish charm and Cornish money dug them out, but it was an unsettled life for Anna and her elder sister, made more so by the outbreak of war when Anna was fourteen. The family had been living in London, but with bombs on the way, Anna, her mother and sister evacuated to Cornwall; her father stayed behind with Anna's teacher, the woman he subsequently married.

'I hated it, my parents parting, and I resolved it would never happen to my kids. When you are left with one parent, you are used as a confidante and I came in for a lot of midnight pacings of the room – it takes a very strong-minded parent not to use his or her children in this way, and it was quite hard on me; but Mum was in her early forties, and that can be a difficult time for any woman. I felt that she was in the right, but I really loved my father – who was in the wrong.'

With all this turmoil going on at home, Anna still managed to do well at school, passing matriculation at sixteen, which was earlier than most. She became an art student, but it was the nights more than the days she remembers; the dances, with new partners every week spilling from the troop ships that came into Falmouth. 'I had a pretty good time and I was pretty irresponsible. I can remember my reaction to D-Day: it was "Damn, that's the end of the Thursday dances," because all the boys were off to France.

'I suppose I was heartless,' Anna says, sounding surprised and ashamed by the realisation. 'I had dozens of boyfriends and I teased them, perhaps beyond endurance; but it was more through ignorance than anything else. I dare say a lot of Jane Austen characters have done the same.'

As the war progressed, Anna tried to join up, but was turned down due to some obscure problem connected with her air tubes. The art college had turned out to be a disappointment, so she left and took a job as a governess before finally opting for office work and the job that was to be her undoing.

'The job was with a firm of marine surveyors and naval architects, and that was where I met my fate, my long-term lover, who was the junior partner. There were three of us in the office, him, the older partner, who was a dear old boy, and me, the typist and dogsbody. We were all extremely happy together for two years, then the old boy had a heart attack and died in the office. It was a shock. I had never seen anyone die before, and I was very fond of him.

'I stayed on, and after another year, the junior partner told me he had been in love with me for a long time. He was a good few years older than me (I was twenty-four and still a virgin, but not for long), and I was flattered, I hadn't dreamed of such a thing.

'I don't think I ever loved him, but I was very attracted to him. We had the office to ourselves, and any man can wear a girl down if he wants to enough. My mother might not have let me work in an office with such an attractive man, but he was a good boss and certainly not the "touch-typist"/"hands-on" type, even if he did make a beeline for me after he'd told me he loved me.

'Then I started getting in an awful state of worry and nerves about this affair; I didn't like taking Holy Communion any more, but I had to or my family would have known. I'm not terribly religious, but I was breaking the rules. The trouble was that he seemed to need me so desperately. He just longed to be able to get free of his present wife and marry me, but there would have been such a scandal, and I couldn't contemplate it with my mother and grandmother living in this small town.

'Eventually I told my mother, and wished I hadn't. She was absolutely, absolutely appalled, and I had a semi-breakdown. I left the job and my doctor told me it was time I got away from my mother as well, after all, I was twenty-seven.'

Throughout her affair, Anna, as well as taking Holy Communion to keep up appearances, also took up with other men, a stream of boyfriends with whom she conducted chaste relationships. Her lover, an extremely jealous man, absurdly encouraged these friendships because, no matter how painful the duplicity, it was the lesser evil compared with the shame of adultery in 1950s Falmouth.

Anna found a new job in a local hotel where she could live in, but the affair was not over. 'He caught up with me and I was sorry for him, but I would have given anything to finish it. He persuaded me to go up to London and get a job there so that he could come and see me and stay overnight once a month. This went on for a number of years until he felt he could ask his wife for a divorce without involving me. He told her the marriage wasn't working and that he was going to a new job in New York.'

The plan was for Anna to join him in due course and then they would marry. Everything seemed set, all the years of waiting and pretence about to be over, and even if Anna was still not in love, she was prepared to go along with what seemed to be her fate. Flattered, pitying and mesmerised, at the age of 34 she was still far from being her own woman, but a tragedy was about to take place that not only made her wake up, but has haunted her to this day. Throughout his marriage, Anna's lover had his mother-in-law living with him, and when the old lady found out that the marriage was ending she blamed herself and committed suicide.

It's not hard to imagine how Anna must have felt when she heard what had happened, but her lover said they had to go ahead with their plan or else all the suffering would have been for nothing; he even had the single-minded audacity to say that his mother-in-law's death would be without meaning unless Anna married him. 'I was still very fond of him, but a bit fed up.' Anna is not a woman to over-dramatise: everything about her whispers 'good form', and as she tells her story the most astonishing part is that she tells it at all.

If it wasn't the suicide back in Falmouth that finally broke the spell cast over her for the best years of her youth, it must have played a part in freeing her, and at about the same time she fell in love with another man. 'I was working in another hotel and so was he. We'd known one another for a year and then suddenly, for both of us, it just happened. I knew this was the man I loved and the only man I had ever loved.

'There was the most frightful bust-up with my lover. He had left his wife and was already living in America and waiting for me to join him. I wrote to him and he came home and tried to beat up the new man. I told him I hadn't meant to do it, but it had happened and what I'd had with him had gone. He went back to Cornwall – he was too ill to return to New York – and I never heard from him or of him again.'

Anna married her new love in 1960. She wore a blue floral shirtwaister with white accessories, and looking at the photo you'd never guess she had a past. She looks as prim and respectable as net curtains, and was married in the Catholic Church by the uncompromising Bruce Kent.

The marriage has worked well, defying Kinsey, but Anna has suffered periods of terrible depression, the jumping-out-of-the-window kind. She gave up her job soon after marriage and thought, 'Oh God, I'll go mad without anything to think about' and did. She had two children in two years, and after the second birth the baby had to be taken into care while she went into hospital for electric shock treatment. 'My mind had seized up and I wasn't safe to look after a baby. I think it was all a throw-back to the affair and the horror of that suicide.' Tony Hancock was in the hospital at the same time, and even if ultimately the treatment failed him, his being there made Anna feel better.

But the depression came back, and there was more shock treatment. Anna lost chunks of memory, became epileptic, had to give up her driving licence. Her husband was stalwart throughout, but didn't really understand about depression, never having known it himself. 'He just sighed deeply and carried on. His idea of sympathy was to say "poor old thing" and leave it at that.' But depression, even if other people do understand, is, by its nature, suffered in isolation. Eventually, after years of torment – if not depressed, then waiting for depression to descend – Anna was given a drug which has finally banished the 'black dog' and given her peace of mind. 'I certainly paid for that affair, one way and another,' she says, 'but my marriage has come up to expectations, barring all the wretched illness. My husband was such a rest, so easy compared with my lover; he's a bit of an MCP, he doesn't think I can drive (the epilepsy has gone and Anna has her licence back), but he's not a possessive man. The affair didn't seem to bother him all that much, although I think he expected me to forget about it too quickly. I went on worrying about it, and hurt his feelings by talking about it. We've had our quarrels where I've said "Right! I'm leaving you", but we've been pretty happy, really.

'I suppose the affair has been a taboo subject, certainly it has with my mother and sister. They were so appalled and it has never, ever been mentioned.'

Even more unmentionable in the 1950s was another kind of affair; in fact, getting found out could still land you in jail at that time.

Jim and Phil met in 1954 in Belfast. They're not married; they can't be, but they say theirs is a marriage just like any other. 'I just quote Virginia Woolf – "it takes all sorts . . ." says Jim, with a theatrical flourish of bronzed arms that look as if they would have managed in the shipyards where his mother saw his future forty years ago. But Jimmy is an actor, quietly successful on both the stage and television, the type who plays hard men, IRA chiefs, the bully boy with the butting bald head and military moustache.

He was fifteen, still a schoolboy, when he met Phil, then twice his age. He'd been brought up in the sort of poverty that was so extreme it became a joke: 'You grew up in a cardboard box? You were lucky. We only had a paper bag – and we had to share that with another family.' Jim's bag was a mean little terraced house beside the Belfast shipyards, peopled by a strong-willed mother, a sister and a darling grandfather who'd spent his life at sea. Father was someone Jim only ever met twice. Grandfather did his best to feed the family; even when all else was pawned, with the help of the shotgun that one Christmas finished off the two resident swans in Victoria Park.

It was grandfather who pushed for Jim to go to the grammar school instead of the yards, who saw how clever Jim was, how artistic and likely to succeed. 'We had to scrape and scrimp to get hold of a second-hand uniform, but I took it on as a challenge and I had a wonderful time, marvellous teachers, and I did very well, thank you very much.'

Particularly well in drama and the arts. 'I played truant to go and watch the ballet and opera, and it got me into trouble, but the headmaster – well, he realised I was gay.' So did Phil.

Phil was 32 and working for the BBC in Belfast. His background was as different from Jim's as either could imagine possible. Phil went to public school, and there was no question of a second-hand uniform; his family was wealthy in the manner of old money and servants. Like Jim, his penchant was strongly towards the arts ('he's a terrible actor' says Jim, in a camp whispered aside), but he was good at science and maths, and sport. 'My uncle was a painter, which is where the artistic bit came from, and there were lots of cousins; always at Christmas we did a play, and at school I started a cine club. At the outbreak of war the BBC was short of people and I got in at eighteen and remained there until I retired.' He started as a radio engineer, then joined the RAF as a pilot for the rest of the war, flying the Mosquitos that bugged the night fighters from Germany, 'bending' their radar to deflect the bomb drops. After the war he moved into production, working on *Children's Hour*, *Uncle Mac*, *Toy Town*, *Jennings at School*. The posting to Belfast was to help set up television.

Meeting the fifteen-year-old Jim is a moment still vivid in the memory of both men. Jim, hungry for contact with the world of art and drama, had discovered a late-night place where others with the same hunger met in the dark to watch television's first arts programme, *Monitor*. 'That night it was something to do with the Age of Kings,' remembers Phil. 'I had arrived late. During the programme my hand touched another hand along the back of a sofa, and we kept hold; but when the lights went up I saw that the other person was wearing a school blazer.'

Phil himself had realised his homosexuality as a schoolboy. He'd had an affair with another boy ('an unconsummated affair,' specifies Jim). 'You'll grow out of it,' his father had said. Phil didn't, didn't want to. He'd had a couple of affairs before he met Jim. A week after the touching of hands, Jim went to his flat, a lavish abode full of mahogany and family silver. Tchaikovsky's 'Pathétique', Jim's favourite, was playing, supper was out of this world, and there was a log fire. 'It was terribly romantic and I just started to cry like mad,' says Jim. 'I was so happy because I had met someone with whom I wanted to spend my life.'

'I was looking for someone my own age,' says Phil. 'But when Jim came up to the flat that first night here was this highly sophisticated young man who didn't appear to feel out of place. I thought it would last six months and then he'd find someone his own age, but he said "no", this was for keeps. I was totally besotted with him. He took me by storm. There was so much love and power.

'Obviously to begin with I was very conscious that I was in love with a fifteen-year-old. It was totally illegal – this was 1954 in homophobic Northern Ireland. I worried about him feeling a "kept" boy, I tried not to spoil him; there was no pocket money.' 'But instead of going up to the "gods", I could sit in the stalls,' adds Jim. Even so, the money and Phil's sports car were not what impressed Jim: 'I just knew that Phil was the person I wanted to spend my life with, who I was in love with.' Homosexual or heterosexual, fifteen is young to know, but Jim has never wavered in his love for Phil, not even during the year they spent apart when he went to America to study drama.

It was a broken ankle that made it possible for them to start living together while Jim was still at school. Jim had a part in *Androcles and the Lion*, but while the production was still in rehearsal, he broke his ankle playing basketball. Phil's flat was close by rehearsals, and it was the single-minded headmaster who suggested that Jim should move in so that the play could go on.

Jim never moved out, even after he won a place at Queen's University. To the outside world, he was Phil's ward, his protégé; his mother became Phil's cleaning lady, but it was twenty years before she knew her son was gay, and even then perhaps she preferred not to take any notice. Grandfather, who had seen the world, said, early on, 'so what'.

From Belfast, Phil and Jim moved to Dublin, then London. Jim, claiming all the artistic rights, swept away the mahogany and the silver; the house they share today is velvety against stone-covered walls, comfy, cosy and chic. For the past ten years, since Phil took early retirement from the BBC, they say they have lived out of each other's pockets with Phil at home a lot of the time and Jim, like nearly all actors, working spasmodically. 'A lot of heterosexual couples have found this difficult, being together all the time, but we get on very well, we like an awful lot of the same things. It seems boring and dull, though not to us, but we've never had a row, never screamed in anger, never had what I would call a "wolfy"; little tiffs, that's all.' 'At the end of the day,' says Phil, 'you have to climb into bed with your lover.'

'A lot of people, heterosexual and homosexual, come to us and ask our advice about their relationships. We are incredibly lucky people. We don't have the piece of paper to say we are married, and we don't need it; the only reason we'd want it would be if it gave us total equality with heterosexual people in things like pensions, where a wife goes on getting half after her husband's death. We're not religious, so that part wouldn't mean anything.' 'I'm terribly anti-religion,' says Jim, 'having grown up in Northern Ireland.' 'I'm not as far away from it as he is,' says Phil. 'Well, you've got a brother who's a vicar,' informs Jim.

A cup of tea is suggested. Jim hovers in the doorway of his kitchen (and it is *his* kitchen – Phil hasn't cooked a meal for years). 'I think it's so important to say "thank you", not to take it for granted that meals and cups of tea are going to be made and put in front of you,' he says. Phil, whose upbringing would make it very difficult for him not to say 'thank you', agrees. He says his parents, between whom he never heard a cross word, were his role models for happy, harmonious living together, and there were homosexual couples at the BBC, who'd been together years and years and knew all about how to make relationships work. 'It's an attitude of mind towards your partner. I don't own him and he doesn't own me. I must earn his love every day, and he must earn mine. Put it this way, my love battery is there to supply the current for him, and vice versa; of course batteries run down, but you can't self-charge them . . . it's in the very simple things . . . when I was fifteen, I asked my mother "What is this love thing between you and father?" She said, "It's the toothpaste tube – not minding about it being squeezed from the middle." Jim's not a tidy person, and I can't stand untidiness, but the thing is not to get niggled by it. Why should someone do everything the way you want it? When you meet someone and fall in love, you suddenly realise you're not number one anymore.' Jim places a mug of tea beside Phil's chair. 'Darling, thank you,' Phil says.

What about the idea that in homosexual relationships one partner tends to play the female role and the other the male? 'I hate using this role thing, and I don't think it applies,' says Jim. 'We fit into our natural niches and it's fifty-fifty division of labour.' 'Jim loves cooking, which, I suppose, is usually the wife's role, but I do all the washing-up and cleaning.' 'And there aren't the same expectations and pressures on us as there are on heterosexual couples. We're not expected to be randy like the husband or chaste like the wife, we don't play those roles and never have, wouldn't know how to – it's easier if you're homosexual.'

What about children? With all that talent for life, love and home-making, wouldn't children have been nice? 'My sister has had five children and having them has had a profound effect on her psyche. Of course, gay people don't have that, we have an easier life. Children are a pressure – I mean, a blessing – we don't have; and for me, being an actor, the financial side isn't such a worry – I don't know how hetero-sexual actors cope when they have children.'

Phil and Jim sit in their velvety chairs, plenty of space between them, yet you only have to be in the room with them to know they are a couple, that there is love there and that feeling of solid permanence that attracts others as if to a life-raft. Only once have they been apart, the year when Jim, as a young man, felt he had to prove to himself that he was not a 'kept' person; when he went to America on the advice of actor Eric Porter and studied drama. He went on a Fulbright Scholarship and an Arts Council grant, and proved the point, although he wrote to Phil every day, sent a tape once a week, and was never in any doubt that he would return. It was 1963, the year Kennedy was assassinated, and four years before sex between consenting adult males became legal in Britain. Everyone over forty remembers where they were and what they were doing when Kennedy died, but it's difficult to set the memory in an era when people in this country like Jim and Phil could still be sent to prison for their love.

Jim loved America, the energy of the place, and he would have liked to have lived there, but Phil couldn't cope with the materialism, the emphasis on what you had rather than what you were, the same concern that had been plaguing marriage experts in Britain, who, having read Kinsey, saw everything British following the American way. Jim came home to London, to the London of the 1960s; but wasn't this to be the time for Britain to take the lead? I seem to remember it that way. After all, we had The Beatles, and they were about more than pop music. It was the time of Super Mac and 'You've never had it so good'; the decade when girls like me suddenly stopped dressing and thinking as our mothers always had. It was when young people became a separate category in society, a new socio-economic group buoyed up by 'purple hearts', hairspray and hype. But marriage was still the thing to do, and living together without it was still a sin and social shame, whether immoral or illegal, although at the time the illegality of Phil and Jim's relationship was still seen as immoral, too.

6 To love, honour and obey any reasonable request

I F CHASTITY WAS under fire in the fifties, obedience was in for a tentative knocking come the early sixties, with both girls and boys beginning to question that bugbear of many a bolshy bride, the awful four-letter word 'obey' in the marriage ceremony, and all that it implied. 'If a wife is willing to be a good wife she should be willing to do anything, but I don't think she should have to obey her husband,' said a young teenage girl, caught up in a 1960 survey. 'He might say to her, "Go and get the coal in", "Put the new spark plugs in the car" or "Go and chop the wood". The wife would get into a mess with the coal, she'd probably chop her fingers off chopping wood, and more than likely ruin the car for life . . . anyway, the woman usually obeys her husband in some things, because even when he says, "Go and make a cup of tea, dear", unless he says "please" I still think it's a command.'

'I think that a wife should obey her husband because the men are supposed to be the bosses of the house and the women are always jabbering like old gasbags, and talking over the fence to another old gasbag, always always talking. Women should cut out the gaff and get on with some work,' a 1960 schoolboy opined. He and his friends were asked what they would do if their wives refused to obey. 'Get in that ruddy kitchen and get my dinner!' they shouted, making swiping movements with their arms. Yet the same boys were said to fill their school essays with exquisite maidens and queenly brides, and weakened over the idea of wifely obedience when it came to dealing with babies, the girls pointing out that not only were they incapable of having them, but also of washing them properly: '. . . they might use Brobat or Parazone or something.' The girls had the last word, suggesting that both parties to the marriage should agree to obey *any reasonable request.*

A group of older teenagers were asked what they thought was the main reason for marriage, and while the majority replied, without hesitation, 'love', some said 'to have a family', and one, memorably, replied, 'to have someone to live with when your mother dies'.

Morals, of course, were still a strong talking-point, with the complaint that the word 'immorality' in the middle of the twentieth century meant sexual misbehaviour, even if the Archbishop of Canterbury was to declare in 1963 that fornication was not necessarily the worst sin, spiteful talk could be as bad. But more concerned with action than words, Ceridwen Higginson, writing in *Christian Comment*, said: 'There may well have never been in all history such an uncharted no man's land for teenagers to struggle through. There is not one positive direction sign left to guide the young unmarried in their relations with each other. Instead there is a sort of Pilgrim's Progress country. On the one hand are the Delectable Mountains, representing good and faithful marriage. This is unquestionably good and desirable. On the other hand is the Quagmire of Immorality and Vice, which is very nasty. In between, where once the boundary ran, is a wide Wilderness. In this region wander the adolescents of today. The Mountains shine but seem a long way off, and the Quagmire, though smelly and repellent, is also fascinating.' Hadn't it always been so? Perhaps not. Paul Johnson, writing in the *New Statesman* in the early sixties, shortly after the *Lady Chatterley* trial, said: 'It is a moot point whether the publication of *Lady Chatterley* will damage the morals of young people; what cannot be disputed is that the trial reinforced the impression that sex is the dominant issue of the age.' Incidentally, the title of Mr Johnson's piece was 'Are Virgins Obsolete?' It is impossible to imagine the question being posed or even considered today, but he concluded that in 1963 virginity was still 'a girl's best friend'.

I think he was right about the dominant issue, and as a virginal twelve-year-old in 1962, I remember trotting along to my local library and asking for a copy of *Lady Chatterley's Lover*. The librarian asked me if my mother knew I had come to borrow this book, and, looking her straight in the eye, I lied 'yes' with all the coming immorality of my generation. The book was brought forth from a back room and I hurried home to wrap its wickedness, and mine, in a plain brown-paper cover. I found the incomprehensible passages by using the Quagmire method, thumbing through until I reached the grubby, dog-eared pages. I took the book to school, a convent from which I was later expelled for other sorts of misbehaviour – and promptly had it confiscated. The Reverend Mother/head-mistress, a saint of a woman, more widely read than I had imagined, summoned me to her study, and there we agreed that it was a boring old book and not worth all the fuss. There again, her being a nun, and me only twelve, maybe neither of us knew what it was all about.

Of greater interest to me a year or two later might have been Joan Biggar's *Dating without Tears*, published by Mills & Boon. Her advice began with how to get a date: 'Little flutters of the hands to add expression to your conversation . . . a smile and a graceful flutter of the fingers will bring him over like a magnet . . . little smiles, a sweet curving of the lips, little wide-eyed glances followed by a modest downcasting of the gaze.'

Having secured a date, how did a girl then conduct herself? Mrs Biggar had several suggestions in the way of opening gambits to stimulate conversation: 'Can there really be such things as ghosts?' was one, another: 'Why does radio reception always seem better at night?' It was better not to try to appear too clever, and advisable to avoid petting on the grounds that one thing would lead to another. But should the worst come to the worst, a sudden switch to serious conversation could fend off unwelcome advances: 'A sexless subject like the Common Market or the leader in *The Times* may stop him pressing his mouth spongily over yours in the middle of a sentence.'

In a similar genre, Barbara Cartland moved on to marriage in her 1960s offering *Husbands & Wives*, another 'how to' book, in which the newly married were exhorted to be content with nothing less than 'the fringe of splendour', to be achieved, you must have guessed it, via the stomach. Vitality being the key, Miss Cartland stressed the virtues of good food for beauty and vigour, and the value of protein foods as sexual stimulants, pointing out that wives in the kitchen had greater power than perhaps they realised. I met the great foodie a decade later when I was a junior reporter on her local newspaper. She was widowed by then, but still brim-full of vitality, and she told me that she had a man every year. I don't know what she gave him to eat, but I was given the most filthy cup of tea I have ever tasted, together with a dollop of honey.

The sixties was the new age of uncertainty, but most young people wanted more than a taste of honey. Couples were marrying younger than ever before, the most common age for women marrying in 1960 was 21, and for men, 22. This was no great change for women, but young husbands were something new. It was a trend throughout all the advanced industrial countries, and due entirely to a buoyant economy, full employment and good wages. Young men felt confident enough to take on the responsibility, which was still primarily theirs, of financing the married way of life. But the closeness in age between husband and wife made it difficult for him to command and for her to obey.

The new young husband in the early sixties was more of a companion to his wife than lord and master. Saturdays were spent looking in the shops together, planning the dream home, which cost a good deal more than the £160 the average couple needed and could afford to spend furnishing their first house. This new male interest in home-making was cited as the main reason for the demise of mother-in-law jokes. They weren't funny any more because everyone was on the same side. 'When you're married and got a little baby, it's something to work for. You've got responsibilities. Before, I never knew what home was. It was always the all-night caffs for me. I'm not all that interested now. The boys are getting married anyway and that,' an eighteen-year-old husband explained.

Among the people who comment on trends were those who thought it reckless to marry so young, and that in some instances it was little more than a sortie in the war against parents. Others, foreseeing the collapse of affluent society, talked gloomily of long-term debt, both personal and national, of family life breaking under the strain. But all this was in the future, and optimistic commentators in the early sixties dismissed the public scandals like the Profumo affair and declared the conduct and morals of the British people to be higher than ever before. A. J. P. Taylor said: 'There is far more real feeling in the present-day love affairs of young people than in the old ones, and they ripen far more often into stable happy marriages. In my opinion, today's younger generation is the sanest and the most moral ever known.'

A.J.P. was being quoted by Dr Ronald Fletcher, who delivered the 1963 Herbert Gray Lecture at the Royal Society of Medicine. The lecture created a sensation because, while congratulating the nation on its high state of morals, Dr Fletcher put forward the notion that marriage should no longer be seen as the only place for sex. He went further: 'The conception of marriage as a legitimation of sex is itself immoral. Now that sex is dispossessed of sinfulness and is regarded as a natural and enjoyable impulse and experience, and now that contraceptive techniques make possible the experience of sexual intimacy without reference to procreation, sexual intimacy and marriage are no longer going to be thought synonymous. It is of the very greatest importance that young people should not enter into marriage on the grounds of the mounting pressure of the desire to sleep with each other.

'Though it is true that people may make mistakes and suffer deception and exploitation in sexual relations before marriage, it is equally true that the same things can happen within marriage. The truth is that people in general never think about the ethics of sex within marriage, only outside it. And their attitude is a rather appalling implication that once marriage has occurred less concern need be felt about these matters: sex is now safely confined, firmly controlled, hedged round with social and legal safeguards. But this, too, clearly involves treating individuals not as ends in themselves but only as a means to what is thought to be a socially necessitous regulation of sex.

'In short, such a conception of marriage, as a kind of social or religious impounding of the sexual impulse, only to be allowed out on presentation of a licence, is itself immoral.'

Dr Fletcher had not finished, he still had the Church lined up for a broadside: sex was no longer sacred, and neither was marriage. 'If there was one sad feature of social policy during

1963 it was the vision of the Church standing in the way of the humane reform of the divorce law on unethical grounds. One can put the matter as simply as this: if the Church maintains with such rigour that true marriage should be founded only on mutual love, how can it possibly maintain with equal rigour that marriage should be perpetuated when that same love has ceased? Is this not a fantastic inconsistency – a religious insistence upon an immoral situation? And is it not, again, a treatment of individuals not as ends in themselves, but as a means only in relation to the idea of an unalterable sacrament? – an idea, it may be noted, held only by a minority.'

The Marriage Guidance Council, under whose auspices the lecture had been held, was quick to denounce Dr Fletcher's ideas, and time has proved him wrong on a further comment about divorce. He said there was no need to be unduly worried about divorce statistics, that there was no evidence to suggest a prevailing desire for divorce among young people which would lead to an increase in the figures if the law were changed. When he said this the divorce rate was running at less than four per thousand marriages, compared with nearly nine just after the Second World War, but more than thirteen by the mid-1980s.

He was also somewhat adrift concerning the Church, if the number of church weddings versus civil was anything to go by. Religious dogma may have been held by only a minority, but the majority of couples – 70 per cent – still preferred to marry in church, and most of the brides at that time, including Princess Margaret, promised to 'obey' their husbands.

Pam was an obedient sixties bride: 'It was just part of the service and I accepted it. Mind you, my husband's not like that, he doesn't tell me what to do.' She and Barry married in 1966, and remember it as 'the year of the World Cup' – the year the England football team won.

Twenty-five years on, Pam and Barry still live in the three-bedroomed semi-detached house they bought before the wedding. It's a homely place, rooms leading into one another without corridors, a vague smell of slow cooking; comfy, organised clutter, a wife who doesn't go out to work. Pam and Barry are Londoners who knew what they wanted when they married, a quiet life out in the provinces, but not too far for visits home. 'We drew a fifty-mile radius and ended up here, north of London. Anywhere south would have been too expensive for us.'

Pam grew up in a council flat. Her father was a bus conductor, her mother a cleaner. Family life was unexceptional, but good, and the only way Pam and Barry wanted their life together to be different was in owning their own home. Theirs was the era when this became widely possible for young couples who hitherto would have expected to take rooms in someone else's house. Finding somewhere to buy was the big thing, dictating the date of the wedding, even the nature of the marriage, often a partnership devoted to mortgage repayment – renting had never so cemented a relationship in bricks and mortar. 'We just wanted to have a place of our own and to get married,' Pam says.

She was twenty when she met Barry. She was working as a secretary to a water purification company in Holborn, and Barry was with the electricity board. They met at a dancing school, Pam's 'Mecca': 'Dancing was the love of my life, I'd go seven nights a week sometimes, otherwise it was the pictures or parties. We weren't into drugs or anything in those days, not like young people today.

'I really enjoyed my youth. We all had record-players – we were well into music, Tommy Steele, we were Buddy Holly fans, The Beatles, Dusty Springfield, they were my favourites. I was never all that keen on Elvis, but he grew on me as I got older. There were little gangs of us and we'd meet in one another's houses and play the number one record.'

Barry's first love was stock-car racing, and, inevitably, dancing gave way to weekends under canvas and the rev and flow of old bangers. When Barry and Pam met, he was going out with her friend's sister, but he was by himself that first night at the dancing school. 'You had your dad's car, the Humber Hawk, remember?

'It really started at my twenty-first. My friend's sister said she didn't really want to go out with him and I said I did. After six months he said maybe we ought to get engaged. When we got the ring [a diamond] we said we would be engaged for a year, during which time we hoped to find a place. It was just coming into fashion to get a house instead of rooms.

'You had to book up a long way in advance for the hall and everything, so we thought we would make it Easter 1966, but as things turned out we got this house sooner than we'd expected. It was £3,400 on a twenty-five-year mortgage. We worked out that it would be cheaper to bring the wedding forward rather than pay both our families to live at home, and pay the new mortgage. We never considered living together before we were married – you didn't do that in them days. Our parents wouldn't have liked it, no, it wouldn't have gone down at all well.'

Pam and Barry paid for most of their wedding themselves. There were more than a hundred guests at the reception and it cost about £250. Pam's dress was £20, and there was a week's honeymoon in Hastings. The total expenditure took all the money they had saved to furnish the house, and the result was a collection of second-hand and make-do and a decision to wait five years before starting a family: 'We decided we weren't going to have children until we'd got all new stuff, isn't that right, Barry?'

In this marriage Pam does the talking. It takes a while for Barry to say much, but he gives the impression of being a good listener, a solid, reliable type to have around the house. Pam went on working for the appointed five years but lost her first baby; her son was born seven years after the wedding. More children would have been nice, three was the plan, but there were miscarriages and then two cats instead. There's never been any question of Pam going back to work; Barry likes her to be at home and so does she – it's how they planned things to be.

'We think we are lucky. When we first got married I didn't think we would last,' Pam says. 'I had the "itch" at three years, then at ten years. To make twenty-five years is pretty good going. I should say seventy-five per cent of the people we know have been divorced, some of them two or three times.

'We used to argue a lot, violently sometimes. I just wanted my own way. I'd rush out of the house for a few hours, go round to a friend. I think it helped, my parents being fifty miles away; if they'd been closer I'd probably have gone home to them and that would have made it harder to have gone back.'

'When we got married we said it was "till death us do part",' says Barry. 'You make a commitment and you honour it. My life is like that – it's the only way I see life, not to give up at the first hurdle – otherwise I'd have given up in the first month. I think you know one another better in the first two weeks of marriage than at any time before, however long you've been together. You have got to want it to succeed and to stick at it.'

This man is stickability incarnate. 'I never thought about the marriage not lasting,' he says, pausing, as if this is the first time in 25 years he has ever considered the possibility. Do they see themselves as romantic, I ask? 'We're not a hand-holding couple, and Barry's not one for walking down the street carrying a big bunch of flowers. It would be nice if he did.'

'I have done sometimes.'

'Only by Interflora.'

But flowers, however they are delivered, can be a lazy way of being romantic. Tireless everyday effort on each other's behalf is more Pam and Barry's style, with the occasional bit of something extra special. When Barry had his 50th birthday, Pam decided to throw a surprise party and went to amazing lengths to ensure that it was a surprise. She hired the local St John Ambulance headquarters, invited all the family and friends, made elaborate do-it-yourself catering arrangements, and then planned an intricate exercise in deceit that had Barry turning up on the night thinking he'd gone there to mend a fuse, and might have had him worried if he'd ever really thought about the marriage not lasting. The party was a huge success, even if Barry was wearing his oldest jacket in anticipation of the darker reaches of a fuse cupboard, and Pam says it was worth all the effort, a night to remember, and, yes, a piece of true romance.

Pam and Barry's son, now eighteen, walks through the living-room several times while I am there. Pam hopes he will marry, but not too young. She says she wants him to enjoy himself first, as if there is some sort of assumption that he won't afterwards, as if her 25 years enjoyably married has been some sort of fluke. She says it will leave a bit of a gap in their lives when the boy goes, when it's just the two of them going along together, her and Barry; but there's always plenty to do in the house, the one they got married for, and the next 25 years, well, they look like going according to plan.

Wives like Pam were suddenly, and patronisingly, hailed as economic miracles in the sixties, as if society already had an inkling of the writing on the wall. 'It may well be generally assumed that married men and women enter into some sort of economic partnership; its character is not, however, made nearly as clear as it might be,' said C. H. Vereker, talking to the Merseyside MGC in May 1960 about the paradox of marriage. 'One of the reasons for this,' he continued, 'may possibly be that wives are not in any precise sense paid for their services. They have their "keep" as it is called, and they may in addition have "pin money" or its equivalent. Their services, however, are not reckoned in cash value; and the whole of this vast and important group of economic activities does not figure in the national accounts. This is, indeed, blessedly anti-inflationary; and this is one of the great things which women do in our society. I worked out once how many women I should need to replace my wife and what it would cost me, were I to pay each of them for her services. I needed about six at a cost of between three and four thousand pounds a year; and all this I now get for what is called "love". The dilemma is alarming. If we were to give up wives and love, either we could appoint cooks, nurserymaids, secretaries, girlfriends and so on, if we had the money, or else sustain a terrifying reduction in our standard of living.'

It was time for another round of correspondence about the status of women. 'I didn't know they had any,' was one attempt to quash the debate. A woman had social prestige only through the status of her husband. Outside the home, she was a shadow of her man. Surveys of the day confirmed this, with one respondent, a college-educated woman, unwittingly pointing to the overwhelming trend of a decade or two hence: 'I get tired of having my few personal contacts outside my family in which I am anything more than my husband's shadow. He does not realise this, fortunately, and one day, when the children are bigger, I may be able to escape, if I am still sound in wind and limb.'

The debate ranged around the uncomfortable financial dependency of wives, which, of course, was key to their status. It was mooted that wives should be allotted an amount from the family exchequer as of right, but the idea fell on stony ground. 'When a husband refuses to consider such an arrangement I feel that his resistance should be respected, not labelled "selfishness", "intolerance", "bullying", etc.,' wrote Mrs Margaret Macfarlane of Doune, Perthshire. 'I believe that it is really difficult for some men to deal with money in this way. Their mastery of the money is inextricably bound up with their pride, their "overlordship" – their very manhood. This may be hard to accept, but before a wife insists upon any financial distribution, she might weigh what she will gain against what might be lost. May I add that I always read about these matters with interest, and profit.'

And getting a job was not the answer. A Derby wife wrote: 'I have just been reading an article in this morning's *Mirror* about marriages being broken up. I think I know the reason why there is alot, there is nothing upsets a child or a grown up, to come home and find no fire and Mother or Wife to greet them, it is this going out to work that does alot of it, I am a Mother of five, I had them all in less than nine years, so you see we had a terrible struggle, they all had a secondary education, and there was no allowances then, but it never occurred to me to go out to work, nothing pleased them more than to see a nice fire and me to greet them, if only to shout at them, in fact my Hubby is still the same, smiles all over his face when walks in at night after being out all day at work, it is alright getting all this money, but it does not buy happiness, the same as we have known for 40 years in May, that is all I can think of, that causes these upsets, I have opened up my thoughts to you, so I will say I remain yours truly, Mother of Five.'

The last word on sixties status came from Lena Jeger, who argued that women and men had been rendered equal by the dark side of science. From the beginning of time, man had protected woman, but the advent of mass means of destruction had made the sexes equally destructible. 'Now brave men can no longer fight to defend us from the greatest dangers – they are as helpless and vulnerable as we are. The bitter irony of truth is that modern science has produced the most significant status leveller of all, for it has thrust on us the most terrible, brutal, absolute equality.'

Did anyone take much notice of this terrible truth? In relation to marriage, I think not; other matters were still more weighty. 'You would be amazed at the number of young women in this country whose greatest wish in life is to be top-heavy,' a sixties 'agony aunt' told readers of *The Listener*. ' "My boyfriend admires these pin-up girls with large busts. Mine is only $32^{1}/_{2}$. I'm sure he will leave me if I can't increase it. So please can you give me a bigger bust? I enclose a stamped addressed envelope." ' But almost by return of post, we all wanted to be thin. Post-war plumpness, the indicator of plenty, had to shrink into mini-skirts and a new era of less wholesome excess.

7 The life and times of the Bigamy Queen

INDING THE Bigamy Queen was not easy. I had an address in the southern reaches of Birmingham, but the directions she'd given me were difficult to follow; right turns were left turns, and, like her, I kept taking the wrong road. And then when I found the block of flats I started wondering whether it was all a wild goose chase, because surely nobody still lived here.

It had started to rain, but I parked the car in another street, away from the vandalised ruin of stacked homes. A smashed wardrobe, crumbly pieces of bricks and mortar littered the pathway, but there was a working lift, a dank metal cage with the stench of stale life, and an incongruously pleasant and helpful man inside who told me he knew how to reach number 65, but not that he lived there, that he was husband number ten.

Pat Hinton, a round-faced Welsh woman in her thirties, opened the battered door of number 65 and led me along a narrow hallway into Shangri-La, or a close approximation. The room is the sort of picture you see in Sunday colour supplements, how to make something out of worse than nothing. Malcolm, husband number ten, has made the room nice for Pat. It didn't take him long, a bit of bricklaying, painting and papering; a desperate veneer over the inevitable decay. Pat says they won't be there long, that it isn't where they want to be, and, besides, the whole block is due for demolition. There's a dog, a gentle, friendly mutt introduced as a child-substitute – Pat found him in a dustbin when he was no bigger than the top tier of a wedding cake, otherwise, it's just Pat and Malcolm in the flat. They've been married six weeks, and on the coffee table there's the bridal bouquet to prove it, a spray of artificial red and white blooms, optimistically shielded against fading by a flimsy sheath of plastic. I've been talking with Pat for half an hour when Malcolm comes in, the man in the lift who didn't say who he was, slight of build, a face brushed with melancholy; he mutters something about always being on the go, mending things for other people. He has a hammer in his hand. Pat is his second wife.

Pat, an aide-memoire on the arm of her chair, is ready to begin the story of her ten marriages, some legal, others not, most of them much the same. She has averaged a new husband every two years over the past twenty, though few of the marriages lasted beyond six months, the majority ending in violence and weary disappointment. Yet hope has never died, and she says it's all been worth it to reach the point where she is now, because this time it's going to work. This time it's true love, and the rest is just history.

Growing up in Wales in the fifties and sixties, Pat had no idea until she was sixteen that her family was not as it seemed, that from the start her life was blighted by pretence. She didn't know that her parents were really her grandparents and that she'd been adopted by them when she was a year old. The revelation came during an argument with her 'sister', who suddenly pulled rank and asked her just who she thought she was talking to. 'I had a carving knife in my hand, and I wanted to stab her. I felt I had been betrayed.'

Her sister-cum-mother had given birth at sixteen, and Pat was to do the same, but not before a tragedy took place that haunts her more than all the failed marriages. Newly pregnant, newly reconciled with her real mother, she voiced a craving for sweets. Her mother, anxious to make amends, to comply with her daughter's every whim, set off with her to the sweet shop. 'We were about to cross the road when she suddenly pushed me out of the way and was hit herself by a car. At the hospital she said "If you leave me I'll be dead when you get back," but I had to go to telephone the family. "I'll not see my grandchild born" were her last words. The bloke who hit her was never caught, but I blame myself for having that craving. When my son was born, he was her double and I couldn't touch him. I felt she had come back to haunt me.'

Pat did eventually touch her baby, and, abandoning plans

to have him adopted, married his father, a tyre-fitter. But within the year, she'd taken the baby back home to her family and run away to join the fair. Her first husband, like many to come, had turned to the bottle and battery.

After her first divorce she married a soldier and went with him to live in Hong Kong. A martial arts expert, he literally got on her nerves, inflicting the sort of torture that gets Amnesty International involved in cases outside marriage. His tastes all round were more exotic than she'd bargained for, and when he brought home another woman to share their bed, Pat informed him that she wasn't inclined towards exhibitionism, and went for him with a pair of scissors. Six months later, and back in England, she took a chance and married number three, hoping for a settled life. That lasted three months, number four, six months, number five, the same. Pat talks of 'binning' marriages. Her sixth husband battered her so badly that she ended up in hospital, her internal injuries so severe that she had to have her womb taken away.

Some of these marriages were legal, others bigamous, but the men weren't to know either way, and Pat never told them. She says they didn't understand her, they didn't listen, but there was always this huge lie blocking any possibility of lasting happiness. Pat would break down and cry, but she couldn't tell her husbands why, and pretty soon they'd give up wanting to know.

Pat blames the Army for her bigamous routine. Seven of her husbands were soldiers, and she says she married them simply because there was no other way she could live with them. The Army does not allow unmarried cohabitation in its quarters, and Pat and her son had no other home. The grandparents who'd brought her up had died, her mother was dead, and there simply wasn't anyone or anywhere else for her. 'You don't get a lot of choice in blokes, living in garrison towns. A lot of them marry to get out of barracks and have a glorified skivvy, that's how it felt.'

The saddest part of Pat's story is the loss of her son. Having found it impossible to give him up for adoption as she'd originally planned, she was eventually forced to let him go when he was eight years old. As a small child he had watched his mother being abused and beaten by a succession of men in uniform, one hardly distinguishable from the other. He had been shifted back and forth across the world and rarely stayed put anywhere for more than a few months. Pat finally gave him up for adoption when she was sent to prison for fraud, and she has not seen him since. He's a grown man now. She's tried to find him, but to no avail. Daily, she hopes he might find her, but she is still moving about too much to be easily traced, and it's possible that no effort is being made.

In the mid-eighties, alone and legally divorced, Pat decided to give the navy a try. She married a merchant seaman, a kind man who did not beat her, but who wanted her to live with him at sea. 'I couldn't cope with it and he couldn't live ashore.' A year after the marriage she was in trouble again and sent to prison for three years on fraud charges involving credit cards.

Three months into her sentence, she was in hospital having a lump removed from her breast, and with the stitches still in, she slipped out of bed and ran off into a snowy mid-winter night, wearing only pyjamas and flip-flops. She ran off back to the Army, to a soldier she'd been writing to in Germany, to another bigamous marriage. Again, he didn't know she wasn't free. 'None of them ever knew,' she reiterates. 'It was none of their business.'

But Pat's life had finally caught up with her. While she was living in Germany she would panic every time she saw a policeman, convinced he was coming for her.

Marriage number eight was no different to the others, as fatally flawed, as inexorably brutal. Pat returned to England and gave herself up to the police; but when she told them about all the bigamy they just laughed and told her she was nuts. 'Eventually I was given six months for each of the four bigamous marriages, but they ran concurrently with the rest of my fraud sentence. I served the three years and when I came out of prison my story hit the front pages of every newspaper. It was BIGAMY QUEEN RELEASED FROM PRISON all over the tabloids.'

If ever there was a story of hope triumphing over experience, it is Pat's. 'I met another soldier, and I really wanted this one to work, but we just couldn't live together. I found out he had been carrying on with someone else and I took an overdose. Three days I was on a heart monitor in Salisbury

Hospital, but he never came to see me. He didn't want to know.' The person who did was Malcolm, a telephone engineer Pat had met in a pub. 'For the first time in my life I had found someone who listened to me, and who understood.'

Pat and Malcolm had been together four years when I met them. They didn't know where their life together was going to take them; both were unemployed. Birmingham was a place they felt they had to be for the time being to be near Malcolm's children, although their mother was unhappy about any contact when she found out about Pat. Normal people don't have ten husbands, and what kind of man knowingly becomes number ten? 'My past isn't that clever. All right, I haven't been married nine times, but the past is the past.' Malcolm drifts in and out of the room he's made for Pat. He doesn't really want to hear her talking about the other nine, besides, he's heard it all before, and in another room there is drilling and hammering to be done. His family has disowned him for marrying Pat. He's been described as 'lovelorn', but it's difficult to tell, and Pat declares herself 'in love' with him, one of only three she's felt like this about. 'I always expected marriage to be a fairy-tale, and I always thought I would find true happiness. Each time I went to the registry office I just blanked my mind away from all the bad experiences. I wouldn't want to go back to any of those marriages and if I had the time again I'd stay single. They say there is a Mr Right for everyone, and it took me twenty years to find him. I think I'm just a very moral person; I believe sex should be private, in the home, in marriage. I've never had any sex problems, only when they've tried to tell me when to have it. I have got a very nasty temper, but a person can only take so much. The women in prison thought I deserved a medal, having so many husbands. Some of them were in there for killing theirs. I think I'm in the *Guinness Book of Records*, but there's been more fuss because I'm a woman. A lot of the law is one-sided. I feel that I can hold my head up – I haven't hurt anyone except myself. I don't think bigamy should be an imprisonable offence unless it's for extortion. I did it as a cry for help. There's probably a hell of a lot of people out there who have committed bigamy but who don't have the guts to come forward and own up.'

Pat wears her crown with unexpected dignity. She's a

tortured soul with a bad temper, someone who's got it wrong so many times she could easily be dismissed as a bad joke, except, that underlying each of the 'binned' marriages was the sincere hope of finding something made in heaven. If she's found it with Malcolm she says it's because of the 'little things', the little bits of caring and loving she didn't know before.

It is difficult to imagine Pat's story belonging to an earlier era, before the softening of institutional marriage. I saw her and Malcolm on television a month or so after meeting them. It was one of those day-time programmes designed around an egotistical presenter, with members of the public put in the studio as props. The subject under discussion always concerns relationships – even if it's 'Hanging' they wheel on murderers' wives and victims' mothers, and there were Pat and Malcolm, up front, her looking as if she'd just been eating a really delicious ice cream – that transitory, lip-sucking contentment; Malcolm with an uneasy, 'what am I doing here' look about him.

'One of the main benefits of television has been that the public discussion of such topics as abortion and prostitution [relationships again, or lack of them] has helped to create a climate in which it is easier for people to acknowledge the existence in themselves of emotions previously swept under the carpet,' readers of the MGC Journal were told more than two decades earlier, in the late sixties. 'It is no longer necessary to pretend all is sweetness and love.'

This new wave of honesty was backed up by a survey suggesting that fewer than one in ten marriages were ever fully and deeply happy, and even those that were didn't get to such a stage of bliss until at least 30 years.

Ignoring these poor odds, in 1967, psychologist Dr James Hemming posed the question 'Is there a future for marriage?' The Bigamy Queen, who was to hedge her bets, had yet to start out on her odyssey, but I think that she and Dr Hemming might have been in agreement. 'Will marriage go and be replaced by a sexual free-for-all? The answer is, of course, it won't,' he said. 'Men and women need to struggle to find that testing, enduring, annihilating and resurrecting bond with a member of the other sex, through which they can discover and transform themselves. They need it as much as they need air and food and shelter. The defeated life is, in part, defeated by the death of the hope of finding such a relationship.' Marriage, he said, had never been more popular, not least because it was taking on a new image that was not about dreary 'settling down', a life sentence for two. Instead, it was being seen as a 'springboard for a fuller life'.

Unfortunately, this still ended in a belly-flop for some. The 1968 Government Survey of Women's Employment revealed that one in six wives were working outside the home in spite of their husband's disapproval, and two in six didn't even get a hand with the washing-up. Communes were hinted at as one way of lessening the burden, but for those not yet ready to throw in the tea-towel, the reality of marriage was increasingly about joining forces to pay a mortgage – even if wives' earnings were yet to be taken seriously into consideration by building societies.

Newly married, late sixties home-owners invariably started out on a new '100 per cent mortgage' housing estate, only to spend the next few years planning their escape to something more 'individual'. Those who didn't make their get-away before the babies began to arrive could find themselves stuck for years, and isolated, not in the individual style planned, but amidst the soulless bricks and mortar of despair. 'There is an absence on the housing estate of any real focal point for community life, such as the warmth and familiarity of the pub just around the corner, for pubs are few and far between on these estates; cinemas and dance halls, theatres and concerts are often non-existent except in nearby towns; there is rarely a little shop along the road to which one can slip when the tea or the bread runs out, and where the latest local gossip can be picked up and exchanged; and the churches are usually built long after the estates are established. The tendency is for the parents and children to stay at home and fall back on the telly in family solitude,' a marriage guidance counsellor of the day reported.

But at least they were able to see how miserable everyone else was finding life with all that honest soul-searching on the telly night after night. Those who got really bored and lonely resorted to 'primitive misconduct' with the neighbours, in other words, eternal triangles and wife-swapping (I've always thought stories about wife-swapping parties apocryphal, but that could be because I've never been invited to one).

One of the main problems for young married couples living on the new estates was that they had moved away from their home towns and the parents and grandparents who might have been on hand to help when the wife gave up work to start a family. 'Bored and lonely, one young mother felt so oppressed by the imprisoning walls of her house, her one-person workplace, that she would take her baby out and walk for mile upon mile around the endless and identical streets of the huge residential estate on which she lived just to be able to feel amongst some other people,' the MG counsellor said. One suggestion was that she should make her way to the local welfare clinic to try to meet other young mothers with the same preoccupations about confinements and feeding problems, but in my own experience such meetings were far too competitive in the realms of potty-training and the like, and only added to the overwhelming oppressiveness of new motherhood.

On the plus side, the isolation of young families from the traditional support system of relatives and friends was said to be creating the fledgling 'new man', young fathers with a keen interest in sharing child care; although this didn't stop the young wives from feeling lonely and frustrated if they were the ones at home most of the day. Many also worried about their own adequacy in child care and home-making, and some saw the root of the problem in education.

'Education – for what?' asked wife and mother Mrs Wendy Whitehead in the MG Journal in 1968. 'The school curriculum, as far as I discovered, was just not designed to equip a girl for the most vital years of her life when her ability and success in this new role of wife and mother would not only determine her own degree and sense of fulfilment, but the happiness of those for whose welfare she would be responsible over a period of many years.'

Mrs Whitehead described herself as one of the 'unlucky' ones to win a place at grammar school. Instead of reciting Latin and French verbs, she thought her time would have been better spent learning the sort of things that could make the difference between running a house and making a home. Girls' education was too stimulating, too geared to the outside world, and almost certain to make the young wife and mother discontented when she had to stay at home. 'As things are at present, when so many doors leading to a realm of opportunity and advance have been opened, to suddenly slam them shut on the birth of a child is understandably sufficient cause for mental frustration and nervous symptoms of the kind which are too frequently analysed by the psychiatrist.' Mrs Whitehead was a 'high-timer': it was 'high time', she said, that society stopped criticising modern mothers who wanted careers, because this was what they had been trained to want. If society wanted them to stay at home – and make a home, a high time was the last thing girls should be taught to expect.

It seems that Mrs Whitehead's advice was heeded, because, more than twenty years on, one of my own daughters is studying 'Child Care' for GCSE, although the motivation is a career caring for other people's children while their mothers continue pursuing career paths inspired via French verbs.

Barbara Cartland, in another of her non-fiction books, *Living Together*, published in 1969, made it clear where she thought a wife should be: at home, if only because it was 'up to the woman to keep sex alive' and going out to work might make her too tired for this task. But reading the many books about how to have a good marriage, particularly the ones about love-making, was not always recommended. 'A couple who are getting on quite happily may come across a book in which practices that seem way-out, or even unheard of to them, are regarded as commonplace. This may make them feel they must be missing something and are somehow inferior to most people.'

Problems with sex, if not solvable through books, meant a visit to the doctor, but not all GPs were sympathetic, and bearing in mind that Hormone Replacement Treatment was as yet unknown as the panacea for flagging libido, one 50-year-old wife asking for help from her doctor was told: 'I can't do anything. It's just that you're past it.'

At the other end, honeymoons were up for scrutiny: were they a good thing, was it better to be at home or away during the first weeks of married life? The suggestion that honeymoons away were wasteful, expensive and artificial, and that marriage stood a better chance of getting off to a good start if the newlyweds stayed at home was met with 5,000 readers' letters to the *Sunday Mirror*. Columnist Anne Allen wrote: 'The one thing that is guaranteed to leave a lifetime of regret is going to stay with relatives, or staying at home with mother. Those who did found it is quite commonplace for a mother to pop in to get something out of the wardrobe. Brothers, and even fathers, simply cannot keep the glint out of their eye or the joke off their lips at the breakfast table.' However, going abroad was also a mistake, adding foreign food and too much heat to the delicate period of adjustment. One couple wrote: 'We slid about in bed like two sardines soaked in oil.' Others had the romantic idyll ruined by hard beds and hissing cisterns, mostly foreign; but there were problems, too, for those who stayed in Britain: 'The idyllic country cottage proved somewhat primitive. The owners, an elderly couple, had the room next to us and they had to come through our room to reach the toilet. The old man seemed to need this almost hourly. Each time he fumbled through he said "Take no notice of me, just get on with it."'

Disappointment was a recurring theme, especially for the brides: 'He left me every evening to go drinking with some men we met.' Another wrote: 'I hadn't realised just how unpleasantly unclean he was, and I am a very fastidious person.' And: 'The sex part was awful.'

'I was still a virgin when I married at 25, although I had been courting for seven years. I was still a virgin when I returned from our four-day honeymoon,' wrote a very disappointed wife, comparing her experience, or lack of it, in the forties, with that of her daughter in the sixties. 'My honeymoon was not, in actual fact, a honeymoon. We had done the right thing, as we thought, and waited for marriage, but when we were married, we found it difficult to unwind after seven years of restraint. It was not until we had been in the privacy of our own home for a few days that we tried to relax, only to find that we were ignorant and not really suited sexually. We have four lovely children, grown up now, yet our sexual life has never been what it should. We are now adjusted, as they say – we've gone without for years! My daughter married last January, and it has all been quite different for her, thank God. They are a sensible, modern, intelligent couple who did not go without entirely before marriage but took reasonable precautions.'

A family planning survey in Liverpool comparing the 1940s with the 1960s reinforced the enormous change that had taken place over the period, and the Family Planning Association reported: 'In 1940 we dealt mainly with women in various stages of anaemia and malnutrition, the victims of chronic pelvic disorders and generally too crushed or dispirited to care for themselves or their children. Now we deal with baby-faced brides of seventeen and smart young wives holding down important jobs and feeling very much equal partners in home and marriage.'

But this equality in marriage seems to have applied only to the young. Middle-aged, middle management couples were still stuck in the mould of male dominance, and the majority of managers' wives questioned in a sociological study thought it right and proper that the main meaning in their husbands' lives was derived from his work, while the main meaning in theirs was him.

Whether this uneven balance in marriage was good or bad depended on what each couple wanted out of the arrangement, and the burgeoning ideas of feminism were to be a new sort of tyranny for the stay-at-home wife content to play second fiddle to her husband's job. If she was looking for reassurance it was there in 1965 from Professor John Macmurray, who gave the NMGC's Herbert Gray Lecture that year: 'I have little doubt that this imitation of men in the struggle for places in a man's society is only temporary,' he said, adding, somewhat ambiguously: 'This doesn't mean that we have only to wait for a time and things will settle back into the old well-known and, for men, comfortable groove. It means, on the contrary, that we have hardly begun to experience the social impact of the emancipation of women, which, I am certain, was one of the greatest steps ever made towards human maturity.' The Professor wanted to point out that women, having won the right to be free, could express this freedom by choosing to continue in their old role; what mattered was having a choice.

Those who decided not only to take a job but to compete

with men quickly discovered that they were still expected to run the home, and in an era when few could afford a housekeeper and many had moved away from the traditional support network of family and friends; but the Professor had an answer to this one: the family, he said, was now too small a unit for the burdens it was expected to carry, and he predicted 'experiments in the enlargement of the family by artificial means – combinations of families in a single home'. The word he was looking for was 'commune', but 'flower power' living was still in bud, traditional marriage was more popular than it had ever been, and a greater number of teenagers were marrying than ever before.

Being 'left on the shelf' was again the big worry, and marriage bureaux were enjoying a boom. It was estimated that as many as 30 marriages a day in Britain were as a result of bureau introductions. Modern city life and the urban culture didn't provide many opportunities for finding partners, except at work. The traditional hunting grounds of church and community groups had brought people together in the past; marriage bureaux were an effective alternative in an urban pluralistic society.

'Our clients and the general public's attitude to the bureau has changed,' Heather Jenner said. She started her famous bureau, the first of its kind in Britain, in 1939. It was aimed at gentlemen working in the Far East who came home on leave to find wives, but with only a few months to meet, woo and wed. 'In 1939 clients used to be much more diffident, or aggressive, according to how it took them, than they are now, and they were terrified that anybody might get to know that they had been to us. Now, the younger ones especially seem to look upon us as just another social amenity, and tell their friends that they have been to us, so much so that more and more of our clients now come to us through recommendation. These younger people too are much more frank about their problems than their elders were and are also used to having things done for them. If they want their teeth fixed they go to a dentist, if they want a husband or wife they go to a marriage bureau.

'Class distinctions have changed considerably amongst the young, too. Education, their way of thinking, and simply their way of life is becoming more important than who their father was. The girls are much better looking and made up than they used to be and more practical; most of them one feels will be perfectly capable of dealing with the problems of life and have been doing so for some time. The men are more tolerant in important things such as whether their wives should work after marriage or not, and in less important ones such as whether she wears a mini-skirt or false eyelashes. Women still say that they like the man to have a mind of his own and that they would like him to be the dominant but reasonable and amiable partner. Men also say that they like a girl to have a mind of her own and to be able to take responsibility when necessary.' Emancipation, it seems, was still under negotiation.

8 Somewhere between bondage and every man for himself

I USED TO WONDER why my grandmother, a woman good at getting her own way, put up with all my grandfather's games; by which I mean the endless bowls matches, hours and hours of watching the dullest game on earth. I wondered about it after I left my first husband because he spent too much time on the hockey field and the cricket pitch. I felt wicked, a bad lot, for what I had done. My husband said 'you knew what I was like when you married me', but it took more than a decade for me to come up with the same retort. Now I venture to think that if one of my daughters married and then abandoned a games-player, she wouldn't have the guilt.

Encapsulated in this family tree, its branches twisting and breaking in the wind of emancipation, is the way marriage has changed during this century; and it's all down to women, hardly to men at all. The uneven balance continued only as long as women allowed their men to get away with it, and when marriage became as unimportant to women as it was to men it was time to invest it with new meaning and purpose. It had to be re-invented, elevated to a higher plane; but the passage has been bumpy, two or three decades of trial and error, and not much in the way of role models.

Girls who married in the early 1970s may have stopped dressing like their mothers, but most were still hidebound by their mums' ideas about being a wife. Where else could they look, and how were they to know that an undercurrent of confusing discontent would surely sweep them up over the ensuing decade?

Olivia was nineteen when she married in 1970, and nothing in her aristocratic upbringing had prepared her for modern marriage. The undercurrent was to sweep her up with a vengeance, and the confusion was, perhaps, compounded by the twenty-year age gap between her and her husband.

Her parents, who were related to royalty, created their own minor scandal when they themselves married. There was no appreciable age difference, but one was Catholic and the other Protestant, and the Catholic family minded. This may not sound like too much of an impasse, but the Catholics had a 20,000-acre estate to pass on, and such acreage tends to have the clout to demand ongoing spiritual heritage. 'My parents rather enjoyed this Romeo and Juliet aspect of their marriage,' Olivia says. 'My father was in his first year at Cambridge and got sent down for marrying. My mother, whose father was a diplomat, was "decoratively" educated. She had a glaze of culture but nothing very profound. Their marrying was a lovely scandal. Everyone was very cross, but my father was the only son and due to inherit this huge and crumbling estate,' which is where Olivia spent her childhood.

'It had mines and moors and rich pastures. There were horses and salmon rivers. It was paradise on earth, and yet all of us [there were five brothers and sisters] were unhappy during our childhood. We lived under a shadow of oppression and fear, which was ironic because we had charming and beautiful parents, who tried terribly hard to be good parents. But they were so unrounded and poorly educated ... and privileged. They had not the smallest degree of self-doubt.

'My father was an idle man, but highly sexual and earthy, whereas my mother was ambivalent about sex. She said how wonderful it was, but banished my father from the bedroom during the curse. I remember him asking her whether he could sleep in her bed and being told he had to sleep in the dressing-room. I think they were faithful, and they were very disapproving of divorce.' A divorce would have been public, but sexual abuse, or good old-fashioned incest, was still a very private alternative in the 1950s, and both Olivia's sisters have talked euphemistically of 'tensions', although Olivia herself remembers nothing.

'My mother loathed her children as they grew up,' Olivia says, seemingly hooked into this horrid childhood as if nothing in her future life could surpass its vivid vileness. 'There was always some unobtainable ideal that was expected but that nobody was very clear about how to achieve. We were not encouraged in any department, but sneered at for not having intellectual achievement. I felt guilty because it seemed that I had somehow mislaid my knowledge. Childhood was a period to be endured.'

The transition to adulthood was to mean further endurance: a brief season as a fat, faint-hearted 'deb'; a spell in France, flower-arranging lessons, then a job with a London estate agent, and home at night to a basement bedsit. The fear of family scandal had been realised through an elder sister's affair with someone Olivia describes as a 'crossing sweeper', and had ended in tears and exorcism, as if the girl had to be mad and 'possessed' to have made such a liaison. Olivia was expected to behave better and hadn't anticipated the opportunity to do otherwise. 'I thought London would be dead at weekends, that everyone would have left for the country, but I was surprised to find it full of people, and parties.

'The whole thing was terribly confusing, and I didn't know what I was supposed to be doing. I had a small allowance that was constantly in danger of being cut off, and I didn't seriously consider having a career. It was the late sixties, and I suppose I "escaped" into marriage.'

Olivia met her husband at a party. He was a well-known actor and she felt she knew him even before they were introduced. He seemed to represent everything she wanted to escape to, but he was 23 years her senior and had been divorced three times. Even so, Olivia felt it was she who had the problem, through the *lack* of a 'past'.

'I wanted to get rid of my virginity, so I consulted my elder sisters and we selected a middle-aged mid-European. One of my sisters invited him to stay in Scotland, and I travelled with him on the overnight sleeper; but he was too honourable, and I didn't manage it with him until the next night at my sister's. He was rather taken aback, but he was very nice to me and I think he thought Christmas had arrived when he realised what I wanted. I was not remotely in love with him.'

The middle European was Olivia's only lover before she married Gerald. She is very honest as to how she felt about marrying him: 'He was a name most people recognised, which

I liked very much. He was a fashionable figure, and I think I was doing what is called "star-fucking". I also felt that my marrying him was endorsed by his having had three very interesting and beautiful wives. I was not in love with him, but I had been festering away in my fettered heap and I was ready to make my bolt.'

What she bolted into was London winings and dinings with the rich, the famous and the royal, with weekends, then increasingly much of the week, in the country. Gerald had proposed to her on Christmas Day at her parents' home, and there wasn't much protest. 'If my daughter was contemplating the same thing I would put in a great deal more energy in "bringing more light", but the solution for girls in the sixties was still to get married. My father suggested we should live together first, but I didn't want that. I must have thought I was in love with Gerald then, but I know now that I have never been in love with anyone – I have never minded about anyone more than myself, except my children. I think I would know love if I met it, and I think I haven't.'

Olivia now describes her husband: 'He is the most extra-ordinary, generous, brave ... I don't think I was any more sinned against than sinning. It wasn't the age difference that undermined the marriage, because Gerald is ageless. He's a "pied piper" and he now has younger friends than I have.'

Two children were born within the first two years of the marriage, but there was plenty of money, enough for domestic help, nannies, a chauffeur, a cook. There was high intellectual nourishment as well, and Olivia, if not in love, felt 'moved and stirred' by her husband. Was she happy during the twelve years of the marriage? She says she didn't know how to be, that she wasn't in the habit, but that some happiness was, perhaps, made. 'We gave each other and other people a good time. We loved the farm we lived on, and our children, and we were frightfully interested in each other. He believed it was possible to decide to be in love.'

Throughout the marriage, Olivia was the stronger partner, the aggressor, with Gerald always the victim, although decisions of any kind were avoided by both of them. 'This is probably why we stayed together so long, but I was so frustrated and bored.' Olivia owns that her feelings of frustration were not really connected with her marriage, that she was experiencing what thousands and thousands of women have gone through when they have realised that motherhood and marriage are not enough. Accordingly, she flailed about until she struck on the idea of improving the farm's efficiency by her own efforts. She went to horticultural college, but did so still shackled by the paranoid, anti-feminist notion that she didn't have the right to be good at anything. Gerald had never encouraged her in any direction, but he was of a generation that didn't see such need in a wife, any more than her parents had considered encouraging Olivia in a career. By the time she was 30, and unfulfilled by the now failing farm, she felt quite desperate for something, although exactly what she hadn't a clue. 'I was incredibly depressed, and cried every day for years on end – gosh, I sound a treat. Financially, things were getting tight, and the marriage was becoming rockier and rockier. Gerald had a series of illnesses for two years on the trot, and the amount of nursing completely wore me out. I don't like looking after people.' But leaving was nothing to do with any of this. Olivia says it was a non-decision, that it was inertia that broke up the marriage. More immediately, it appears to have been Digby.

'I had been unfaithful a few times with "safe" people – more as a pastime than anything else. Then Gerald went away to work in Australia, and I had an affair which ended badly. I'd had to sell the farm, which I loved, and to someone really horrid. I went out to Australia to spend Christmas with Gerald because he had always been my friend and I wanted to be with him, but when I got there I found that he had fallen in love with a man. I could tell because he glowed, as you do when in love. For the first twelve hours I said how pleased I was for him, but then I started to shake, literally, and went into the deepest shock. I just had no resources left. I was very thin and nervous anyway and thought life could be sustained on Marlboro and vodka. I had been dropped from a great height by my lover, and suddenly I felt disgust and betrayal over what Gerald was doing – we'd had a good sex life at some point.'

Banished to the guest-room of the house Gerald had rented, Olivia slept alone, while Digby occupied her place in Gerald's bed. She endured the situation for only a few days before leaving the new love-nest and a concurrent orgy of drug-taking. But getting home at such short notice was to involve taking a circuitous route and several 'plane trips, during and in between which Olivia managed to have sex with three total strangers, one after the other. Almost as soon as she arrived back in England she crumpled up completely and was carted off to The Priory – 'that's the smart people's "bin" '.

More horrors were in store. It seemed that children from Gerald's previous marriages had been sexually abused, and he had been 'sacked' for buggery from both public school and university, although this last revelation was not new to Olivia. She says that she knew about it before the wedding, but maybe it had suited her to forget at the time; maybe it had merely added to the overall *avant garde* attraction of Gerald. With circumstances altered, and Gerald back in England accompanied by his new lover, and Olivia stuck in hospital, abandoned by hers, old sins had lost their frisson. 'Things between us were not tickety-boo. The relationship took a serious dive and never really recovered, although I felt the affair with Digby would pass, and it did.'

Throughout this period, Olivia's children, ignorant of what was going on, were cared for by her sisters. Their lives were about to change as well, but through Olivia's new marriage, not their father's way of life.

Three weeks before her marriage to Gerald, Olivia, displaying all the fretful flakiness of the overbred, had decided she was in love with another man twice her age. 'He was a friend of Gerald's, and I remember in the registry office, thinking "this person has got to appear and save the situation".' In the event, she had to wait sixteen years, but she says: 'I married my second husband in a fantastically heady rush.'

Olivia's second marriage began with a Catholic wedding, the Church having managed to convince itself that the first marriage had not really happened. Olivia's new husband, who had not been married before, viewed the marriage as part of a hiatus in his career; he had given up a top job and was looking for a sea-change in his life. 'We had known one another sixteen years, but we didn't at all. "Good egg wifeliness" was how he saw me. I think I knew somewhere that it was a mistake, but by this stage I was pretty well addicted to mistakes. He fucked people like other people drink, just to forget and ease the pain. He never looked at me again after we left the church on the day of the wedding, he was so appalled by what he had done – getting married.'

The marriage was a disaster and lasted only two years, during which time Olivia's children suffered in a way they never had before. 'My son was touchingly excited and pleased about the marriage, but my husband was sarcastic, cutting and dismissive, and this poor little boy – he was fourteen – just shrank. He was very badly dented. As for my daughter, she found my husband repellent. The atmosphere, I can tell you, was just neat! My new husband was a nice, good man who had turned into a monster.' There were drinking bouts that ended in drying-out clinics, then more drinking bouts, and so it went on, yet, almost as soon as the marriage was over, they were to be seen at parties together, dancing, fondling, overtly affectionate. Why did they do this, I asked? It was just for show. Did they get a kick out of it? Oh, no – that would have been so bourgeois. The distinction was lost on me.

'I had asked him to leave. He was quite happy going mad – he was used to it – but I actually felt my life was threatened, I was so full of anxiety and fear. I couldn't eat and I was sick all the time. He threatened suicide quite often. It was a dreadful cycle of dependence, but when I asked him to go, he went with relief. He had thought marriage and children were going to solve everything, but his "uppers" and "downers" were more reliable. I think he hated me because I found out how inadequate he was. He wanted a child, but I didn't want one with him. He started to drink "to die" on the honeymoon – he managed to turn over the car at ten in the morning, but I daresay he would have an equal number of stories about me.'

Throughout all the drinking, drug-taking and abuse, there is one single incident Olivia says hurt more than most. Her second husband rarely bought her anything, but one day she came home to find a passion flower waiting for her on the table. It was her favourite, and she was so pleased, not just with the plant, but that he had thought to buy it for her; but then she saw another, identical one half hidden on the floor behind a table leg. This second plant was for an old flame. 'You weren't meant to see that one,' her husband said. Olivia, a moment earlier lifted to heights of happiness, then understood the mean cruelty behind the incident.

Olivia says the age difference with her second husband was very apparent, while this was never the case with Gerald, perhaps because he had been married before. Would she marry again, I ask? She has been alone for five years and rather likes her life this way, but tomorrow night she is dining with the other man who dropped her from a great height, the lover she lost just before going to Australia. Would she really consider marrying him? 'He's nasty enough,' she says, and I notice that her eyes have suddenly glistened. She has a good job now and if she keeps at it she has a very real chance of fame and fortune, yet she would give it up if there had to be a choice between marriage and career. 'I used to think it would be the height of chic to be double-divorced by thirty and working in the media; but I don't think work is sacred, and I am much more serious, more thoughtful about marriage than I was in 1970. I try not to be a masochist, but I'm aware of the tendency. I'd be a much better bet now.'

Olivia may not be typical of the 1970s bride, yet what she went through will strike a chord with the many women who subsequently realised they needed to establish their own identity separate from marriage, who found themselves wondering what marriage was all about and how much was in it for them. But the experts of the day saw it coming, and in 1970 the discussion was no longer about housing, money, sex, or in-laws; 'relationship' was what mattered. The basics having been largely sorted out as a result of the country's improved standard of living since the war, there was space to worry about quality. 'We have reached the point today at which people are less and less willing to tolerate a mediocre marriage,' marriage expert David Mace wrote in the MGC Journal in 1970. 'The traditional functions of the family – mutual protection, economic security, co-operative production of food, vocational training of children, and so on – have more and more been taken over by the community at large; and the major function of families today is to provide emotional security and fulfilment, and a sense of personal worth, in a vast and complex world. Failure to achieve a good relationship in marriage therefore means a major disaster today, comparable to a failure to beat off the Indians or raise enough crops for the winter in the past.'

As always, the experts blamed the problems and failures on ignorance and proclaimed society at fault for not preparing young people, for allowing too much romance and pleasure-seeking during courtship, rather than sitting them down and explaining how the rows and misunderstandings were bound to come, and how these should be seen as some sort of masochistic learning experience rather than the end of love.

'We are doing a deplorably poor job of preparing young people for marriage,' David Mace said, 'but the problem is not just one of lack of knowledge. At least equally important is the tragic fact that many of these people are utterly confused about what marriage involves, because they have been furnished with no good models with which to identify. I find that those who come to me for counselling, surprisingly often, say they wonder whether marriage may not be greatly overrated. They are sceptical about what it has to offer. They even say they have never seen a really good marriage, and ask me whether such a thing exists. They admit that they cannot regard their parents as models, because in some cases their marriages ended in divorce; or if not, they communicated clearly to their children that they were living together in a state often far removed from warm affection, and sometimes no better than impatient toleration of each other.

'If one has no personal experience of observing a good marriage function, how does one learn the skills necessary for this delicate task? How does a man know how to deal with his wife in a thousand complex situations, if he has never watched another man skilled in the art? How does a woman know how to function as a good wife if she has no concept of how the role is played, because she has never seen it played?'

To be fair to David Mace, even if he did talk about men dealing with their wives, and women learning to be good ones, he blamed much of the 1970s marital upsets on men not wanting to get too involved in their marriages. 'The attitude is widespread among men that, while one must devote a certain amount of special effort to the business of courtship, once the girl is won and safely corralled in the split-level suburban home, the husband can again give his full attention to his previous preoccupations – his work, his men friends, his sports [bloody hockey again], his hobbies. This concept is fortified by the fact that boys in our culture are not prepared for in-depth relationships with anyone, and particularly not with the women in their lives. They are raised to consider that the manly role is that of rugged independence.' The modern marriage problems started when women recognised the undercurrent of discontent as their own desire for something a bit more rugged, not in their husbands, but in themselves in shaping their own destinies.

Mace, however, saw wives endangering marriage by demanding too much of their husbands' time, enforcing too much togetherness, too many nights of the week at home instead of out with the lads and in the pub. His last word on the ideal marriage relationship for 1970 – 'relationship in-depth' that should depend more on rarefied quality than the quantity of time spent together, was to cite the union between Harold Nicolson and Vita Sackville-West (although Mace refers to it as 'the marriage of Harold Nicolson'). 'People who have a good relationship *want* to spend time together, and find ways and means to do so; but they also recognise each other's rights to spend time in other ways, because they have no fears, anxieties or suspicions that their spouses will develop wayward tendencies as soon as they are out of each other's sight. An excellent example of this was the marriage of Harold Nicolson, the distinguished English writer and commentator. In his memoirs, edited by his son, appears the following letter he received from his wife: "I was always well-trained not to manage you. I scarcely dare to arrange the collar of your greatcoat, unless you ask me to. I think that is really the basis of our marriage, apart from our deep love for one another, for we have never interfered with each other and, strangely enough, never been jealous of each other. And now, in our advancing age, we love each other more deeply than ever before." '

Pretty words, but history has fingered both Nicolson

collars, and when it comes to wayward tendencies few could have held a candle to Harold and Vita. Their son, Nigel Nicolson, published *Portrait of a Marriage* four years after David Mace's article in the MGC Journal, and all was revealed: Harold's description of Vita as being 'like a jellyfish addicted to cocaine' when she fell into the hands of her lover, Violet Keppel; and Violet's commentary: 'Marriage is an institution that ought to be confined to temperamental old maids, weary prostitutes and royalty.'

The same year, Nena and George O'Neill published *Open Marriage: A New Life Style for Couples*, exposing the 'impossible' demands of traditional 'closed' marriage, and setting out new guidelines – living for the moment, open and honest communication, flexibility in roles, open companionship, equality, identity and trust – all of them tried and tested years before by Harold and Vita and others with the money and manners to get away with it, among them Naomi Mitchison, who described her experience of open marriage earlier in this book.

Yet what the O'Neills were talking about in the 1970s was somehow different; maybe because they were expounding a new way of marriage for those who couldn't really afford it, emotionally or financially, when it all went wrong. There was talk of a taboo on tenderness, and a new consumerist view of marriage: 'Divorce is to be recognised as a hazard of life, not as proof of inadequacy and failure. No one is condemned for changing jobs along the road of life. If the possibilities of one job dry up for a particular individual, then the sensible thing is to make a change.' Those who didn't in the 1970s were suffering from apathy or lack of courage; a first marriage was often merely a learning process to be gone through to give subsequent attempts a better chance of success. Yet 'divorce and live happily ever after' seemed to make about as much sense as prescribing an enema for the starving, with people like Desmond Morris saying there was a desperate need for more warmth and humanity, and the medical authorities worrying themselves sick about VD and abortion resulting from cultural pressures towards dehumanised sexual activity, moral ignorance and inability to develop loving relationships. The very word 'love' had taken on a different meaning that was no longer much to do with relationship. The pop culture was blamed, the dear old Beatles accused of using imagery and words designed to depersonalise sensuality in an ugly and cynical way; and the magazine *Oz* went completely beyond the pale with its ads showing a naked couple having intercourse with the slogan, 'It's a fuck of a song, man!'

It seems that there were two extremes, the taboo on tenderness at one end, and the utter rejection of mediocre marriage at the other. Of course, most people were still bumping along somewhere in the middle, having been told that disenchantment was inescapable – the conclusion of an exhaustive study of 1,000 marriages begun in 1939. Sociologist Robert Chester confirmed this cheerless finding: 'Contemporary ideals of marriage might lead us to hope to find warm companionship and emotionally full relationships. Instead, the research accounts seem to speak of relationships which are low in satisfaction, sexually arid, defective in communication, and perhaps either devitalised or merely passively congenial.'

The alternative to all this drear was serial monogamy, not Bigamy Queen style or on a trial and error learning curve plan, but properly paced for the three periods of married life, beginning with *romantic* marriage for the young, with no presumption of permanence, and no babies. This would be followed by *parental* marriage with an assumption of permanence at least until the children were mature, and then there could be *post-parental* marriage, in which the emphasis would be on the needs of the latter half of adult life. Chester was quick to point out that all three marriages could be between the same people, but on an 'allowed to stay on for good behaviour' basis rather than as of right.

Another escape route for those disenchanted with the whole idea of marriage was communes. This didn't mean groups of couples, but more a 'three musketeers' approach – all for one and one for all – with, in one instance, everyone piling on to a twelve-square-yard mattress in an effort to feel fully collectivised. But it didn't work, and within a year broke up into couples.

The more marriage was knocked, the more popular it became. In 1970 the number of new marriages was approaching half a million, more than 25 per cent up on ten years earlier. The increase was chiefly due to couples marrying younger and younger – the great majority under the age of 24 – but also due to remarriage of the widowed and divorced, particularly among couples too old to have children. This all pointed to the popularity of marriage for its own sake, rather than for the practical purposes of founding and funding a family. Marriage no longer mattered in the old way, but in the new thinking it mattered a lot more. Underlying the trend towards quantity was the search for perhaps unattainable quality. The disenchantists could shout about it, but nobody really wanted to hear. Let them keep their twelve-square-yard mattresses, their planned serial monotony; better to have loved like Harold and Vita than never to have risked your all.

Bucking the trend of so much marrying were the seventies voices of dissent saying it shouldn't and couldn't last as an institution. Eva Figes predicted the 'back-benching' of marriage largely because she saw it as a false haven for the insecure. 'I personally believe that we should educate people to think that the only security is within themselves and not in their interpersonal relationships. The only idea of a secure place that I can think of is Wandsworth prison.'

Figes said that young women in the early seventies were still marrying for security and to get away from Mum and Dad, and young men were still marrying for regular sex. My own memories from this time, comments from friends who were marrying, rather confirms these reasons for the wholesale bolt to the altar. I think it was love that was 'back-benched', and according to Figes it never stood a chance: 'We are all fairly highly educated with very diverse expectations, but most of us, if we're honest, know that the companionship of one person in large doses is simply not enough. Every marriage is a happy one until you know the people really well and then you begin to see what goes on underneath.'

Like other commentators of the day, Figes based her opinions and predictions for the future direction of marriage on Britain's high standard of living and attendant high expectation of life in general. We had the time and leisure to concentrate on our emotional lives, on our sex lives too, and regular sex – as in readily available – was boring: 'Now I myself do not believe that the erotic element can be or should be contained within a marital relationship, and of course immediately you recognise this you're in trouble when considering marriage at all. I believe the idea of regular sex is about as exciting as masturbation. I believe that sex within marriage usually either becomes dull or dies out completely.'

Figes shared the learning curve idea of marriage, seeing it as something to go through before you reached full maturity; divorce, if seen in terms of failure, was, perhaps, a good failing, and not an end, but a beginning.

Assuming all such ideas to be firmly rooted in Women's Liberation, the critics countered with 'what price personal fulfilment?' On a 'give and take' theme, a Scunthorpe correspondent in the MGC Journal suggested: 'Freedom in marriage surely finds itself somewhere between bondage and every man for himself.'

Angela Willans, Mary Grant of *Woman's Own*, was rummaging through marital expectations at the same time that Eva Figes made her pronouncements. Falling in love, Angela said, was wonderful, but not much to do with marriage. Society needed to tolerate more sexual and romantic experience before marriage – a different angle on the learning curve theory, and less costly.

The expectation of emotional togetherness in marriage often led to frustration and misery, she said. 'It's the idea of two people becoming as one – yes, as someone said, and the husband's the one.

'It seems to be the general expectation of marriage that it will end loneliness by ending aloneness. But no one insists that you should be able to live with yourself before you take on the lifetime job of living with someone else – sometimes I wish this was somehow possible. For this ability to be at peace and at ease with oneself is, in the end, the only answer to loneliness. It can be very devastating indeed, my letters show me, to expect marriage to be an answer to loneliness and to find that you can be more lonely in marriage than you ever were when you were alone.'

Similarly, there was high-minded comment in the sixties that it was unwise to marry until you could live without sex, which may have had something to do with Angela Willans' idea that marriage in future would be a much smaller area of people's lives. More seriously, marriage was probably heading for the margins because it was no longer a male-dominated institution, the husband no longer automatically the head of the household. Other institutions have tended to lose their importance as soon as women have achieved parity within them. A good example is the Church: the ordination of women in America has, according to the ordained women themselves, downgraded the priesthood and with it the Church, and the same will happen in England. What's the betting on disestablishment before the end of the century, now that women have been granted priestly parity?

But marriage was still going strong in the seventies, and for the first time this century there were more men than women of marriageable age. Heather Jenner said this changed the whole pattern of traditional courtship. In cars and women, the modern male still preferred the smooth working model rather than the merely glamorous, she said, whereas seventies girls were demanding the impossible. They wanted equality but at the same time a strong shoulder to weep upon.

Jilly Cooper, in her 1970 book *How to Stay Married*, put all the theorising into perspective with some straight-from-the-shoulder advice for young brides who had already found that equality had a long way to go: 'If you amuse a man in bed, he's not likely to bother about the mountain of dust underneath it.' 'Do take the stew off the gas before you start making love.' And, 'The curse should be renamed the blessing – every row two weeks before it arrives and a week after it's finished can be blamed on it.'

Both a curse and a blessing, marriage, all the experts agreed, had become extremely demanding and difficult because its future depended on quality not necessity.

9 The loneliness of the long-distance stunner

'YOU'RE BORING, stupid, uninteresting, and you haven't an ounce of love in you.' Hazel, a woman in her mid-forties, with two almost grown-up sons, remembers precisely the words her husband used nearly a decade ago to explain why he was leaving her.

I hadn't eaten with Hazel the evening I went to see her, but I couldn't but help with the drying-up; is there anything more lonely than washing-up alone, more poignant than a kitchen sink scene with the drama all gone? There's a tea-towel pinned to the wall like a tablet of stone. 'The Kitchen Prayer', it says, and goes on like a cheap greetings card, blessing pots and pans, a wife's duties and a man's. There's a postcard too, depicting an eighteen-week-old foetus in colours too bloody to sustain a stare.

The house where Hazel lives is the sort of place men buy for their wives and children after the divorce, a mean, shabby little house squeezed into a terrace in a rough road where children of all ages play in the street until it's dark. The cars, those that go and those that don't, bleed slimy pools of oil over front gardens, the pavement, anywhere they can find a space. This is a road where people don't plan to stay, but spend a long time in the planning.

It's not that far from the area where Hazel and her husband were born in south London, but when Hazel was seven her family moved to a new town north of the Thames. They'd been living with her maternal grandmother, and the rows were such that they were prepared to take a house in a strange town, just to get away. But powerful love-hate relationships don't go away like that, and granny moved with them. Years later, Hazel's husband accused her of marrying him only to escape, but people look for that sort of reason when they want to end a marriage and need to shift a bit of the guilt on to the one that's being left.

Hazel met Martin on a blind date in 1966 when she was nineteen. It was the era of darts in dresses, pointy bras, structured hair-styles and the remnants of Beatlemania. 'I didn't like him,' she says. 'He was not good-looking. I didn't fancy him and I wasn't going to see him again.' But Hazel's friend told her Martin was really keen, and his friend was telling him a similar story.

After a couple of years Martin had 'grown on' Hazel. 'I found I was talking about him all the time. There was this lady at work who said, "You keep on and on talking about this Martin, you must like him a lot." I realised then that I liked him more than I'd thought and that night I telephoned him and said I had something to tell him. "I think I love you," I said, and he said, "What? Only 'think'?"

'He went on holiday to Spain with his friend, and I went away with my friend. When they came home his friend told mine he didn't want to go out with her any more. It rather spoiled the holiday. I said to Martin I supposed he didn't want to go out with me any more either, but he had been sending me letters every day while he was away. He asked me to marry him while we were at a friend's wedding. I was the bridesmaid and he said he wanted a word with me. I thought he was going to call it all off. He had said he didn't think I loved him, but I'd said I did.

'We argued a lot during the year of saving up. It was the tension of the wedding, getting the flowers and the car. It came to a head one night and I said we shouldn't get married. I gave the ring back and he went and sat in his car – he had one of those little bubble cars. He just sat there for a while and then he drove off and I thought, "Oh, what have I done?" But my nan said we should walk round the corner, and there he was. He lifted the roof of the car and told me to get in.'

From the beginning of their relationship, Martin was always telling Hazel that he didn't think she really loved him, but maybe he was looking for something different from the quiet, enduring type of love she had to offer. Theirs was a 'beauty and the beast' match, and when Martin left Hazel for another woman, he said, 'I bet you never thought any one else would ever fancy me.'

The wedding was a rowdy affair, with Martin's friends from London hiring a coach for the day, getting lost in the new town and holding up the ceremony. For Hazel, this beginning might have been seen as a pointer to the way the marriage was going to be, with Martin continuing his almost nightly drinking sessions with 'the boys' for years to come.

Their first home was a rented flat in an old house and the plan was to save for a place of their own before having children. But things didn't work out like that and both the boys were born while they were still in the flat. Hazel soon found herself in the sort of situation that makes women leave: stuck at home all day and every evening, alone with her first child, and wary of a husband who had taken his first swipe at her following a drunken homecoming. He was full of remorse and tears, never-again promises, but Hazel was always frightened of him after that. 'I just let him rule the roost – I wasn't one of these women who stand up for themselves – and a lot of the time he was very loving. I'm making him out to be such an ogre, aren't I?

'The trouble was, if we did go out together we didn't really have a lot to say to one another. We were all right in a crowd, but not on our own. He put on a show for his friends, but there were just grunted monosyllables for me. I suppose what really did it was when I became pregnant the second time. We'd been trying for another baby and I must have been about eight weeks when I lost it. It came away in the loo and I saw it, the little baby in its sac. I hadn't even known that I was pregnant. I brought it out in my hand and I said to Martin "Do you want to see what I've got?" It happened again a few months later, but that time I just told him I'd lost it. He carried on eating his supper and, later, he went out as usual.

'I thought about leaving him, but he said if I ever did I couldn't take his son. He was very domineering, but I stayed because I took my vows seriously, for better, for worse; I thought perhaps all men were like him.'

Until Hazel had stopped working to be at home with her baby, the £10 a week she earned had been put aside for the deposit on a house. They had lived on the £20 a week Martin earned, £5 of it going on rent. The initially unplanned family meant that by the time Hazel had her second child there was only £600 saved towards a house. But Martin was about to seize an opportunity to start his own business, and overnight the £600 was gone on a speculative deal. The gamble paid off, and suddenly, the money was there to buy a house; the £600, doubled, trebled . . . 'I thought it was going to be a new start,' Hazel says.

Fifteen years into their marriage, Hazel felt things were better. There had been the attempts at wife-swapping with the next-door neighbours, the hideously embarrassing scenario of three willing participants but not Hazel, mindful of the cold, too close, light of day to be faced across the garden fence the next morning and forever after. Martin had stopped going out every evening, but fell asleep in the armchair instead. He was working hard, building the business, and Hazel didn't feel she should say anything about his disinclination to wash, 'and he always said deodorants were "poofy".

'They say it's always the wife who's the last to know. He used to go out a couple of evenings and play squash. It was the barmaid. I should have realised there was something going on when he started buying new underwear and better clothes – he'd never been interested in clothes. Then he said to me "Tell me the truth, do I smell?" It didn't even click then, when he started using deodorant.

'I'd been out all morning collecting money for Guide Dogs for the Blind. I came in and started shouting and hollering – I was doing that a lot. It was a Saturday and I went upstairs to change the bed. He came up after me, told me to stop what I was doing and tell him what the matter was. We hadn't been making love very often, and I asked him then if there was anyone else and he said of course there wasn't. Then he burst out crying and said we should kiss and make up. He came home a month later and said "You do know I've been seeing someone."

'This is the best bit. He suggested we should have a weekend away without the boys, but after taking them to their grandparents he took me into the pub to meet the barmaid. He wanted to know what I thought of her. He even made arrangements for us to go out for a meal, the four of us, her with her husband. When he told me about her, I said, "Oh, that's why you've started using deodorant," and he said, "Trust you to think of that." I told him I didn't want him to go, even though there was me with my moods and him always dropping off to sleep.' So began the worst bit, the period of indecision for Martin. At first he said he would stay, but that Hazel was not to tell anyone about the barmaid, not if the marriage was to have a chance of surviving. There were family outings as there had never been before, a holiday in Spain, a new bathroom, a car for Hazel; but Martin didn't stop going to the pub: he said people would guess something had been going on if he stopped.

'I couldn't stop losing weight; not being able to tell anyone was terrible. I used to say, if you can't trust your own husband, who can you trust? In the end I had to tell somebody so I told his mother when we were out blackberrying, and she told me his father had been the same.

'I thought about following him when he went out in the evening, but who was there to babysit? One night he asked me how much the housekeeping cost, and I thought, ooh, good, he's going to give me a pay rise, but I think he was just working out whether he could afford to keep both of us. He spent that year getting everything right, so he could leave. When he went, I 'phoned up his mother and said "he's gone". It took me five years to get over it.'

How did she know, I asked, know that it was five years? 'It was five years before the pain stopped – it was a physical pain. I think you can die of a broken heart. Unless you've gone through it, you can't know what it's like, all the worry of what's going to happen, how you will cope, the awful feeling of rejection. There was no sense of relief. I still loved him, you see, and I wanted him back.

'He moved into a caravan with her and he still couldn't decide. When he came to see us I would be on my knees, begging him to come back, and our younger boy kept pleading with him, "Please Daddy, please Daddy, please come back." He said he would, and I got all his favourite foods in, but when he came he didn't have his suitcase, and it was that night I knew he wasn't going to come back. In the morning I sat in front of the mirror making this funny noise. I said I couldn't go on. My father said he was going to kill him.

'Not knowing why was really the worst part, after all I'd put up with and not saying anything; not getting fat, not letting myself go. What had I done wrong? He told me. He said: "If you really want to know, you're boring, stupid, uninteresting, and you haven't an ounce of love in you." I said: "That just about covers it all." He said the barmaid wasn't as pretty as me, that she bit her nails, but he could talk to her for hours.'

While Hazel's father thought about killing Martin, she thought about killing herself. 'I had some pills, but then I thought, if I take them, he'll have won; he'll have her and the boys. Getting a job was what saved my sanity. It was only the provisions counter at Tesco, but it gave me back my confidence.'

Throughout their marriage, Hazel says Martin was always one of those husbands eager to put his wife down, to undermine and belittle in front of other people. Often, this can mean that in the 'victim and aggressor' stakes the roles are reversed at home, but with Hazel and Martin there was never any doubt who had the upper hand. Martin was a bully, given the chance, and Hazel gave him plenty. Even a decade after their marriage was over, he would snap up that chance: at a family funeral, an occasion Hazel was dreading because Martin would be there with his second wife, he openly criticised her appearance in the proprietorial manner of a bullying husband, asked for a kiss and was unpleasant when he didn't get one.

He has looked after her financially, but at a price, the lingering sense of ownership allowing him to make passes at her, to tell her she should lower her sights to find another husband. She's looked, but without much enthusiasm. 'I don't fancy anyone. When you've been hurt like that it takes a long time to get over it, but, yes, I would consider marrying again one day. I could live another forty years, and that's a long time to be alone. But I've got a good job now, and I'm happier than I was when I was married to him; I don't have to ask his permission for my life.'

Until fairly recent times, the last 100 years or so, the British wife, married or divorced, depended entirely on her husband's magnanimity; and if she had tried to leave him he would have been quite within his rights to have kept her prisoner. Equally, a man like Martin would not have found it quite so easy to divorce – if you can call what he and Hazel have been through in any sense easy.

Unlike marriage, divorce started out as something available only to the privileged few. Before 1850, on average there were fewer than two divorces a year in England and Wales compared with 150,000 today. To get out of a bad marriage 150 years ago involved a private Act of Parliament for each individual case, and the expense alone restricted the rigmarole to the very wealthy. Even after the Matrimonial Causes Act of 1857, which made the process more accessible, there were still only about 200 divorces in a year, predominantly among the well-to-do. It was not until after the Second World War that divorce became a remedy for the working class and 70 per cent of the 30,000 petitions involved manual workers. Of course, the great divorce revolution was still to come, the bloodstained seventies and eighties when the divorce courts became marriage abattoirs engaged in wholesale slaughter.

How did it all begin, this carnage? Was it that wicked old fatty, Henry VIII, with his lust for Anne Boleyn? Apparently not. If anything, the Reformation regularised an even bloodier state of affairs.

Christian ideas about the permanence of marriage had developed as a reaction to Roman times when divorce became common and part of the general moral decline that was to undermine an empire. Yet, as the centuries rolled by, the Christian ideal suffered a similar, though less honest undermining. From the outset, Christians had a great list of forbidden unions which made about as much sense as the old Sunday trading laws. A man could not marry his grand-daughter, but there was nothing expressly prohibiting marriage with a daughter. An uncle could marry his niece, but an aunt could not marry her nephew. The reasoning behind this last one was that such a marriage would reverse the natural order of authority, aunts being seen as formidable authoritarians.

The list grew, and by the time King Henry started fancying Anne Boleyn it was always possible for Christian marriage to be annulled if you looked hard enough for a prohibiting kinship. And it went beyond blood ties: the third cousin of a godchild could not marry the third cousin of the godfather; and to have had sexual intercourse with a distant cousin of the person you eventually hoped to marry could render the marriage void.

Bearing in mind the closeness of communities in the Middle Ages and the much smaller population figures compared with today, it was a miracle that anyone was able to find a valid marriage partner. That they did, probably keeping the possibility of a prohibiting kinship as a useful get-out in the event of things turning sour, indicates that nothing much has changed in our approach to marriage, only that modern-day divorce is less hypocritical than Middle Ages annulment.

Couples who discovered kinship before their marriage but still wanted to wed appealed to the Pope for dispensation to marry; and unless they were brother and sister or equally closely and incestuously related, the restriction was lifted, but at a price. The Vatican was raking it in, and by the time King Henry applied for his annulment from Catherine of Aragon on the grounds that she had previously been betrothed to his brother, trafficking in annulments had become such a scandal it made the Reformation seem like a breath of fresh air.

Until fairly recent times, divorce, like marriage, favoured men; wives committed adultery, while husbands merely strayed. Until 1925 the children of a marriage were regarded as the property of the husband. Society had no mercy for wayward wives. In my own family there is the story of a great-uncle who sent his wife home from India after she had flirted with a junior officer. The 'flirtation' was no more than too much of a kindly smile, but my aunt was never again allowed to see her three children. It seems that until this century things had not progressed much from Old Testament times, when a wife could be cast aside for burning her husband's supper, although now it has gone full circle in the United States, where divorce actions today can rest on a wife's cruel insistence on feeding her husband the wrong breakfast cereal, giving a whole new meaning to complaints about not getting your oats.

The greater cause of marital breakdown in Britain this century has been war. The First World War brought a sudden increase of 1,500 divorce petitions a year, but after the Second World War the number soared to an increase of more than 20,000. Disruption to family life and greater readiness to divorce were the reasons given; moral laxity may have crumbled the Roman Empire, but it was the other way around in twentieth-century Europe, cause and effect reversed. In 1947 there were 60,000 divorce petitions; too many marriages had been hastily made in the hell of war.

Peace brought renewed hope for marriage, and at the end of the fifties the *News Chronicle* printed a story with the headline THE DIVORCE BOOM IS OVER and a prediction that there would be fewer and fewer broken marriages. We've managed to defy this fairly convincingly, but by 1958 the number of divorces had dropped to 25,000. The *Chronicle* optimistically attributed its prediction to the stand of the Church concerning marriage and divorce, and the increase of marriage guidance.

The Bishop of London, writing about 'Divorce and Forgiveness' in the *Daily Mail* in the mid-fifties, said: 'Our welfare workers could tell of significant instances after the war. A soldier has returned home to find that during his prolonged absence his wife has had a baby by another man. After the first shock of grief and anger he has been induced to take his wife back. Sometimes she has brought the new child with her. In course of time not only has the wife been completely restored to her husband's affection, but the child is treated by him as if it were his own. This, I acknowledge, is a somewhat exceptional case. More often the child would be cared for by one of our societies, but the ultimate reconciliation between husband and wife is not exceptional, and it is for that that I plead. To some it seems a quite startling idea that unfaithfulness in married life can ever be forgiven, so childish is our ignorance when face to face with fundamental questions.' The greater change since the Bishop wrote this would appear to be the position of the child, who seems to have come a poor second to the marriage. The illegitimate birth-rate had reached a peak in 1945 – one in ten – but if anyone thought sex outside marriage to be a twentieth-century phenomenon, comparable figures had been recorded in the 1880s.

Having a child was a good way of saving a failing marriage,

123

according to a mother of seven daughters, Lady Hawke, commenting in the *News of the World* in the early fifties when moves to allow unilateral divorce after seven years were begun. The issue was debated hotly in the House of Commons because, although it sounds to us in the nineties no more than a technicality, at the time it represented the first step towards a sea-change in our attitude towards divorce. In the 1950s divorce was still very much about right and wrong, guilt and innocence, and the idea that a marriage could simply fall apart without either party being particularly at fault was impossible as far as the law was concerned. Divorce was always bad, always about wrongdoing; to see it as a remedy undermined not only marriage, but a society founded on the family. 'Divorce is not only a symptom of broken marriage, but the germ of the disease itself,' Richard Wood (Conservative, Bridlington) told the House. 'It could only be granted for insanity or a matrimonial offence,' Sir Patrick Spens (Conservative, Kensington South) insisted. The moment we went beyond that, he warned, it was only a matter of time before we got down to divorce by consent, producing more and more broken homes.

L. Wilkes (Labour, Newcastle-on-Tyne) agreed. Working-class wives who had spent their youth bringing up their families should be protected from divorce at the husband's whim after seven years. 'Innocence and guilt are really being made to disappear in a kind of vague shadow.'

The pattern of divorce petitions in the fifties showed more wives than husbands taking the initiative. They sued on the grounds of adultery, desertion and cruelty, in that order, twice as many for adultery compared with cruelty. In 1958 there were 350 husbands who sued their wives for cruelty, but what form the cruelty took is open to speculation. At about the same time in America a husband was able to divorce his wife because she had cruelly hidden his fishing-rod. My first husband might have had a case involving that hockey stick, but I don't think he would ever have lived it down with the team.

Cruelty, adultery and desertion seem to have been the principal grounds used for divorce in the fifties and into the sixties, but there were several others available. Madness could be used, so could epilepsy and VD, and a husband found guilty of raping another woman. Wilful refusal to consummate was another cause, and this could extend to refusal to have intercourse without contraceptives, sparking considerable debate about the meaning and purpose of marriage in twentieth-century Britain. Sodomy and bestiality featured as well, although in the case of T. v. T. reported in *The Times* in 1963, the wife was refused a divorce on the ground of sodomy because her husband managed to convince the judge that she had consented. On appeal, this decision was overturned after it became clear that the husband had tricked his wife into the act by telling her it was her duty, and that everyone did it. The duty bit was a lie, but hasn't sodomy long been a favourite British pastime?

Whatever the grounds, it seems incredible to us now that the sordid detail of marital breakdown had to be picked over to such a degree, that people who wanted to get out of a marriage had to make up stories and perjure themselves before the courts with contrived confessions of adultery. The only people who benefited from such a system were the private detectives hired to scrutinise hotel registers and sit outside bedroom doors beyond which two strangers whiled away the night playing cards – we've all seen it in the old black and white movies.

Yet there was real and valid concern behind the reactionary arguments against changing divorce law. The fear was that divorce as we know it today would lead to couples parting and families being split up when there was no real breakdown in the marriage, just lack of effort to make it succeed. Here I will stick my neck out and suggest that this is exactly what has happened in the vast majority of cases, at least those that don't involve violence and abuse. Would I have divorced? Would my friends – about 50 per cent of them – have divorced if it hadn't been so easy, if we'd had to wait and then go through some sort of degrading pantomime or public confessional?

The law can't be blamed; after all, it does no more than serve society, and attitudes towards marriage and divorce were already changing long before the law caught up. In the late fifties and early sixties, 'modern' couples were said to be divorce-minded and to regard marriage as a temporary affair with no degree of permanency, so said the Bar Council in their evidence to the Royal Commission on Marriage and Divorce. At the same time, a national marriage survey was looking into why couples parted. Teenage brides stood the least chance of avoiding the divorce court, but it didn't make much difference whether their husbands were the same age or old enough to be their fathers. The survey also showed, contrary to what you might expect, that marriages between people from widely differing backgrounds were no more likely to fail than those between couples with similar upbringings. The problems started within marriage, when one partner developed ahead of the other, when they didn't grow together, but apart.

By the end of the sixties, the country (more specifically, England and Wales, because Scotland's laws have always been a bit different even if the trends are the same) was so ripe for divorce law reform that even the Church had come up with a few ideas in the form of a report entitled 'Putting Asunder'. 'What the public wants is quick, cheap, easy divorce,' a woman journalist said at the press conference the day the report was published. But the Church, ever mindful of 'right' and 'wrong', was worried about misbehaving marriage partners 'getting away with it', and urged the country not to allow divorce by consent. If marriage was to maintain its importance in society it couldn't be too quickly or too easily broken, and some sort of 'inquest' ought to be part of each divorce hearing to establish why the marriage had died.

A member of the Archbishop of Canterbury's committee that produced the report, barrister Quentin Edwards, warning against quick and easy divorce, said the law should not favour hurt pride: 'An injured spouse might, on reflection, prefer to adhere to the marriage for the time being in order to give the other a chance to return to the joint life. These opportunities are likely to be lost if relief can be obtained too quickly.'

Others saw it differently. The Lord Chancellor, Lord Gardiner, said: 'Surely our common sense tells us that adultery, desertion and bad conduct at home are often symptoms of matrimonial collapse, rather than the disease itself. Keeping a man or woman married as a punishment is an odd conception. It will do no harm to the happily married to allow unhappy marriages to be decently buried; and their burial may enable those unhappy spouses to enjoy, in their turn, the blessings of a happy married life.'

Individual joy or sorrow aside, Parliament and the Church were both concerned that the old divorce laws had become almost as scandalous as the sale of dispensations and annulments by the Pope 400 years earlier. Otherwise decent people were knowingly deceiving the courts with farcical confessions of non-existent adultery just to get out of marriages that had died a natural death. Everyone knew that this was what was happening, including the judiciary, and such a state of affairs could do nothing but undermine the law and bring it into disrepute. Things had to change, but few of the reformers could have foreseen the deluge of divorce that would ensue; nobody could really call a divorce-rate of one in three progress.

After the reform, which came into effect at the beginning of 1971, making irretrievable breakdown the only ground for divorce – even if the cause of the irretrievability still labelled the partners guilty and innocent – the land of marriage became rather like the Soviet Union after the demise of communism: there was a rush to freedom, then people began to find that they were out of a job, short of money and rather lonely after the lights had gone out and the rest of the world lost interest. The walls had crumbled, but the landscape of new beginnings was bleaker than expected, and some started to think that the old order wasn't, after all, quite so bad.

The more cautious reformers had issued warnings. 'Divorce begets divorce. It is *a* solution, but it becomes *the* solution because it is available. People tend to want things that are available. There is a dangerous belief that divorce is a cure for matrimonial unhappiness – bury the marriage, and you live again – but this is far from true in many cases: divorce simply results in loneliness, despair and serious financial hardship.'

Lateral thinkers of the day decided that the problem was not divorce, but marriage. It was too easy to marry and ought to be made more difficult. Couples should register their engagement and have to wait a while before being allowed to marry. During this cooling-off period they should be made to read handbooks about sex and hire purchase agreements. And to avoid shotgun weddings, it was suggested that illegitimacy be abolished, although public opinion was already moving along the lines of better a bastard than a bad marriage. Counselling should be virtually compulsory – as it already was if you wanted a church wedding – and the hope was that 'people will come to view marriage consultants in the same light as they view their doctors'. Unfortunately, it all sounded more like the dentist, and the good intentions were consigned to the 'unrealistic' file.

While Church and State had been pontificating over reform the annual number of divorces had doubled in ten years, proving that the law was merely about to catch up with the trend; but some people were questioning whether a court of law was the right place for divorce proceedings; wasn't it rather too grave and sledgehammerish? Perhaps the same could be said for marriage: too heavy and loaded for a new generation trying to do its own thing, and the prophetic prediction in 1970 from the Divorce Law Reform Union was that not only would young people live together unmarried, but that society would accept it.

Yet public opinion, while redefining the parameters of morality, still preferred a bad marriage to divorce. 'If a married couple without children are very unhappy and both feel that there is no chance of getting the marriage back on the road again, which of these should they do?' asked a national opinion poll at the end of the sixties, 'Seek a divorce/get expert advice/separate/continue to live together/live together but lead separate lives.' Less than half the poll answered 'divorce'.

Over and over again, the statistics for divorce have shown that marrying too young is at the root of the problem in the majority of cases, but at the end of the sixties the country indulged in a peculiarly perverse piece of radical reform. It reduced the age of consent from 21 to 18. Again, it was a move designed more to protect the law than to maintain the law's protection, and it was argued on the grounds that parents didn't need the knuckle-duster of the law to dissuade their children from early matrimony. The way things were going it might have been wiser to have raised the age to 30.

Increasing divorce was set to cost the country a fortune, not only in Legal Aid, but to the Health Service. Divorce was supposed to bring relief of suffering, but more often it caused greater misery. A sample survey of 150 women who petitioned for divorce between 1967 and 1970 showed 130 of them experiencing health problems. They said their hair was falling out, they had abscesses, asthma, emaciating weight loss, chest pains and tummy ache. There were terrible headaches, dizziness and skin rashes, along with overwhelming feelings of hopelessness, desolation, shock, bitterness, failure and insecurity, while, ironically, 'cruelty' was no longer in the vocabulary of divorce law. 'It is a sobering thought that we give from Exchequer funds £42,000 annually to the Marriage Guidance Council and we spend between £3 and £4 million annually on divorce costs,' William Wilson MP said in the Commons at the end of the sixties.

By 1972 the annual number of divorces had risen to nearly 120,000 – more than four times the figure of a decade earlier. With all this misery going on, what was the Church doing to alleviate the suffering? The answer was not a lot. The very title of the Church's contribution to the divorce law reform debate, 'Putting Asunder', rather summed up the sniffy attitude. Two-thirds of all marriages were still taking place in church, yet when they fell apart the vicar was the last person a lot of people thought of approaching for comfort and advice. 'I was absolutely at sea,' said one wife, a regular churchgoer whose marriage ended in divorce. 'There were all the practical problems I had to cope with as well as the emotional ones.' It was to friends, not, on the whole, church people, that she turned for help. She didn't go to the vicar, even though she was deeply distressed about the religious aspects of her marriage breakdown. More to the point, he didn't approach her. 'I thought he would be shocked and embarrassed if I confided in him. I felt so ashamed. There were other clergy I knew and respected enormously, especially one, but by that time he had been made a bishop. I would have liked to talk to him, but I knew he was always terribly busy, and it didn't seem fair to bother him. Anyway, what could I ask him to *do*, other than listen to my woes, and one couldn't ask a bishop to do that.' I am inclined to think that if the bishop had been a woman the story might have been different, but we have yet to see if the upper echelons of the priesthood will seem more accessible when women are there.

'Technically, I was the innocent party,' continued the

religious wife, 'but I didn't want that distinction emphasised, and it seems to me that the Church does emphasise it. I felt we were both guilty of violating this sacred thing, marriage, and that it was a kind of guilt I should carry with me for the rest of my life. It made me so miserable I couldn't bear to think about it. So in the end I shied away from the Church altogether, and turned to a psychiatrist friend – who I knew was agnostic – in the hope that I'd get a rational explanation of what had gone wrong in the marriage, and some practical suggestions about how to cope with life. Of course he was terribly easy to talk to, very down-to-earth and quite unshockable. He explained my feelings to me. He also happened to know a good deal about the technical side of divorce, and recommended a first-rate solicitor. I doubt if many parsons could have done all those things.' They probably could have, but an image of approachability seems always to have eluded the solemn, grey-clad, grey-complexioned male clergy of the Church of England.

The vicar was not alone in failing the abandoned wife; his congregation didn't help, either: 'Even the smallest bit of practical help – like the occasional offer of babysitting – from someone closely connected with the Church would have given a kind of reassurance at a time when one is so ready to see rejection that one sees it everywhere. I can only think that people don't realise this, or they couldn't behave in such a seemingly unchristian way.' Churchgoing, then and now, does seem to be an insular and tunnel-visioned activity, and maybe it should not be expected to be a social service: surveys have shown that people with marital problems are more likely to write to a newspaper agony aunt than to press the doorbell at the vicarage.

While the Divorce Reform Act 1969 did a lot to help lessen the stigma of divorce, it was only a beginning. In my family, and most others, being married was like eating your greens – you had to eat the lot, however sick they made you feel; you stuck with them and kept at it, meal after meal, until the bitter brassica taste was acquired and appreciated. It was all to do with virtue, doing the right thing and accepting what was perceived to be good for you whether you liked it or not.

When the rebellion came it was inevitable that many of us

rebels would develop a perverse longing for cabbage once it was no longer on the menu. Getting divorced wasn't quite the liberating experience imagined; it was still squalid, made more so by the headlong rush. 'Oh my God – it's like a jumble sale! It's like queuing up for a jumble sale!' one petitioner told a researcher as she waited outside the courtroom. Once inside, there was bewilderment, even disappointment, at the lack of judicial interest in the individual marriage. 'It's supposed to be a matter of satisfying the judge, but to me, he didn't take much satisfying.' What a let-down. There had been all that fuss over reaching the point of no return, and when it came to the moment, nobody wanted to know about the wretched marriage itself. It was like spending years in rehearsal for a play and then finding there was no proper performance at the end. It was unsatisfactory. It didn't do anything to assuage the bitterness, and it wasn't a bit like it had been when you not only got the chance to tell all, but were obliged to do so.

By the beginning of the eighties, a million couples having divorced during the seventies, there was nothing new to tell, nothing brave, *avant garde* or rebellious, about ending a marriage. One-third of all marriages ending in divorce were said to be in trouble in their first year, and a third of all marriages were heading for divorce. The cost in terms of misery was summed up in a single gruesome statistic: the suicide rate of divorced people was six times the average; and the cost in fiscal measure added up to £40 million a year for the taxpayer.

As long as marriage remained the only licensed activity not subject to any test of competence, the casualty rate would never decrease. So said the MGC experts, especially David Mace, that founding father of marriage guidance in Britain, who moved on to the United States but continued to cast pearls of wisdom across the Atlantic. Marriage guidance, he said, should be more exactly what it called itself, guiding people through their married lives from one year to the next, beginning with special classes prior to the wedding, followed by regular monthly meetings during the first year of marriage, and annual check-ups thereafter. My own feelings about this sensible approach is that its chief advantage would be to warn prospective spouses against marrying anyone who even suggested such a course. 'I believe,' wrote Mace in 1980, 'that these procedures would make the best possible use of marriage counsellors by enabling them to apply their skills in situations where they were not dealing with already advanced conflict, but helping couples to learn procedures for negotiating obstacles to growth. Working in this way should be much more rewarding for the counsellor, who would be building up lasting friendships with couples striving to maintain successful and creative relationships. And those who came for help in an advanced state of marital discord could be enabled to sit in groups with other couples whose marriages were working well, and who could provide them with models of the kind of relationship they were seeking.' Presumably at the end of it they could sit a GCSE in Smugness.

Needless to say, the idea didn't catch on in Britain, and the casualty rate continued to grow until the mid-eighties, when it reached one in just under three, where it has held fairly steady ever since, suggesting that we have reached the divorce-rate plateau beyond which there would have to be a basic change in our attitude and approach towards marriage. By this I mean the idea of serial monogamy becoming the expected and accepted norm, replacing the current ideal of marriage for life. Reasons for divorce over the past decade would tend to confirm this trend, even if it's not the way most of us would choose to plan our married lives. Although the majority of divorce petitions are still down to adultery, surveys have shown that infidelity is not seen as the ultimate crime in modern marriage; being boring is worse, exceeding violence and anything else that, at least, keeps you on your toes. Being boring, and 'growing out of' are the big ones.

It's also well proved that we don't give up on marriage, even if we more readily discard partners. Since 1979 over a third of all marriages each year have included at least one remarrying partner; but practice doesn't necessarily improve performance, and the failure rate for second marriages is higher than for first.

A major strain imposed on second marriages has been the financial provision for the first family. In 1982, two years before The Matrimonial and Family Proceedings Act (MFPA), £1 million was owed by defaulting husbands in jail for failing to pay maintenance, and half of all orders were in arrears.

Divorce law reform of a decade earlier had made divorce easier, but for some men, more expensive. The ending of reliance on marital 'fault' as the only basis for divorce meant that some 'wronged' husbands had been ordered to support ex-wives, who, under the old law, wouldn't have got a penny. After the initial reform, some such husbands found themselves bringing up the children single-handed yet at the same time having to pay thousands of pounds a year to their ex-wives; and if the husband married again, his second wife had to share the financial burden of her predecessor as well as care for the children. Bitterness and martyrdom had a field-day, and the new Act aimed to end this unfair 'meal ticket' aspect of the financial arrangements.

'The tendency is still to treat wives as helpless, unable to work and dependent,' the MGC reported, yet only 5 per cent of working husbands had a wife not working. The MFPA aimed to encourage self-sufficiency for both partners by applying the bulk of maintenace to children of the marriage. Yet there were loud voices of dissent, chiefly from MPs Jo Richardson and Harriet Harman, who were concerned that any change in the law would benefit only middle-class men, while all ex-wives would suffer. The logic of this was a little obscure, but based on the notion that the rich and the poor would be equally unaffected for diametrically opposite reasons, and only those in between would notice any difference in the variation of a maintenance order. However, the ex-wives, at all three levels, might suffer, unless, according to the two MPs, there were substantial changes in social security legislation, tax law and opportunities for training and employment. Richardson and Harman were criticised for seeming to challenge the 'children first' ethos of the new Act, but this was a misleading and underhand swipe at their motives. It had taken centuries for women to reach parity with men in the marriage stakes, and as far as divorce was concerned, universal equality was as fresh-faced as a decade. The MFPA unwittingly presented an opportunity for a bit of 'nibbling away'.

The new Act wasn't just about money, it also dealt with the length of time marriage had to be endured if, as was sometimes the case, it proved to be a big mistake from the word go. Instead of three years, the sentence was reduced to one, although the religious factions cried foul, claiming that one year of suffering was too short and didn't give marriage a fair crack of the whip; yet quick divorce had been possible under the old law if 'exceptional depravity' could be demonstrated, or at least, convincingly proved. 'This curious provision in the law seemed to suggest that there was a condition of "normal moral depravity",' observed one bemused commentator.

Those who objected to the new timing were reminded that in Scotland there was no time bar at all. During the parliamentary debate Nicholas Fairbairn cited the case of a bridegroom who, on his wedding day, celebrated to such excess that he was incapable of exercising his customary prerogative, and so the bride spent the wedding night with the best man. Under Scottish law the groom could have commenced divorce proceedings immediately, although Jo Richardson and Harriet Harman might have suggested that the bride should be the petitioner. Either way, the point of the story was that timing made little difference as the incidence of divorce in Scotland was no higher than in England and Wales.

Whatever the intentions of the MFPA, it seemed to encourage new focus on the plight of divorced men rather than divorced women. Studies and books were published about the suffering of men, how divorce had not only robbed them of their children, their homes and much of their income, but had also destroyed careers and friendship networks, and led to low self-image. In other words, men in the 1980s generally had more to lose than women; the sunny new horizons beyond divorce were largely for female viewing in an era still bathed in the expansive theory of feminism.

Perhaps this is why three-quarters of all divorce petitions are brought by women, even now, in the so-called post-feminist era: the future still looks better the other side of marriage. The men, presumably, tend to accept this, too, because fewer than one divorce in a hundred is defended to any degree. The number of decrees absolute in England and Wales is currently running at a little over 150,000 a year, a little over 12,000 in Scotland, which is higher than a decade ago, but lower than in the mid-eighties. Relate, as the National Marriage Guidance Council has called itself since 1988 in order to spread the net wider, reports that divorce in Britain has been on a fairly even plateau for some years, nudging up slightly, but not alarmingly so; although our divorce-rate is one of the highest in Europe at more than one in three, or, annually, $1^1/4$ per cent of all existing marriages. David Barkla, the fount of all knowledge at Relate, says he doesn't know why we should be more divorceable and divorcing than our Community neighbours, but my own theory is our changeable weather and the irritability it engenders. Coupled with this, and setting aside feminism and easier divorce law, I'd say it was also to do with television and the constant drip-feed of high drama in the everyday settings it is so easy to identify with. The only way to make television 'soaps' interesting is to have the characters lurching from one emotional crisis to another, and maybe we feel deprived if our own lives don't reflect this. This sounds flip, but don't we tend to see the whole world through television these days, so that scripted people, places and situations seem more real than reality? It could be that I am putting the cart before the horse with this home-spun piece of theorising; but I've got another idea that equally blames television: we stay up too late watching it and are too tired for sex.

There are all sorts of reasons why people don't get on, and blaming television is probably unfair; the notion is even shot to pieces by 50,000 divorces a year that are due to adultery. Most of the others are down to unreasonable behaviour, a couple of thousand caused by desertion, 40,000 as the follow-on to separation ... the figures don't vary much from one year to the next. There's been talk of 'no blame' divorce, the nearest to which under the present law is separation, but it could be that we are not yet sufficiently civilised to cope with such an idea. We like to be able to apportion blame, it makes us feel better about the essentially destructive nature of divorce; even so, I was amazed to discover that private detectives are still doing a roaring trade in matrimonial investigations. Hadn't all that gone out with the Act?

The Cambridge Detective Agency is three floors up, there's no lift, and I passed a dirty ashtray on the landing. I realised too late that I was wearing my mac, the one with the big, turned-up collar. The office is in an attic, but it is shared with a marketing consultancy and is far from dingy, and the chief detective is a long way from looking shifty. Former policeman Vincent Charles Johnson is a blue-private-eyed stunner, smartly dressed, well spoken; he could be in the movies. Instead, he handles between 40 and 50 cases a week, 60 per cent of them matrimonial. 'Years ago, you had to catch people in the act, leap out of wardrobes, but things have changed. A lot of couples these days have amicable divorce.' Those that don't may meet Mr Johnson when he serves legal documents on them; most of his work is on behalf of solicitors, but 15 of the 60 per cent is surveillance, and even if crouching in wardrobes is outmoded, the work is still pretty cloak and dagger.

'People still want evidence of adultery for their own peace of mind,' Mr Johnson tells me, although I am at a loss to understand any sort of peace this knowledge might bring. 'We had a client recently who'd had her suspicions for fourteen years. She was damn sure her husband was seeing someone else. He was away every Tuesday and Thursday, allegedly working. We followed him to a village in the Fens and a house where he let himself in with a key. We called our client and she turned up with a suitcase. The woman at the house opened the door to her and was wearing skimpy clothes, but denied that the husband was there.' He was, and subsequently admitted that he'd been having an affair for the entire period of his wife's suspicions, during which they had lived in various parts of the country, but had always been followed by the mistress. 'Our client didn't know why she had waited so long to confirm her suspicion – it had been eating away at her, but now she's pleased it's all settled. She's going through the angry stage, and they will divorce.' This particular piece of surveillance cost £250. Mr Johnson charges £18 per hour, 40p per mile, and an extra £7 an hour if it means staying up late. 'I don't like matrimonial work, it's tacky,' he says, 'but, if I like the person, or feel sorry for them, then I'll do it.'

Sometimes the work is dangerous. There was the Norfolk lumberjack with a chainsaw, the bruiser in the Kung Fu outfit, and the heartbroken husband who stuffed a twelve-bore shotgun into Mr Johnson's mouth. Mostly, he talks his way out of tricky situations, but sometimes it's a case of a quick sprint back to the car: 'I had a doctor the other day who tried to stab me. His eyeballs started rolling about in his head and he raced to the kitchen and grabbed a carving knife. He slashed it in front of me – I was only serving him a document, and this is a doctor, for heaven's sake, running at me with a bloody carving knife. He stabbed my car, and then followed me in his. I didn't tell the police. The way I see it it is perks of the trade; I do enjoy the odd situations, the rush of adrenalin.'

Other times he has been better prepared: 'The solicitor told me one chap was a knife maniac. "He'll stab you," he said. I went home and took off my suit and put on some really rough old gear. I tied several copies of *Cosmopolitan* round my chest inside my jacket and I looked like the Michelin man. In the event, the chap I went to see was OK, but just as I was leaving, the string broke and the magazines fell on the floor. It was very embarrassing.'

Then there was the husband leading a double life. Mr Johnson followed him to London and eventually discovered he was planning to fake his own death and disappear with a new woman and a great deal of money. The man's wife accepted Mr Johnson's report of what was going on, but she wanted to see for herself: 'It's curiosity, and sometimes it's better if there's a direct confrontation. People will swear blind they are not doing what they're accused of. In this particular case, all the various bank accounts were frozen pending the divorce.'

Some of the people who climb the three flights to Mr Johnson's office, he cannot help. 'I won't take people's money under false pretences. I had a chap who wanted me to find his wife. He got out a single thread of material and put it on my desk. He said his wife would be wearing a dress made of the same stuff. I didn't take the job on.' Distraught, beside themselves with misery, others will ring up in the middle of the night: 'My husband's gone off to see another woman. He's driving somewhere around Royston in a green VW Beetle.'

Most clients know what their husband or wife is up to before they enlist the services of a private detective, they just want the proof so they can do something about it. 'It usually comes down to the sex angle, the lack of it, and the husband or wife coming home looking happy. Most are right about their hunches.' And it has nothing to do with female intuition – there are as many men as women climbing Mr Johnson's stairs. The men he is asked to watch are many and various, but the women – 'the adulterous woman usually plays in a darts team on Tuesday nights'.

10 The discovery of sex and the tyranny of the orgasm

ND THEN THERE WAS the lady who asked her librarian for a copy of the *Calmer Suitor* ... Repression, it seems, typified the British marriage in matters sexual until fairly recent times; it's only in the last twenty years or so that British wives have noticeably staked a claim to orgasmic levels of satisfaction, rejecting the 'think of England' acceptance that had sustained generations of women through the 'beastly' part of marriage.

Marriage expert Dr Wendy Greengross told a medical meeting in London in 1976 that the days were over when she asked women patients if their sex life was satisfactory and they replied: 'My husband is very good like that. He doesn't trouble me much.' Women, Dr Greengross proclaimed, were learning that they could enjoy sex and go on enjoying it a lot longer than men.

This would seem to present something of a conundrum, conjuring up the possibility of licentious behaviour on the part of sex-crazed old ladies whose husbands had run out of libido; indeed, dissatisfaction with the British husband's performance was confirmed in 1974 by *Woman's Own*, whose survey among more than 1,000 British wives revealed a depressing level of disappointment when it came to love and sex. A year later, the MGC conducted their own survey, and a third of the married couples who took part said they were experiencing sexual difficulties, with almost the same number admitting infidelity. This was compared with a survey conducted twenty years earlier, when infidelity featured at only 50 per cent of the 1975 level. Other surveys resulted in similar findings, the British marriage, particularly in middle age, had become a limp affair, without much sex, with nothing to talk about, and surviving on little more than grudging companionship and, on a good day, passive congeniality. Women were to blame for discovering orgasms and wanting lots of them. Their husbands couldn't cope with the pressure of demand and impotency rates soared.

Sex was at the top of the agenda for public discussion as never before; but it was all so frank and meaningful, so earnest and such hard work. If there had been an element of fun in the promiscuity of the early seventies, the sexologists of the late seventies and early eighties drowned it in their dedication to the orgasmic cause. Our culture was said to be paying the inevitable penalty for denying sex so vehemently for so long; and by 'so long' was meant centuries of sex-negative religion as espoused by Christianity, wherein celibacy holds the moral high ground. By contrast, Islam is counted as sex-positive, and the Hindus, well, they were the ones who thought up all those different positions – 729 at the last count.

What was needed to add verve to the British marriage was more anger. Couples who became too cosy together, too passively congenial, had got it all wrong; conflict had to be accepted as a key element in the sexual relationship and glossing over it only killed desire. At least, this is what we were told by an American psychiatrist, but the idea of cross lovers didn't really accord with the British expectations of marital bliss, or the more jaded view expressed by Jill Tweedie writing in the *Guardian*: 'Pity the poor marriage counsellors, the sex advisers who continually grapple with people's sexual problems based on high expectation for a mundane activity. In come the couples who, after years of marriage, say the lust has gone out of their union. Do the counsellors say "naturally", or "of course it has, you twits"? Not at all. Brainwashed as the rest, they scratch their dedicated heads and recommend sex clinics, grotesque positions, and peculiar undies. Why not, they say, have sex in the middle of a field for a change? Or do it on the bonnet of your car or in a plastic dustbin? What they never say is the truth, that sex is better than a smack in the belly with a wet fish but not a whole lot better.'

One seventies solution, proclaimed like a newly discovered panacea, was the infidelity already tried by 30 per cent of the

MGC survey. Too much was expected of modern marriage, satisfaction in all departments – economic, social, procreative, emotional and sexual. The load was too heavy, the modern couple likened to a bridge meant for five-ton vehicles but now expected to carry enormous lorries of 30 tons or more. As a result, faithfulness was no longer to be viewed as a clear-cut concept; it could indicate priority of choice, but without excluding a bit on the side. In other words, being unfaithful didn't have to threaten the stability of the marriage, in fact it could help sustain it by lessening the load. But what of jealousy? Apparently, this was no more than a culturally induced emotion found only where marriage was regarded as a cage outside which sexual relations had to be an automatic threat to everything.

Denying jealousy sounds a bit like the propositions put forward by the Flat Earth Society, but there was another curse on the horizon, another spoiler for those who had found logical and convincing reasons for infidelity. AIDS had yet to come into our vocabulary in the mid-1970s, but we should have known there would be something to stop the free-for-all. Even so, the crusade for greater freedom continued, with experts talking about the stifling of our normal sexual drives due to society's unjustified fears about the implications of promiscuity. We were told that before long the act of copulation would not involve any risks or hidden dangers; but the last risk to be abolished would not be unwanted pregnancy, or venereal disease or any other physical danger, the last risk would be psychological, because we took it all too seriously.

Doctors, perhaps suspecting that the worst was yet to come, were accused of not wanting to see VD eliminated and of exaggerating the dangers of the Pill, simply in order to discourage promiscuity. The Pill, if it did encourage promiscuous behaviour, was also at the root of the emasculating problem mentioned earlier. Women not only enjoyed greater sexual freedom but there was also the wider emancipating effect. Able to limit their families and take up careers, British wives gained in self-confidence and economic self-sufficiency. Husbands were dangerously close to becoming redundant in the traditional power-broking role of provider, and as their usefulness diminished, so did their self-esteem and sex drive.

Made in Heaven

The 1970s sexual seesaw had catapulted women into the ascendant.

Reflecting over two decades of answering readers' letters, agony aunt Georgette Floyd, otherwise known as Clare Shepherd in *Women's Realm*, wrote in 1978 about how the balance had tipped. 'Instead of letters from unjustly treated wives, today I am more likely to get a letter from a man who is crouching in a bedsitter while his wife and family enjoy the comfort of the home for which he is paying a huge mortgage, another man is visiting – and the very poor husband has committed no matrimonial offence at all.' Perhaps this was the problem. Letters from the earlier decade had included complaints from wives who claimed that their husbands were 'beasts' – often, according to Georgette Floyd, when he was acting in a fairly normal fashion; but sexual ignorance on the part of women had given way to voracious appetite: 'Now the problem is not so much trying to help a woman to enjoy sex but trying to get her to accept her own and her husband's limitations.'

Floyd went on to say that one of the most noticeable changes in the letters was the growing complexity of family structures: 'At one time the women who wrote to me would say they were either married or single. Now they say they are not married, but living with a man; married and living with another man; single and living with a man married to someone else.' The content of the letters had also hugely changed from the 1960 twilight days of innocence when one in five wanted to know the Facts of Life – 'always with a capital F and a capital L, as if they were asking for the New Testament'.

Twenty years on, the reading list could keep you up all night. The plethora of sex manuals, route-planners for voyages of self-discovery, how to, what to, when to and who to books, was in danger of rendering the subject too technical for comfort. Reviewers complained of unmitigated boredom, of being fed up with the pictures of shaggy-haired couples hanging from chandeliers; and if in bed, it was always a four-poster (so conveniently well appointed for bondage). There were great tomes devoted to the elusive G spot; chest-aching volumes penned by people with names like Cockshut; learned theses scorning the muscular torso and big penis (women were more attracted by slimness and small buttocks); there was even a treatise on the expansion of male nostrils during coitus.

One of the most famous of these books, Alex Comfort's *Joy of Sex*, was superseded in the late seventies by *More Joy of Sex*; from climbing to mountaineering, readers said, with additional advice on the etiquette required for foursomes. The suggestion was a nice dinner to start with, followed by mattresses in front of the fire and the assurance that, once undressed, everyone would instantly relax, but with the rider 'Don't, at any price, give an exhibition – it's insensitive.' I've never been able to work out whether group sex is for people with problems or those who don't have any troubles at all; whether it is a fillip for flagging libido or just another thing to try.

By the beginning of the eighties, married couples had become so confused about the whole business, so over-exposed to conflicting expert advice, explicit eroticism and the boundless possibilities for sexual gratification, that the only retreat was into 'marital sexual dysfunction', the 1980s terminology for a headache.

MSD as a recognised and treatable condition sprang from the work of Masters and Johnson, the American couple who took sex into the laboratory in the sixties. This was nothing to do with test-tube babies: it involved observing copulating couples, volunteers who didn't mind an audience, albeit a serious one in white coats. From their observations, Masters and Johnson identified four male dysfunctions and six female ones, all of them more or less to do with either erections or orgasms, or lack of them. More to the point, M & J had developed treatments, and in the mid-seventies these were adopted in Britain, the MGC securing government funding for a trial run. The treatments involved theory sessions with therapists combined with a programme of homework – rather like evening classes for late developers. Couples progressed from fairly simple exercises, generalised touching and stroking, through to 'mocks' and then, with all the theory in place, to the real thing. Some jumped the gun, 'they broke the ban on intercourse three weeks running', one therapist said of a couple receiving treatment. This same therapist noticed that male clients troubled by premature ejaculation tended to arrive early for their treatment sessions, while those with the opposite problem sometimes didn't turn up at all. Whatever their problem, all who did attend were assured that there was no 'British standard orgasm' to be achieved, and no marriage guidance recommended position for intercourse.

'When a pendulum starts to swing it is difficult to get it to come to rest in the middle,' wrote Celia Haddon in her book *The Limits of Sex* published in the early eighties. Masters and Johnson had led us to expect too much from sex and 'the tyranny of the orgasm' had caused unnecessary disquiet among couples hitherto perfectly satisfied with whatever they were doing; they had been made to feel inadequate, even unhealthy, and all in pursuit of the technicolour dream at the summit of the mountain.

For those with no head for heights there was some comfort from a 1984 MGC survey among young people asked what they really wanted from marriage. Sexual satisfaction featured fairly low in their priorities, with trust and 'someone I can talk to' at the top of the list. The girls, for all the female sexual emancipation gone before them, rated sexual satisfaction much lower than the boys; there again, the girls had yet to discover the longevity of their concupiscence compared with that of the boys, or so Dr Greengross would have it.

Meanwhile, among the married, sexual dissatisfaction, or rather, the voicing of it, continued to grow, with two in five couples in the mid-eighties admitting to having experienced sexual problems. The less forthcoming went to the family doctor complaining of headaches, rheumatism, palpitations, fatigue, bowel disorders, excessive flushing and perspiration, skin rashes, anxiety and tension, asthma, eczema, peptic ulcer, angina, migraine, apathy, weight loss, insomnia, all manner of ills beneath which lurked a bad time in bed. Doctors said it was a 'chicken and egg' syndrome; bad sex, bad marriage, which came first? Either way, some patients had turned to drink while others preferred Valium, coined 'the over-40s' marijuana'.

For those who turned to marriage guidance it was, according to some, about as much use as consulting a Luddite's crystal ball. Despite the MGC's bold experiments with sex therapy in the mid-seventies, counsellors had not really latched on to the idea. It was a bit like the old joke, the one where the machine-gun salesman turns up at the battlefield, but to no avail – the general is too busy with his bows and arrows. It was all part of the 'British Disease'. People wanted the wonderful sex they kept hearing about, they wanted their marriages to be successful, but when they asked for advice they got the hit and miss stuff that applied to an earlier age. Sex therapy was the new cure-all, but it was still being used as something separate from the main business of marriage guidance.

This is well illustrated by the experience of Jane and Lawrence, who sought help from the MGC in the late seventies. Theirs had been a turbulent marriage from the start; both had been married before, and the high expectations that had caused their first marriages to founder looked likely to destroy the second. Jane wanted absolute security, while Lawrence wanted absolute love. The problem was that Lawrence's quest meant that he was chronically unfaithful, totally undermining Jane's sense of security.

Separately and together, they went to more marriage guidance sessions than either could remember, and somebody was even unkind enough to tell them they'd had more than their fair share. Eventually, sex therapy was offered, but not at the usual place where they went for counselling – instead they were sent to the local hospital.

'We only had one session, but that was because the woman we saw was about to retire,' Jane told me. 'We didn't talk about sex at all, but that one session was better than all the rest had been, in fact it was very good. Lawrence opened up in a way he had never done before. He was much more in touch with his emotions and he actually broke down. The therapist made him realise that his needs were too great and that it wasn't sex, it was love that he needed because he hadn't had much affection as a child.

'I remember that it did something to me, too – my heart went out to him, he was so vulnerable. We must have been putting up barriers with the ordinary counsellors.'

The ordinary sessions came to an abrupt and bizarre end during a fund-raising soirée in aid of the local MGC. By a cruel twist of fate, the cellist providing the evening's musical interlude turned out to be Lawrence's latest mistress, a jealous and overt woman unfamiliar with the etiquette of adulterous love affairs.

Sex therapy, if it had got round to that, might in time have worked for Jane and Lawrence, but it was too late for them; too late for their local MGC as well. (More of Jane later, post-Lawrence and into a new relationship initiated via a computer.)

The trouble was, British gut feeling was never to catch up with the new attitude towards sex as a proper topic for open discussion and a good, clean, wholesome pursuit; I remember a neighbour of ours telling me he had no vices 'other than that indoors'. Vice or virtue, there were those who saw danger in public debate about sex, in the single-minded search for earth-moving, star-seeing satisfaction; it was undermining the family, and in so doing, the stability of our society. The time had come for a swing to the 'moral right', the return of Victorian values and the subjugation of self to the wider brief of family life.

To some, this repression of self would always be especially difficult. While the rest of us had been discovering sex, undermining our family values and generally rocking society's boat in the main stream, there were those still marginalised in the bywaters of sexuality, in the muddied pool of gender dysphoria. Don and Val are a case in point, an outwardly ordinary middle-aged couple with sons and daughters, friends and neighbours, and a quirk of Don's character that makes them different.

'Nobody can accuse me of wearing the wife's clothes,' Don tells me as he unpacks the shopping, moving about the kitchen with purposeful step and the domesticated certainty of where everything goes. At a guess I'd say he is a generous size 20. He has arrived ten minutes into my interview with his size 12 wife about what it's like being married to a transvestite.

Don is, by any reckoning, a big man. His hunting ground is limited to Evans Outsize, frocks that could be pegged out on a campsite and sleep two. He's a big, bluff Scot, with a voice as deep as the glen and an aura of overpowering maleness; but this is Don as Don, wearing jeans and a heavy navy sweater, his thinning hair windblown, steel-framed spectacles above jowly features. With a little help from make-up, a wig and a close shave, the same face becomes Doris, but it's hard to imagine, impossible to think he can do anything about that look around the eyes, you know, the way a man who knows about women looks at them. There again, perhaps this is what it's all about, although nobody has come up with any sort of definitive explanation for why hearty heterosexuals like Don feel compelled to spend part of their time masquerading as the opposite sex.

More than 60 years ago Don's mother gave birth to her illegitimate baby in a remote and close-knit community in the Outer Hebrides. Having a baby out of wedlock wasn't so bad a thing – any increase in the sparse and dwindling population was welcomed except it would have been better if the child had been a girl: a boy had to have a name to carry with him through life and into coming generations. It didn't matter that everyone knew the baby was a boy, but outward appearances were all important, and supposing a stranger came by? Don was put in a dress, and at the age of five, when his father, a military man, reappeared, it was something of a surprise to discover that the little girl was a boy.

Absent fathers are cited as a possible cause of transvestism, but so, curiously, are gas masks. To have been dressed as a girl is perhaps too simplistic, too obvious an explanation, especially as most men of Don's generation wore frocks until they were out of nappies, and only one in 80 British males is a TV (the transvestite term for what they are). Actually, one in 80 sounds rather a lot, about $3^3/_4$ million of the adult male population; more to the point as far as this book is concerned, many of them are married.

Don says he didn't start cross-dressing until his first wife stopped being nice to him. While he was at university and, later, in the Army, a commissioned officer, it never occurred to him to wear women's clothes; then, finding himself alone much of the time, with long periods of working abroad and nothing much to look forward to when he got home, he discovered that the only way he could really relax was to go into his other self, Doris. Wherever he was in the world, in a five-star hotel, in a tent in the desert, Doris was always on hand, unfolded into reality via a pair of frilly knickers and a see-through nightie, because who was Doris kidding, only Don, and he'd seen it all before. He says he felt he had created a partner within himself, the partner his wife had ceased to be.

She didn't know about Doris, the knickers or the nightie, and the ending of the marriage had little to do with clothes; Don never trusted her with his secret because he didn't want anyone else to know: 'Basically,' he says, 'I'm a pretty strait-laced person.'

Perhaps it was the climate of the times, more probably the nature of Val, Don's second wife, that decided him to take the risk and tell. As it happened, Val found the knickers first, before there was a chance for the telling. At the time, she was 3,000 miles from home, about to start a new life with a man she hardly knew. Don had come into her life while he was visiting his son at an East Anglian airbase and staying in the Fenland village where Val had lived most of her life. It was a pub meeting, and love at first sight for Don. Val, fifteen years younger, says she didn't see him as 'potential relationship material', just a nice, intelligent man who was good company.

Val was not yet 40, had been married twice, brought up two children, and become a champion darts player – serious darts, promising fame and fortune. Don pressed his suit, and within weeks Val was boarding a plane for Kuwait where she was to join Don and discover Doris. 'It was Valentine's Day 1984, and I stayed out there for the rest of the year. During this time I found out he was TV – I just found some underwear in a drawer.'

Another woman, albeit a big one, might seem like the most obvious conclusion to draw, but Val didn't think so. Maybe she sort of knew already, through Don's insistent interest in her clothes, in his choosing and buying for her a complete new wardrobe for the Middle East climate. Don says this was simply because he wanted her to feel fine and confident as she got to know the other ex-pat wives whose husbands were his subordinates.

Outward appearances, the good opinion of others, these were as important to Val as it seemed they were to Don. Val had been brought up in a family guided by monochrome morality; there were no shades of black and white in the way one behaved, no room for doubt when it came to what other people might think. 'My childhood was based on an era that had gone. What other people would think governed my mother's life, and you didn't wear make-up and stockings until you were eighteen as far as she was concerned,' which meant these adult accoutrements arrived after the birth of Val's first child and the disastrous early marriage.

Both Val's children were grown-up by the time she arrived in Kuwait and discovered make-up and stockings anew. 'I can't remember whether it was hours or days before I said anything to Don. I was in a state of shock and became quiet and withdrawn. The whole idea of it just didn't fit in with the man I had met and travelled all those miles to be with. I suppose I was still governed by appearances and the discovery hung over me all the time – I liken it to finding out, several years before, that my son was epileptic.' 'Oh, come on!' roars Don, but Val is insistent: 'Look, darling, I'm talking about how I felt.'

With an outrageous stab at practicality, Don claimed at the time that he found the frilly stuff more comfortable than Y-fronts. 'I'd had every intention of telling Val before she found out, but it was a pretty tough admission. I loved her and I knew there was every chance of losing her.' So why didn't he just stop doing it? 'There was no question of giving it up. It's a safety valve that I need.' Later during our talk he was to compare it with women who power-dress at work but need to change into something more comfortable in order to relax at home; but this seemed to me more on a par with my own compulsion to wear an apron in the kitchen, feeling vaguely naked, ill-at-ease and vulnerable without it. Surely there is something deeper and more mysterious about Don's compulsion?

When Val discovered Doris she thought about leaving, but she was a long way from home and she still loved Don. Making friends with Doris was another matter, and a bitter battle began: 'I fought "her" for a long time. The other ex-pats had an idealised view of us as a couple and I was worried about losing my place in the group if any of them found out, but we didn't live with them, Don had chosen to live with the Arabs.'

Val says she began to cope with Doris by seeing her as a theatrical character played by Don: 'There's a great deal of the thespian in TVs, and rebellion. Society puts such pressure on boys from the start, a pressure that isn't inflicted on girls.' These days, back in the village of her birth, Val spends much of her time on the telephone, talking to TV wives, telling them how she came to terms with it. She and Don operate a helpline, today's accolade of acceptance for every sort of deviance. They are both involved with the Beaumont Society, Britain's self-help group for TVs, their wives and families, but in a sense, transvestism has become more a way of life for Val than for Don. She is fascinated by and committed to the cause, if cause it is, and is as ready with the leaflets and 'your questions answered' pamphlets as the purveyors of *Watchtower*. It's the sensible, British way of coping – the if-you-can't-beat-'em-join-'em approach that props up male obsessions and pursuits wherever you look, and in a milder form produces cricket teas.

None of this is to say that Val has found it easy. She resented Doris, not only because three was a crowd, but because this feminine persona on the part of Don seemed so greedy: 'He had got everything as a man, career success, the whole lot, and there he was, wanting to be a woman as well.'

'What's for you won't go past you,' interjects Don, who has a liking for proverbs. 'We [TVs] have no choice. It's a compulsion, no, it's a need, not something I would ever choose.' But for Val there was a choice, and it took her three years, a dive into alcoholism, and professional help to make it. 'Val was the one who was confused. Really, the TV hasn't got a problem, it's the partner.'

After the year in Kuwait, the year of nobody else knowing, Val came home alone while Don went on to Saudi Arabia, a country he deemed too repressive for a Western woman, although Doris, used to purdah, went with him. At home, Val's confusion turned into despair and a lot of drinking. When she decided she'd had enough, she looked for professional help and was told, perhaps predictably, that the problem lay in her own past, the upbringing that had dwelt in the reflection of what other people might see and think. 'I learned that I had to discard perfectionism, and all of a sudden it didn't matter what other people thought. If I had never met

Don or had a partner who was TV, I'd have come to the same conclusion about life.'

Don came home and Val married him – and Doris. 'Sometimes I feel that she is trying to take my role. She can be overpowering, and I feel that there are three people in this house, not two.' Val's children, having accepted Don, had less trouble with Doris than might be imagined; when Val's daughter married, it was Don she asked to 'give her away' although with the proviso that he didn't upstage her in a frock.

The neighbours know. The house is squashed into a terrace and too narrow for such secrets; besides, Don and Val are friendly, outgoing people. It would be hard not to like them and there has to be a vicarious cachet in having such interesting people next door, although Doris remains more private than public. Going out is limited to special weekends when the Beaumont Society will take over an entire hotel. Don says the society's membership is rather heavy with ex-military types, steam train buffs and model-makers, but the meetings are said to be not unlike those of the Women's Institute. Perhaps this is partly because they are as much for the benefit of the partners as the TVs, the reassurance of knowing they are not alone.

Val has embraced Doris along with Don, the woman in the man and the man in the woman, the bluff Scotsman who sometimes comes to bed in a nightie; but it is always Don who makes love to her, there's nothing funny about Doris.

Why so manly a man as Don should want to pretend to be a woman is, by all accounts, inexplicable, although the general drift of the earlier part of this chapter could be seen to provide a clue. Certainly the sexual focus for the past twenty years appears to have been on women, on female gratification. So it continues. Orgasms are so good for us, women are told in the 1990s pages of glossy magazines; they relieve tension and stress, the everyday bogeys of modern life; they are a far better remedy for pain than taking a couple of paracetamol. When the 1990s wife tells her husband she has a headache it's quite likely she's giving him a come-on rather than a turn-off and is expecting more than a cup of Horlicks and a bit of peace and quiet.

The sexologists are still at it, too, counting orgasms, though goodness knows why. Women can reach well over a 100 at one sitting, while the male record stands at just sixteen. There was some old buffer on the radio the other day talking about the count, how he'd watched hundreds of orgasms and still found them thrilling; but what I want to know is, who are these people who don't mind being watched?

11 A sort of emancipation

I F SEX WAS the big discovery of the seventies, work became the major theme of the eighties. From our vantage point of the caring nineties we can see that work became more sexy than sex but ultimately as damaging and wearisome when practised to excess. Must success cost so much? This was the question taxing marriage experts who saw the institution under threat yet again, especially in dual-career marriages. The old adage that behind every successful man there was a good woman underwent an androgynous change to become 'behind every successful executive there is a good relationship'. But with so many good men and women both working, the strain was bound to tell – at work and in marriage.

On this basis it was suggested that industry and commerce should contribute financially to the work of marriage guidance, to pay for the repairs, the damage that work had caused to a relationship. The more cynical observer might see this as just another piece of Total Quality Management hoodwinking – keep everyone happy, and the happiest of all would be the shareholders.

The modern version of bigamy, we were told, was simultaneous marriage to one's family and one's work, but the concomitant problems were often greater than those connected with the conventional version of this particular duplicity. For a start it wasn't recognised as a crime, but the pain and suffering could be just as acute, and the neglect even worse. The workaholic manager was inclined to switch off his 'sensitivity valve' when he got home, and hardly notice his wife and children. His joy, sorrow, anger, pleasure and fun were all suppressed through his preoccupation with work. But this bigamous businessman began back-tracking when he reached his mid-thirties; successful or not, he paused to see what he had been missing at home, that is, if he still had one.

Continuation of the marriage had depended almost entirely on his wife's capacity for adjustment, on her willingness to sacrifice herself to husband and family; but what happened if she had an equally demanding career outside the home? Some experts thought it would be impossible for the marriage to survive, that one of the partners could spread themselves thinly, but if both tried it the whole enterprise would become transparently unworkable. Others disagreed. Two people could be happy together if they were both fulfilled in their work, but they had to be able to talk about it, to express their feelings, share the problems, relieve the stress. This sounds fairly obvious, but for the British marriage, increasingly dual-career, it wasn't quite so straightforward: there was the stiff upper lip to be dealt with.

Here, of course, could lie the root of all our economic ills, because if you couldn't express your feelings at home you were unlikely to be giving your all at work. You might have thought you were doing your best, but to achieve that extra edge the lip had to have crumpled at home.

For those prepared to invest in their marriage, whatever the motive, the eighties remedy was a 'behaviour change programme'. A regular daily 'intimate time' would be prescribed, its premeditated efficacy making it about as appetising as a bowl of All Bran. Eating habits were also part of the regime because the wrong food could be a source of serious relationship stress. There were the dreaded workshops, communal stretching, shaking, shouting, laughing and yawning; meditation, bio-energetics, psychodrama, guided fantasy and various games such as huggybear, trust fall and steamroller. If anyone got fed up they had to shout 'life is wonderful', again and again, until they believed it, or it didn't make any sense. Relationship refurbishment was one of the terms used for it, and even if the wacky methods achieved no more than various degrees of embarrassment, making the effort was probably what counted.

None of it was made any easier by the uncertainty of who should be doing what in marriage in the 1980s. 'Intellectually we now give assent to the sharing of roles in a marriage, but emotionally it remains true that for most people the expectation is that the working wife will cook the dinner and do the washing at the weekends,' wrote the Bishop of St Andrews, Michael Hare Duke, at the beginning of the eighties in *Crucible*, the journal of the General Synod Board for Social Responsibility. 'Society has not yet made up its mind what the differences really are. Is it biology or culture which marks out a wife for a particular pattern of life? The very fact that we are in a transitional phase puts its own pressure on marriages because couples today lack the assurance which comes from conformity to a universally-held pattern. To be able to question so many assumptions about marriage seems on the one hand liberating, and yet in another way it leaves people with the task of making decisions for themselves which may, at least in the short term, seem more emotionally exhausting than being a conformist.'

While there were still plenty of conformist marriages about – 'conformist' equating with husband-dominated – the Bishop was talking about the scenario created by the emergence of 'new' women. Unfortunately, 'new' men had yet to be invented on a socially acceptable scale, and here lay the impasse, creating not so much a problem for women but a crisis for men. Male status, for centuries linked to power, finance and breadwinning, was seriously under threat; women were able to duplicate the traditional male role, but it didn't work the other way.

Male reaction against this pending powerlessness showed itself in all sorts of ways, in violence and rape, in alcoholism, depression, in incest, even in graffiti. It could also be seen within the Establishment, in the Church's tardy response to women wanting to enter the priesthood. As I have mentioned earlier, in countries like the United States, where women have long been fully ordained, the job has lost status. Turning this syndrome on its head, the only answer for the hapless husband of 'new' woman was to upgrade housework and child-rearing.

Former England cricket captain turned psychoanalyst Mike Brearley cited names as the last bastion for men: 'My hypothesis is that we men claim this right to bestow our names on women and children, and women (largely) go along with it, as a compensation for the fact that we are unable to give birth ourselves.' He added, candidly, 'I remember that over the weekend during which we discovered that my wife was pregnant I found myself drawn to wear the sarong that had for years lain unused in my drawer. The sarong is a long wraparound skirt worn by men in Indonesia. My inclination to wear it just then was, I am sure, my way of identifying with my wife's womanhood and also my envy of her for it.'

If the solution to the male crisis lay in giving new status to what had traditionally been women's work, men had another think coming if they assumed it was going to be a pushover stepping into the nursery and the kitchen. Redundancy had become the great fear on all fronts, and many women were loath to give up any of their domestic territory. For those who did, marriage in the 1980s was an unstructured affair with neither party quite sure what to do next or how much was expected of them. (I'm inclined to think that the crux came when the lavatory needed cleaning, but I would say that, wouldn't I?)

As the eighties progressed into the boom years of the economy, the male crisis sort of went away for a while. Husbands were assumed to be increasingly involved with the family largely because they were more evident at the birth of their children; but research carried out in the mid-eighties showed still how little they were doing in the way of housework. After a hard day's work, even not so hard a day, they weren't expected to have any energy left for cooking, cleaning or child care; they were fit only to sit back and recharge their batteries because this was the way men were programmed, not least by the generations of women in their families. Still tainted by this old programming, their wives, home from an equally taxing day at work, would get on with whatever needed to be done, all the while muttering that it was more trouble than it was worth getting him to help. Besides, the working wife and mother of the eighties was still wrestling with guilt assuaged only by this juggling act with jobs. The old programming put the responsibility for home comforts entirely with her; I know, because I was there.

By 1984 working wives had become the rule rather than the exception, finally quashing the long-held belief that 'marriage gives a woman the best chance to leave her mark in the world'. If anything, marriage now hampered her chances, she was so busy trying to keep everyone happy, at work and at home. Sole breadwinning wives tended to find themselves in a particularly delicate balancing act, bringing in all the income, but having to be self-effacing about it, not only to soothe the vulnerable male ego, but to cope with prejudice from other members of the family and society in general. A 1984 survey among couples where the wife worked and the husband stayed at home revealed the way excuses had to be found for so unconventional an arrangement. Most of the husbands said they were at home for a purpose, to study or to undertake some special, but unpaid project: 'I'm not really dependent on her because my savings pay for my studies', 'she isn't strictly speaking the breadwinner because she is bringing in only just over half the money, my grant is almost as much', 'I don't think of myself as looking after children because I'm always doing something else as well'.

If the husband was disabled it was easier; and if the wife had been married before and experienced unhappiness in a traditional marriage this seemed a good reason for being unconventional the second time around. But in one extreme case, family and social pressures had made life so difficult that the couple had to leave town.

Money was one of the trickiest areas, with the wives feeling ambivalent about having, or exercising, their implicit power, and the husbands not wanting to talk about it at all. Yet on the positive side, there were the wives who could really enjoy their work, free of guilt about the care of their children because their husbands, rather than outsiders, were looking after them. And there were the husbands, brave prototype 'new' men, who discovered a lateral development in their self-confidence by successfully taking on a caring role. However, the most essential item of domestic equipment was a tumble-drier, because the hardest part of all for the househusband was pegging out the washing, or rather, being seen with the peg-bag.

Increasingly through the eighties, marriages consisted of joint breadwinners and everything appeared set fair for a new era of partnership and equality wherein the old stereotype roles for husband and wife were no longer relevant or practical and before long would seem as quaint as any other outmoded tradition; but it didn't quite happen that way, at least, not for everyone. Post-feminism came along, and so did going bust after the boom; and as the state of the economy, more than anything else, influences social change, there were some women who retired hurt. They retreated to the safety of domesticity and waited to see what might happen next – from proactive back to reactive in less than a decade. This is not meant to diminish the role of the housewife or househusband, but for women who had tasted the new role-merged marriage, going home was like a kind of disenfranchisement.

Some had set out with that idea mentioned earlier about marriage giving a woman her best chance etc., but then they'd become radicalised. Slipping back, they found frustration and resentment rather than the elusive home-spun contentment that was the myth of generations past.

Laura has made these transitions, from housewife and mother, to budding tycoon, and back again. A plump, pretty woman in her forties, she is married to an MP, John, who she met in the early seventies. The family lives in the Home Counties, within easy commuting distance of Westminster – which sounds like estate agency blurb; but Laura's husband was neither estate agent nor car salesman, he's old Establishment, good and proper. The point about the geography is that he is able to come home each night, yet Laura is lucky if she gets more than five minutes a day of his attention. 'Take today,' she says. 'We woke up at six, and that's when I get the only time to talk to him. He takes the children to school, otherwise he doesn't see them at all, and I don't see him again until the small hours, 1.30 a.m. at the earliest. Fridays and Saturdays he's in the constituency, which leaves Sunday as the only day off, but only half a day, because after lunch he's dictating letters. The only way I can really get his attention is if I drive with him to the constituency. I do miss him terribly.'

For the past decade Laura has sat at home with her children and waited for her husband to lose his parliamentary seat, the waiting punctuated by the occasional trip abroad and moments in Westminster when she has brushed sleeves with the great and the powerful. She is a woman who has succeeded and failed in a career of her own, and now hovers in the shadows of her own self-doubt, subsumed within a supporting role that seems at odds with her self-assured manner.

Laura grew up as a child of the diplomatic service in a household where everyone knew their place, master and servant, and what was expected of them. Her husband, John, had a similar upbringing, and they met while he was still studying law, and she was filling in the time between leaving school and getting married. 'I was working as a secretary and I wasn't any good at it, but I was mixing with people of the same background and I think you have an idea of the milieu you want to be in; but in a sense, background didn't mean anything, it was knowing how to handle people, anyone.'

Handling John was a piece of cake. He fell in love with Laura long before she decided to fall in love with him; in fact she didn't allow herself to be in love with him until some time after the marriage. It was as calculated as that, and if she wasn't marrying for money, it was certainly for the best chance.

Deciding to get married was done in a roundabout sort of a way: 'We were walking in a ploughed field and he asked me how many children I would like when I was married. At some point in the conversation I said that the man I introduced to my father would be the man I married, and he asked me when I would be introducing him. I thought he had probably proposed, and I thought about it for a while. It all depended on what he gave me as a present that Christmas. This was very important to me; if it had been jewellery I would have felt "purchased", but it was an orchid and that was perfect.

'Our families seemed to think there might be a wedding and I'd heard that his mother wanted to know, so I 'phoned John and told him that the answer to his mother's question was "yes". I wasn't in love with John. I had fallen in love before and been hurt, which was why I wasn't going to fall in love until after the marriage – it was a year or so after. I wanted my head to rule my heart.

'I liked John, and I was determined that I would make him happy and that I would be happy with him. I knew he was head over heels in love with me.' Laura somehow manages to get away with saying things like this. With her experience of head ruling heart I asked her what she thought about arranged marriages. 'They are no good because one partner is nearly always too young, but "introduced" marriages, yes, they work.'

John and Laura had become engaged six months after being introduced, and married six months later. 'It was 1973 and we had the whole thing – in the Abbey, it was a very good wedding, although John's parents were ghastly beforehand; they wanted to know everything to the last detail while the wedding was being arranged. They seemed too meddlesome and it took ages to get on with them, but they have come to appreciate me over the years. They used to take enormous pleasure in teasing me, and it could be upsetting.'

While Laura is a 'neon' person, the type who can enter a room and make you feel that the light has just been switched on, John is perhaps more likely to make you momentarily consider whether or not he has given you permission to switch on anything. He is a big, heavy man, who makes ordinary size furniture and houses seem inadequate for their purpose. Stern of countenance, commanding delivery, straight and true, he's one of the 'men in grey suits', and perhaps there's comfort in the thought that he is among those who have power over our lives if power there has to be. 'He's big and soft, a big teddy bear,' Laura says, but she is talking about the man only she sees. We are presented with an undemonstrative man who, nevertheless, takes charge and dominates the proceedings.

Laura knew when she married John that he wanted to get into parliament, but it was ten years before he won his seat. 'I kept him back. He could have been an MP a decade earlier, but I had just had a baby and he was new in his profession, and I think, no I *know* if he had gone into politics at that time then the marriage would not have lasted. The strain would have been enormous, but he didn't know until years later that I had prevented him being offered the earlier seat.' Spouses, apparently, can be approached in these matters before an offer is made. Laura is vague about how John reacted when, eventually, he found out what she had done.

Ten years on, he told her it was now or never for getting into Parliament, and she told him, and still does, that he isn't to cry on her shoulder if it all goes wrong. At the same time, she tells him he isn't to cry on anyone else's, either. 'I told him from the start that he could not play the field, otherwise I would leave him with the children to look after.' Laura's uncompromising attitude towards a hypothetical eventuality is possibly as a result of her mother's experience of marriage, which involved putting up with a great deal of infidelity; although her father's philandering was perhaps understandable given her mother's idea of the ideal husband: 'She told me he should be a homosexual, and then I would not have to put up with the messy side.' (Even more bizarre was her mother's advice never to use a man's bath towel if she wanted to avoid becoming pregnant.)

'Politicians are not sexy,' Laura says. 'They haven't got the energy. If there's a little trollop of a secretary who is readily available, well, it's the power game, isn't it, but they are not more sexy than other men. There are five divorces going on at the moment in the House of Commons, but it's the long hours. Stress is what does it. You hope, in your heart of hearts, that your husband won't get in at the next election, but there are some women who get so immersed in it all that they couldn't live if their husbands came out of politics.

'Sex life does suffer. You have your normal desires, but your husband can't be passionate when he comes home at 1.30 a.m. It demands a great deal of faithfulness. I have had passes made at me, but I haven't been tempted.' Has John had passes made at him? 'I don't think he would know if he had. He hasn't got time.' Yet Laura talks a lot about scenarios for unfaithfulness, perhaps thrilled by the possibility of temptation because John seems so very much not the type, and there's a whiff of complacency because of the old imbalance of love. He had a flat near Westminster when first he got into parliament, but soon decided he preferred coming home every night. 'Friends think he comes home and we make mad, passionate love, but he really is too tired.'

A couple of years ago Laura did consider separation, such was the loneliness, the frustration, but would her life have been any different without the five minutes a day with John? Separated, in a sense, they already were. 'We had some tremendous quarrels, but it would have broken my heart. I broke my leg instead, and that put things into perspective.' How is not quite clear, and Laura goes on to talk again about the five MPs' divorces happening as we speak, marriages splitting up, children attempting suicide because their parents are never there, MPs telling their spouses to go out and do their own thing just so they can go on doing theirs. '. . . the bottom line is the power and glory, and for the wife there is the pride, but I don't like this "goldfish bowl" situation, having to take criticism from complete strangers because I'm in a position I haven't even put myself in. Still, I suppose it's a way of life you have to accept, and now, if John was not around, it would be like cutting off a limb.' Besides, in the hallway of the family home there is a large, framed cartoon picturing the others in the goldfish bowl, all the powerful and glorious beavering away in the Palace of Westminster: 'He's a jolly nice chap, and so is he. He's a shit. Those two are homosexual, although that one's married. He made a pass at me.'

The pass happened abroad. MPs' wives occasionally accompany their husbands on trips overseas – Laura says it makes a break from the dullness of being at home – but on this particular occasion she would have preferred to stay dull. The pass-making MP had tried it on with most of the accompanying wives, and when it came to Laura's turn and she told him where to get off, his rejoinder was that if she wanted her husband's career to progress, this was not the way to help him up the ladder. 'I lost my temper and told him that I would be the one who decided whether my husband went up or whether he didn't.' I, for one, believe her, but there was a time when the decisions Laura was taking were about her own life, about the manufacturing plant she owned and ran, about striking deals in far-flung countries, concerning herself with business plans, market forces and profit margins. But, at home, her child was drawing pictures of abandoned-looking houses – abandoned except for the small and forlorn face peering from a window. Nannies came and went, John was busy with his own career. Laura's business foundered and her factory closed. It's a period she prefers to forget and a way of life she won't try again; and who's to say it was better than having time on one's hands for faithless fantasising about troublesome trollops?

* * *

'Change moves slowly,' wrote school teacher and marriage counsellor Ruth Barnett in 1983. 'The myth of the stronger male persists in spite of statistics showing the greater longevity of women and various forms of male vulnerability. Sadly, many girls still see themselves as destined to live in their husband's shadow and choose low-level careers that will fit in with what they see as their primary function to keep house and look after the children. It is not yet widely acceptable that a man should give up his job to move house when his wife is promoted in her career but the converse is expected of women. Nor is it yet a real choice for fathers to give up their jobs to stay at home and look after babies. Employers still expect mothers not fathers to take time off to look after sick children. In many subtle ways women's work is not respected and valued as highly as that of men. Few people as yet seem to be able to choose their career and lifestyle independently of gender-loaded social pressures.' She, too, commented on the way women appeared to resist encroachment by men into what they regarded as their own exclusive domestic domain, 'perhaps for fear of being shown up as less competent even there.' Oh! Oh! Why did we keep shooting ourselves in the foot? Barnett said religion still had a lot to answer for with its humiliating and debasing attitude towards women, its championing of male superiority; but here was an opportunity for a new and worthwhile mission, to encourage the flock to understand the differences between the sexes while accepting their equality.

Elsewhere, it was suggested that a lot could be learned from the way homosexual partnerships worked. Gay couples were way ahead in the field of dual-career unions, power sharing, and negotiating domestic tasks and other responsibilities. Equality of biology doubtless gives homosexual partnerships a head start, while for the rest of us, however equal in every other respect, when it comes to child-bearing we still tend to capitulate to the old order.

Jeff and Paula married in 1982 after living together for three years. Both had interesting jobs, were career-minded, and hadn't particularly thought about what would happen when they had children. A decade on, they are living in a nice old-fashioned house with two children and a dog, and while

Jeff's career has blossomed, Paula stays at home, feeling guilty about the part-time job that takes her away from her children a few hours a week.

Paula grew up in a small and isolated village, 'one pub and a telephone box'. She was a late child with three much older sisters. Her father was a driving instructor, her mother never worked. Paula's ambition was to be a nurse, but when she saw a clerical job advertised in the local paper she couldn't resist the chance to earn some money and independence. With little or no training, she nevertheless did well from the start and quickly gained promotion. She liked the work and after a few years it became clear that she was in line for a management job.

She had met Jeff when she was fifteen, and he only a few months older. His family had lived in the nearby town for generations, his father was a lorry driver for Sainsbury's, and his mother was a cook. 'I was a latchkey kid, but I don't think it really affected me. I had an elder brother.'

Jeff had already left home when he and Paula decided to live together. He was sharing a rented house with several friends, and there was nothing unusual in Paula joining them and she and Jeff openly cohabiting: this was the early 1980s when cohabitation was not only acceptable in society but, in practical terms, easier than it is today: there was more rented accommodation available, houses were cheaper, even allowing for inflation, and sharing a mortgage, due to a curiosity in tax regulations, cost less for couples who weren't married. But society's nonchalance didn't help Paula's father, who was devastated by her move and refused to accept the situation until a wedding date was fixed. Jeff's parents, a generation younger, had no problem with the arrangement and had been more concerned before Paula moved in to keep a check on their son: 'My parents were worried about the moral aspects, and maybe they did have cause – I would be concerned about my children.'

Buying their own house prompted the decision to marry: 'It was my decision,' Paula says. 'I thought I made that decision,' Jeff says. 'It was a full white wedding in church – I believe to a certain extent,' Paula continues. 'I love the tradition.' Jeff says he has no religious belief but didn't mind marrying in church; he and Paula were quite prepared to follow tradition to the hilt, even to the extent of exchanging vows according to the old order, with Paula promising to obey. It was the vicar who steered them away from such talk: 'He read us the old marriage vows and it was all about bestiality,' Jeff says, 'otherwise, I wouldn't have minded the "obey" bit – I would not have abided by it, would not have expected her to, anyway.'

There were 100 guests at the wedding, then three days' honeymoon in a tent pitched outside Ilfracombe. 'It was a tough year. I had just started my own business, and we had a hefty mortgage.'

The far-sighted vicar had also asked them about children, but the idea hadn't really caught on. Children were part of the tradition, but not yet. Before they'd had a chance to think about it Paula was pregnant. 'I was very upset. I knew I was in line for the job I wanted and I discussed the possibility of taking maternity leave then going back – it's what I would have liked to have done, but after the baby was born I felt too guilty at the thought of leaving her.'

'Money was tight, but Paula working full-time I would have thought a bad idea,' Jeff says.

'It wasn't so bad at home for the first eighteen months, but then I started to get bored.' Paula began a long series of part-time jobs, none with a future, all poorly paid. She says that one day she would like to resume her career, but not until the children are older; she and Jeff have never considered a child-minder, nanny, nursery or au pair.

While child-bearing and guilt have been dictating the course of Paula's life over the past few years, Jeff, who began his working life as an electrical engineer, now holds a powerful position in an international company. He spends 50 per cent of his time in France, and sees himself as a European. (Does Paula feel the same about her identity? 'Yes, since Jeff's had this job.') Jeff says that being away from home so much of the time doesn't present any problems, although he was very concerned about his absence having a detrimental effect on the children. 'I don't think they miss out,' Paula interjects, 'it's you, you're missing them growing up.

'I've got used to him being away, I've adapted my life

around it,' she says. Any sharing of domestic tasks has long since fallen victim to the way things are. Jeff used to help, but he laughs when I ask about it now. A more loaded question is whether he could have adapted his life to fit around Paula's career. At first he says 'yes', but in the same breath changes his mind. 'You'd have been extremely bored – he'd have been looking for other things to do all the time,' Paula says. 'I felt because I was the woman it was my place to stay at home and fit in with what he was doing. It sounds old-fashioned, but I do feel guilty if I'm not with the children.'

Paula has gone upstairs to put the children to bed. I ask Jeff who makes the decisions, and he says it's a matter of consensus: 'There are some areas where I say she can have what she likes, but others where I say I want my own way. I like to think that we talk things through.' Jeff gives every appearance of being a good, kind and honest husband, but about as far removed from 'new man' as any of his forebears – as far removed as Paula is from 'new woman'. Both say they feel they have a much better marriage than either set of parents, and Paula begins to quantify this by talking about dinners not always having to be on the table and kettles sometimes allowed to go off the boil. It is clear that they are happy with one another, that the tradition suits them. They think marriage as an institution has a good future; all their friends are married, all of them, without exception, cohabited first, but more to the point, not one of the wives has carried on working since having children.

Despite all the moves in the seventies and eighties towards equality of opportunity between men and women, the old inequalities between husband and wife seem largely to have been perpetuated, if not through external prejudice then by personal choice, though doubtless influenced by family, friends, employers and society in general. Too much and too little is expected of both wife and husband, and while everyone knows that equality of opportunity and responsibility is, ultimately, the way forward, the reality awaits economic pressures in the form of a dwindling workforce come the turn of the century.

Perhaps the only way for a married couple to achieve true

equality would be if none of the external influences was present, if neither had to be a breadwinner, neither be responsible for domestic tasks, society was silent, and the rest of the family simply didn't exist.

Walter and Dora Mace fell in love with he was 92 and she 91. Dora got out of her wheelchair to walk down the aisle, and like many modern weddings, the whole thing was captured forever on video. When I went to see Walter and Dora four days after the ceremony, they were watching the first showing, surrounded by the silent old ladies and gentlemen who share their home. It was this very silence that brought Walter and Dora together. They were the only talkers in the home, two lonely, lively-minded old people, who'd both enjoyed long and very happy marriages. 'All the others just sat and looked at one another all day. We were the only two that talked,' Walter tells me. 'What about? Oh, the weather, the First World War. I was wounded on the Somme when I was eighteen years old. The weather still affects the wound.'

In the bedroom they now share at the old people's home two beds have been pushed together, two armchairs put side-by-side. It's mid-July, but Walter tucks a blanket around Dora's knees. There's a bright blue budgie singing in a cage, given to Dora by her neighbours when she had her 90th birthday, before she came to live at the home, before she had Walter for company.

'Something drew us together,' Dora says. 'We just melted together. Wonderful, it was. That tea-time, I'll never forget it. He said "Will you marry me?" and I said "Don't be so daft." But he repeated it, and I said "Yes, I will marry you." '

'We waited five or six months. Why? Well, we were so happy, weren't we, mate?'

'I'm not "mate".'

'There we are, I fell in love with her. We were two lonely people.'

Walter was married for 62 years first time round. Much of his working life he was chauffeur to the Lord Mayor of London, but even in his spare time he liked to drive. 'That was a nice little car we had, wasn't it, mate?' he says to Dora, merging the marriages, because the only car they've been in together is the Rolls-Royce that brought them home from the church. They had a Rolls each to get them there, the result of a newspaper appeal that brought half a dozen offers and heartfelt public delight in the discovery that romance never dies.

'Something old, something new, something borrowed, something blue,' Dora recites as she watches herself standing beside Walter, with the video camera seemingly resting on the minister's shoulder as he talks vows. 'I had an "old" dress on, and I borrowed the hat and veil . . .' Dora was in the WAAF until she married the first time. Her husband was a commercial traveller. It was too late for children. Walter never had any either. 'My wife had a baby that died in the womb.'

Walter and Dora are very sure of their vows, very positive in the way that they make the exchange. They won't say 'till death us do part,' and the minister has to give up trying to make them. There are shiny new rings on autumnal fingers that rest intertwined on the arm of Dora's wheelchair. Dora keeps looking at Walter in a way that makes me think of my grandmother, who fell passionately in love with my grandfather after nearly 60 years of marriage. 'I'm besotted,' Dora says. 'He's a lovely, lovely man, who never puts a foot wrong, and I love him dearly.'

'And she's a lovely young lady, and we're going to have a wonderful life together.'

12 Pride and prejudice and nothing much changes

Whence an older woman marries a younger man, the world at large sees something odd and out-of-tune with the way things ought to be. Doubtless, it's all to do with reproduction, although my grandmother and all three of her sisters married younger men and all had children. A great friend of mine had a father twenty years younger than her mother and the tragedy was his death at the age of 50, while the mother, now in her nineties, has spent the past twenty years alone.

When it's the other way around, the young bride and the mature groom, the image is more romantic than sad, and if there is any grief it's likely to be restricted to the bride's mother. 'Tragic, tragic' another friend's mother growled through her clenched Belgian teeth during the exchange of vows between her thirtysomething daughter and new son-in-law, a man in his sixties. The sad irony was that my friend's father had died in his thirties, and her mother had been alone for close on 30 years.

Marriages where there is a big age difference have problems to do with conflicting attitudes caused by the generation gap – tastes in music, clothes, friends; but the greater pressure comes from without, especially when an older woman has married a boy. You might think that society's prejudice against this sort of union would have eased in these more liberated times, but nothing much changes when it comes to bucking the biological system, and my own, inadvertent prejudice must have shown itself the night before I met Steve and Val. 'You are not to say anything about short trousers,' my daughter had insisted, rather like *Fawlty Towers* and 'Don't mention the war'; but it was Steve and Val who mentioned them first because that's what nine-year-old cub scouts wear, and Steve was about that age when he met Val, or Akaela as he called her then.

Steve and Val sit together on one of the two matching sofas in the designer living-room of their terraced home. His hand rests on her knee, fingers reversing back into heavy tattoos and a friendship band woven from black and red silks. Val wears an identical band on her wrist. 'No, I wasn't Akaela when we first met. I was Kaa the Snake, Akaela's assistant.' She was also a married woman of 27 with a four-year-old son.

Val had grown up in north London, where her father was with the Post Office and her mother worked in a factory. When she left school she got a job as a telephonist, and married in 1971 a man five years her senior. 'He was quiet, but dominant, and I liked him when I married him, but soon found out I didn't.' The marriage was to last nearly fourteen years, most of them miserable, painful and sexless.

Steve, now a self-employed painter and decorator, grew up in the same area, the son of factory workers who fought all the way through their marriage and the divorce courts and drove their son from the house with their ceaseless quarrelling. 'The back-biting was awful. They had a ten-year drawn-out divorce and I spent ninety-nine per cent of my time out of the house from the age of eleven. I just wanted to get away from the arguments.'

Scouting was the best escape both Steve and Val could find in their separate, yet concurrent attempts to flee domestic strife, although Val's husband followed her into the movement and the initial friendship was between Steve and him. As a teenager, Steve was always around to help pitch tents and arrange activities for the cubs. He became a frequent Sunday-luncher with Val and her husband, and was friendly with their son.

'My first real memory of Val was at camp, singing campfire songs.' 'It was August 1985,' Val takes up the story. 'I took the Venture Unit to Switzerland with my husband. The marriage was going through a very sticky patch and I found a friend who I could talk to, Steve.' 'You wanted someone to talk to and I wanted someone to sing songs to,'

Steve says. 'He would sit and talk to me round the campfire after all the others had gone to bed, and then one day he took me to see a waterfall and I slipped. I know it sounds stupid, but when he grabbed me to stop me falling I just felt there was something between us.' To the outside world that something was an eighteen-year age gap, but to Val and Steve it was quickly a realisation that they could not live without one another.

'My husband knew there was something going on and he confronted me. When he found out who the other man was he gave me a plastic bag, told me to put my things in it and go. I went round to Steve's house and when his mother came home she said "you've got a girl here" and he said "not exactly". She was divorced by then. She asked if we were both sure about what we were doing and then she let us live with her for the next six months.'

It sounds incredibly straightforward, but of course it was not. For a start, Val was to lose her son. Twelve years old at the time, he was devastated by his mother's behaviour and she has never seen him since that day, the day of the plastic bag. 'I was like his big brother,' Steve says, but Val's son couldn't have been more horrified if this had been literally the case.

Her son's reaction was undoubtedly the hardest part of the affair, and perhaps made the way other people responded seem nothing in comparison, but there was plenty of hostility. In going against the natural order, Val and Steve were to experience society's censorship at its most primeval. 'You fucking old whore' former friends and neighbours would shout, winding down their car windows in the busy shopping streets of this north London suburb.

'But all my family accepted it,' says Steve, who was eighteen at the time. 'The only exception was my eldest sister, who thought Val was on a meal ticket.' Among the others who did not accept it were the majority of Val's friends and the local scouts, who drummed them out of the movement and had both stripped of their scouting warrants. Their crime was to have done something 'unnatural'.

'It was not the sort of thing to do. Val's former friends thought it was fine to have a toy-boy, but not to run off with him. The attitude was that she could have her fling, but keep it quiet, not tell anyone.'

'We didn't want to live a lie,' Val says. 'My mother didn't take it well. She said I was disgusting and all the old curses came out. Then she didn't speak to me for three years, but I kept on sending her cards at Christmas and for her birthday and that sort of thing. The third year, her Mother's Day card arrived late and she rang me to complain, and after that it was all OK.

'People gave us six weeks, six months, one friend said a year. It cuts down your social life, being sent to Coventry. We had nasty 'phone calls, people crossing the road when they saw us. We always felt people were looking at us, although that bothered me more than it did Steve.' Val worried a lot, that what had happened might be wrong for Steve, that he might feel forced into the relationship, that one day he might leave her. 'I loved him so much, it was a feeling I had never had in my life before.'

After their first six months together they had saved enough to buy a place of their own, even though Val had been ordered to pay maintenance to her husband for their son. The court had looked on her harshly and it had been suggested that she pay maintenance for her husband as well. She and Steve moved away from north London to a town chosen for the anonymity it could afford them and property prices they could afford to pay; but if they were escaping hostility, curiosity would always be their neighbour. 'The first home we bought was a one-bedroomed flat, and the neighbours thought it was incest. Lots of people think Steve is my son, but what do you say? You don't go around introducing yourself with "Hi, I'm so-and-so and I'm married to a toy-boy." At one time I felt upset about it, but now the wicked streak in me comes out and I love it. Some people, when they find out, say "good for you", and others, especially the girls at work, want to know what it's like; they mean sex, but they won't say it.'

Val then tells me that the first time she and Steve made love she cried because it was so good. She and her husband had not made love for nine years because Val had found inter-course painful, but with Steve there has never been a problem, not even after the discovery of cancer and removal of a breast

– a notorious sexual confidence-killer for any woman. The discovery of a lump came a month after Val's mother died. The old lady had spent the last months of her life living with Steve and Val in their terraced home and died there. 'You were grieving for your mother and over the operation,' Steve says, 'and we found we had to start all over again. Sexually, you thought I wouldn't find you attractive any more, and I had to convince you that I did.'

Val can't bear to look at herself since the operation, but the physical change has made no difference to Steve's desire. He married Val when she was 40, after they had been together three years. He was 22.

The wedding was a quiet affair, but the honeymoon was spent with 120 scouts. Despite their 'unnaturalness', the movement took them back and most nights of the week they are out 'scouting' or their house is full of young people. Their one sadness is not to have been able to have children of their own. What about fostering, I ask? 'We've thought about it,' Steve says, 'but we already do the biggest fostering of all with scouts. Kids just don't notice the age difference, and we wish that other people would be like them and accept us for what we are.'

In the place where they live now this seems to be the case, although there will always be those unforeseen moments when society blinks and takes a cold second glance. Banks and building societies assume mistakes have been made when forms have to be filled in. There is disbelief, then the sniff of a freak show. 'The psychologists don't give couples like us much of a chance,' Val says, 'but my stomach still churns and my heart leaps when he comes home, when I hear his key in the door. Yes, it's nice.'

I wondered how they coped with the differing tastes that divide generations, Radio 1 versus Radio 2, that sort of thing, but they say they have never found anything to disagree over, other than elements of scouting. Most of their friends are young, and the tendency is to see them as a young couple. When they moved into the house where they live now, the next-door neighbour offered advice as to how potatoes should be cooked, but Steve was eating Val's potatoes when he was still in short trousers.

* * *

Made in Heaven

In the great tradition of deviant romantic love, Steve and Val's story is not so different to the one told by Thomas Hardy 100 years ago in his book *Two on a Tower*, in which the older woman and the younger man have to flee society and hide away in a tower. I loved that story, and the 'unlikely alliance' is a winner for most novelists, even if in reality such liaisons have a slim chance of surviving in our day-to-day culture, where fingers are still kept sharp for the pointing.

Leaving aside the age gap between Steve and Val, her initial interest in scouting points to a very British way of alleviating marital neurosis – doing something useful for others and trying to develop community feeling. I wonder whether this is why worthies are so often bad-tempered, and for no apparent reason; after all, only the lucky few get a boy scout.

Another residual area of prejudice affecting the British marriage is class. More arresting than the older woman with the young man is the plum-in-the-mouth accent accompanied by dropped aitches. It only works if the partner without the aitches is exceptional in some way – rich, beautiful, famous; if not, then nobody can understand the relationship. 'Dropped aitches never in themselves destroyed a marriage,' according to one marriage expert, 'but the little niggles add up.' He also wondered whether it wouldn't have been easier to counsel class-conscious clients in Jane Austen's time, when people had a clearer idea of what they were letting themselves in for if they married across the class barriers.

The most publicised examples of class-crossed marriages coming up against problems are those between members of the Royal Family and commoners. They might speak the same language, but differing attitudes and expectations seem irreconcilable: witness the Duchess of York, branded 'unsuited to royal life' or 'HRH (failed)'. 'The strategy of royalty in this democratic age has been to widen the circle within which it was acceptable for its offspring to marry,' reported *The Sunday Times* in March 1992. 'The royal families of Europe used to marry each other, but as the supply of eligible partners from foreign royal families dried up in the modern world – leaving only toytown royals of a Ruritanian character in Europe's backwaters – the British monarchy was forced to turn to its own aristocracy to perpetuate its line. Those it chose to bring within the royal fold seemed pretty posh to plain folk; but to the royals they were commoners who had to be made royal. That necessary experiment, born of changed historical circumstances, has now clearly failed.'

The Royal Family has got it all wrong. If they've run out of other royalty to marry they should have a rummage round among the other superstars, people who have already experienced what it's like to be rich and famous. On this basis, the Duke of York would have done much better marrying Koo Stark.

Whatever the expectations of the Yorks it seems that one or both cheated on the bargain or didn't understand exactly what the deal was. In this they were far from being unique among present-day marriages. David Barkla of Relate told me that the confusion can begin with the wedding ceremony, especially as some brides still choose to include 'obey' in their vows. 'I have had correspondence from men who get terribly upset because they think they should be the boss – because St Paul apparently said so. These husbands think their wives have cheated on the bargain to honour and obey.' And some have, the wives who want it both ways: to do as they like, but still expecting their husbands to be the providers.

When I asked David Barkla what sort of problems people brought to Relate these days compared with decades past, he put communication, power and authority at the top of the list, adding that nothing had changed, they were the same old problems. Social skills came next, then adultery, unemployment, alcohol, in-laws and children. What has changed is that everyone these days thinks they experienced abuse in their own childhood.

'Cheating' wives, the women who expect the freedom of modern marriage without their share of the responsibility, are, perhaps, the biggest danger and the worst predators on the holy estate. The autocratic husbands are clearly and rightly focused for attack, but the assault is weakened by the existence of 'new *fallen* woman', the post-feminist wife who doesn't play fair by the egalitarian husband.

Television was blamed in the seventies, for propagating the idea that success consisted of the provision by the man of consumer goods for his family, and that failing in this respect indicated failure in a basic and essential part of his role. I remember an extreme example of this when I was working as a news reporter and spent a grisly hot summer's day stationed outside the terraced home of a man who had been working night and day to satisfy his wife's insatiable appetite for white and brown goods. The poor man was so exhausted he'd been unable to provide satisfaction in any other departments; his wife was having an affair and it was the unfortunate wife of the lover who happened to be in the house the day the man finally cracked. He stabbed her, more times than it is decent to remember, but I recall the heat of that day because she had run out into the street and the hideous residue of her death had coagulated and fried on the sun-baked tarmac of the road.

I attended the court case. The sentence was life imprisonment, although it might have been less, even non-custodial, if the victim had been the wife. Some husbands do get away with murder, both literally and with the other, slower kind that kills the spirit. Jane, mentioned in Chapter Ten, was just about finished off by the extraordinary arrangement her husband got her to agree to and managed to sustain for some years.

Lawrence is a quiet man, in dress and manner. His voice is the only immediate attraction, but it doesn't take long to be charmed by him. He seems, and to a large extent is, a thoroughly nice man, the typical understated English gentleman. He's clever too, but doesn't parade it. Jane describes him as 'a hard act to follow'. They first met in the street, one of those maybe misunderstood moments – he said he thought she was someone he knew, she told him to piss off – and they ended up having a cup of tea together.

'I thought, "this man is really old", but he was only eight years older than me. He had a smart car and wore a suit, and he lied about being separated. He came on very strong and I thought that I had completely captivated him. I remember thinking "this man represents an enormous amount of security". Within two days he was saying he knew I was going to change his life altogether.' She didn't. His life was literature, work, wife, children and mistress and remained so, even if the last three parts were to be played by a new cast.

'It didn't take long to discover his polygamous tendencies, but I really thought it would stop.'

Both had been married before, but Jane did not have any children from her first marriage. The first time she had married very young, before she discovered ambition and dissatisfaction; the marriage had drifted apart like a fondly remembered school friendship. There was a half-hearted affair going on between Jane and her boss, but this was sidelined into 'not really counting' because she didn't fancy him, just liked him too much to be unkind.

Lawrence, of course, found it very unkind, and this is perhaps a blind-spot area for Jane, who is genuinely perplexed that he was jealous when the sideline continued. Selective sexual sophistication can be rather naive.

Jane and Lawrence lived together before they married; it was a throwing things, bodice-ripping sort of relationship that developed to a Tom and Jerry level of predatory interaction: 'I couldn't get away from him – I wanted to – I would move out – he would come and fetch me.' Marriage, perhaps, was the answer, and a date was fixed; then Jane realised it clashed with a seminar she wanted to attend. 'Lawrence was very cross. A couple of months later I discovered that I was pregnant. He was convinced it was not his child, but we did get married – after the seminar.'

Lawrence, Jane says, changed after the wedding, although it may have been at the moment of securing her. 'Having wanted me so much, despite the silly affairs he had all the time, I think he might have met someone else at about that time who he felt he could be more happy with. We didn't marry very happily. I felt very insecure and I desperately wanted to make a happy life for the baby.

'After the baby we seemed to be in tune for a while. I suppose I was more gentle – one of the things he had complained about was that I wasn't – he wanted a lot of stroking, but it's hard to do this when you're feeling so insecure.

'The marriage never stood much of a chance. We had moments of blissful happiness; there was always drama, always something happening – I was never bored with the bloke, there was something there.' The Tom and Jerry routine began again after the arrival of another baby, culminating in Jane's leaving with the two children and going to live with another man. 'I really felt I had been buggered around, and

I'd found someone else to look after us. Lawrence was devastated – even though he had someone else. He persuaded me to come back, he was all I really wanted, him and for the marriage to be good.' Jane has admitted that the man she went off with fell the wrong side of the Nancy Mitford code of U and Non-U, although she knows this wouldn't have mattered if she'd loved him as she did Lawrence. Irritations cultivated in the seedbed of snobbery are the acid test of true blue British love.

Lawrence met Geraldine, Jane is not certain when. She didn't know for some time, only that there was someone who it seemed presented a greater threat than any of the others. 'I knew there was someone. There would be all sorts of ways of knowing he hadn't been on his own, but if I challenged him he would turn on me, always denying it. Maybe I knew it was the big one. When it did come out, he said that of course I knew and had known all along, as if it was somehow my fault. He said he was going to stop seeing her.

'I was really frightened that time. I knew it was hard for him to break with her. He was terrible to me, especially when we were with friends, which wasn't like him. Then I found estate agents' particulars in his pocket – no, sticking out of his pocket; it was just when I thought it was going to be all right. He said he had gone to tell her it was all over, but she had told him that she was pregnant. I flung him out.'

Now, this is the good bit. Lawrence telephoned Jane the next day and said that his secretary had come up with this wonderful idea: he should live with Geraldine during the week and with Jane at the weekends – forever. What is even better is that he managed it for nearly three years.

'I was wild. I had affairs, but it was all so debilitating. I was made to feel like a non-person, and I was accepting things that made me hate myself. He absolutely loved it – having two women, an insurance policy always there. I was so stupid, I always made sure the fire was lit when he was coming home. There was constant drama, she'd lost the first baby, then she was pregnant again and said she would have an abortion, then it was adoption. The only weapon I had was lighting the fire.'

As the third anniversary of this tortuous arrangement drew near, Lawrence took Jane to Brazil for a holiday. 'We had the most wonderful time and we were as happy as we had ever been, but the day we came home he rushed off to have lunch with Geraldine. That afternoon I told him he had to choose. I don't think I knew it wouldn't be me.'

Lawrence now lives seven days a week with Geraldine and their child; Jane lives with someone she met through Dateline. The computer made sure he was the faithful type, and familiar with the Mitford code.

How prejudice can destroy the chance of happiness. An aunt of mine turned down a marriage proposal because her lovesick suitor absent-mindedly licked the jam spoon when she took him home for tea. The man she married instead had impeccable manners but no penis. She died a virgin.

Perhaps a better chance of having a successful marriage is to make a cold-blooded choice involving pride, prejudice, the Mitford code and a medical; to marry without love, only liking. 'Marrying because they fall in love is a passport to disaster for hundreds of thousands of couples,' wrote an MGC tutor in an article about her own highly successful 30-year 'loveless' marriage. 'We did not marry because we fell in love, but for a variety of other far more pragmatic and unromantic reasons. Society, it seems disapproves of thoughtful, serious and sensible reasons for marrying, and clings to the concept of marrying for love. In view of the horrendous divorce figures, perhaps it is time we seriously questioned this concept.' I don't know why, but it seems somehow subversive to advocate such a change, especially if you are not only a marriage counsellor, but a tutor of counsellors as well. It's not often that sensible things are subversive, but the idea of sensible marriage strikes a chill in the heart, a great zonking toll of boredom in the breast; enough to make one want to break out and do something rash – which is what people who marry without passion are surely liable to do in due course. The tutor counsellor admits this is exactly what she has done: 'I seem to have saved the soaring, turbulent, feverish experience for men I could not marry since I was safely and happily married already. Perhaps I have had the best of both worlds?' Perhaps she has, the smug so-and-so, but what about those men she couldn't marry, how did they feel about it?

She says she has never been jealous or possessive of her husband, who she married because they shared the same interests and, that most damning piece of faint praise, appreciated each other's sense of humour. She appears to have viewed marriage more as a bolt-hole from the rest of her life rather than as a framework for the whole of life the way most people use it. '. . . as a secure and loving base from which to set out on the search for ourselves and to which we can return in order to recover from the inevitable storms and buffetings outside.

'Despite the excitement and the elation of falling in love, this has felt an uncomfortable and dangerous situation to me – something about being out of control, losing individuality, no longer being mistress of my own fate. I'm deeply distrustful of what falling in love does to me and surely I can't be the only one who feels this strongly enough to have rejected it as a basis for marriage?' She may have it right, but her way of love and marriage on separate planes depends heavily on everyone else involved being prepared to play ball. To a degree, it worked for Naomi Mitchison in Chapter One, and all that's changed is that it's no longer seen as quite so *avant garde* to talk about it.

Marginally worse perhaps than sensible marriage is marrying for money, although some might say that the latter is merely a version of the former. In January 1992, *The Sunday Times* headlined a story TROPHY WIVES, indicating another prejudice that doesn't change, although, judging by the pictures of the husbands, the young trophies earned every penny of their newly acquired wealth. Some were happy to tell the reporter their own age, but scuttled off when asked about the age gap. If it is something to be ashamed of, the 1984 Matrimonial and Family Proceedings Act made sure they wouldn't gain by it unless they stayed the course – to be kept in the manner to which one has become accustomed is no longer the rider to being dumped, and the article made it clear that the wives were more likely to be dumped than to do the dumping in this particular version of loveless marriage.

Perhaps the greatest underlying prejudice against marriage continues to be the assumption that it is a relationship destined for conflict. The following item, spotted in a school magazine, neatly sums it up: 'Former pupils will be interested to know that Stanley Groom and Lorna Andrews were married last week. This brings to an end a friendship which has continued since they first met fourteen years ago.'

13 Made in heaven and elsewhere

I F YOU ASKED ME to find a role model for the ideal modern marriage, Howard and Sally would be my first choice. They married in the late eighties after living together for two years. He's 34, she's 28, and they are as close as can be possible to 'new man' and 'new woman', yet neither seems aware of this, it's simply the way they are. It's as if all the pain and struggle of marriage in Britain over the past three decades has finally metamorphosed into this new type of relationship, unburdened by the old prejudices and role restrictions, yet retaining the best of the traditional ideas of what marriage is all about. Perhaps this is why, despite the huge difference in age, thinking and experience, Howard and Sally reminded me of Fred and Nellie in Chapter One. It could also have been an accident of seating, that Howard and Sally positioned themselves side by side in a pair of chairs not unlike those of Fred and Nellie, in the sitting-room, by the window, and that they seem so much a pair themselves, talking the way couples who appear more one than two do, taking up the slack between each other's words, hearing the thinking, knowing the drift. It's careful and respectful, but at the same time easy and unforced.

None of this is necessarily automatic to a good modern marriage, any more than it was to the sort of union anticipated by people of Fred and Nellie's generation; you're just lucky if you have it, although the trite explanation would be that you have to work at it.

In most respects, Howard and Sally are a very ordinary couple, and I don't think they'd want it any other way. They fit perfectly the specification for 'new' wives and husbands as defined by advertising agents Lowe–Howard–Spink in their much publicised 1991 report 'The Balance of Power', which studied the impact on family life of women working. The LHS 'spec.' says that new wives and husbands haven't completely reversed their roles – the men are not wimps, neither have the women become Amazons; nor have they merged into one and both become androgynous hybrids. The men are still masculine but have gained greater emotional openness, and the women are still feminine, they respond very positively to images of traditional femininity, but they have also learned how to assert themselves and express their needs more directly. There is greater mutual respect and happiness (I'm only quoting here, because I can't imagine how greater mutual respect and happiness could have been gauged). LHS reckoned in 1991 that 10 million households had become 'self-regulating', in other words, 20 million adults had successfully renegotiated their roles in 'new' wives' and husbands' terms of equal opportunity to develop careers and look after the home.

For Sally and Howard, as I've already intimated, it wasn't a matter of renegotiation, they started out 'new', although both come from pre-renegotiation families. Howard is the eldest of five children. His father is an architect, his mother a secretary, although she didn't work while the family was growing up: 'They were much more traditional at our age. My mother is a grafter, always on the go. When we were kids she'd fall asleep in front of the telly by 7.30, absolutely exhausted, but she would never ask for help, just moan about having to do all the work.'

Sally has one brother. Her mother is a teacher, her father an engineer. She remembers her parents as firmly entrenched in the old-fashioned roles of husband and wife, her mother cooking and cleaning, father breadwinning and gardening, and with no trespassing. More acutely she can remember the total lack of communication, the impression of two people sharing a living space and nothing else: 'The roles were too rigid, the common bond the house, the car, the daughter, the son,' Howard says, as if he'd been there too. 'There were arguments,' Sally says, 'but I never thought the marriage would end. The problem was that their attitudes changed about marriage – Mum had wanted to be a wife and mother, but later she wanted to share the responsibilities.' Both Sally's parents are now remarried, but the divorce was bitter, and it had a deep effect on Sally even though she had already left home. 'It made me think about marriage more than I had before. I knew I would want it to be for life – there would be no question of giving it a go with the idea that there was always divorce if it didn't work out.' Neither she nor Howard had given much thought to marriage when they were younger, how it might be different compared with their parents' way of being married.

Howard and Sally met when she was only seventeen. They were both in the Venture Scout Movement and Sally was still at school. Now she is a town planner and on a higher salary than Howard, who works in marine research and spends weeks away in cold places tagging seals.

Soon after they met, Howard bought a house, Sally went to college, and 'after a few years we sort of slipped into living together'. Neither set of parents objected, nor did anyone else – by the late 1980s the term 'living in sin' sounded about as archaic as the making of honest women. Sharing a home, married or not, elevated people to accepted coupledom – certainly as far as the scouts were concerned, because Howard and Sally were forthwith allowed to share a tent as well.

The only people who had difficulty coping with the new arrangement were Sally's grandparents. 'They didn't know how to introduce Howard to their friends, and they didn't come and visit us until we were married, but I don't think we invited them. They were a strong motivation for our marrying.'

'We'd lived together for two years and there'd been no major friction,' Howard says, in that understated way sensible men and women give explanation to matters of the heart. 'And we'd learned from my parents' divorce,' Sally adds. 'Howard won't let me sulk, the way my mother did with my father.'

The wedding, unlike those of the majority of their friends, was not in church. They were, and are, believers, but they weren't churchgoers when they married and both have a sharp nose for hypocrisy. The wedding guests were family and the day was low-key and off-white, with a healthy disregard for the minutiae of superstition, the old, new, borrowed and blue.

Yet, why did they marry? Why bother in this day and age? Making grandparents feel easy is surely insufficient reason? Howard says it's about being more committed, and for Sally it's the same, except she's never told Howard until this minute, as we sit here, how she thought about marriage at the time of her parents' divorce, how determined she was to get it right first time and to marry for life. Howard is touchingly pleased, and how strange but normal it is that we don't tell one another these things in the ordinary course of a lifetime.

Neither has she told him why she decided to take his name rather than keep her own. When they discussed it she said it was to avoid muddle and confusion, today she admits it was more to do with pride in being married. Sally says she believes in the tradition of marriage, and that the traditional ways are returning in society, but I think there's been some editing. Sally and Howard plan to have children, but there is no assumption that it will be Sally who gives up work. For a start, she's earning more, and the house they live in now is heavily mortgaged; it's approached via a steep drive, and you can feel the struggle. 'Besides, you wouldn't want to be stuck at home all day, would you?' Howard says. 'You never know what you are going to feel like until it happens,' Sally answers. 'I say I would carry on working, but I don't know. Most of our friends who have children, the wife works part-time, one or two don't work at all.'

Howard says he would be quite happy to stay at home with the children as long as he could be doing something constructive at the same time – this is a fairly large slip and dent in the 'new man' image, in the 'new woman' too, because Sally merely comments that 'you can't look after a small child and do something constructive'; and of course she's right, if you see it that way. What's different about Howard and Sally compared with their parents and grandparents, and Fred and Nellie, is that they are looking at options that will suit them as individuals rather than allowing themselves to be restricted by the old assumptions according to gender.

David Barkla of Relate, who has spent a lifetime delving into marital assumptions, proffers a less emancipated picture, saying that the housekeeping role, whether allotted to husband or wife, has yet to lose its stigma in society; and while it is not so amazing these days for husbands to keep house, they still don't get invited to coffee mornings.

Shifting husbands like Howard even further out of focus, not long ago, on the BBC radio programme *All in the Mind*, psychiatrist Professor Anthony Clare talked about 'new man' being little more than a myth. I don't know about that, even my own is 'newish', and would probably be more so if I let him. But how many women choose a partner on the basis of his 'newness', even though it would seem to be an essential element for successful modern marriage?

Dateline, Britain's (and the world's) largest computer marriage bureau, must surely offer the best chance of getting it right, yet of the 198 questions asked of new members, not one alludes to 'newness'. 'Interests at home' cover listening to music, reading, gardening, being with children (but not looking after them), cooking and entertaining (but not hoovering and washing-up). Well, they wouldn't, would they? After all, romance is what they are selling.

Those of us who know nothing about computer dating tend to have rather fixed ideas about the sort of people who do. 'Desperate', 'lonely', 'ugly', 'older women', 'shy', 'washed-out'. These are the words used on Dateline's own video, the one they send to people who enquire. They are words from the 'man in the street', interviewed at random in the early part of the film, before you get to the fond gazes of later footage, the couples who talk about how they could have wasted a lifetime looking for the right partner, but managed to short-circuit the system by getting a computer to do it for them.

Barry and Jean love to see people's mouths drop open in disbelief, lumps of potato fall from forks at dinner parties, when they tell how they met through Dateline. 'Does it really work?' the gobsmacked guests enquire. 'What a silly question,' Barry says.

'When people accuse me of exploiting loneliness I say, yes, I am, in the same way people who make bread exploit hunger – that usually shuts them up,' says John Patterson, Dateline's founder, who claims shepherds, lords, solicitors and airline pilots are among his clientele.

'I, personally, like to meet someone who is more intelligent than myself,' says a pretty, dark-haired woman on the video.

'I found it very difficult to get talking to women,' says a pleasant-looking man. 'You're programmed to get on with one another,' says Jean. 'He's the other half of me – I would probably have married someone else, but the agency does a lot of the ground work for you.' 'It's the genuine way to meet,' says someone else. 'The match is perfect. I'm so happy.' It all sounds a bit like Billy Graham. Everyone is kind and caring and has a tremendous SOH (sense of humour); nobody is mean and exciting.

John Patterson founded Dateline in 1966. He was 21, suitably qualified as a graduate in mechanical engineering, and had recently returned from a holiday in America where he'd seen the romantic possibilities of computer science. It all began with the Harvard University freshmen's ball. Shy and awkward, the new students had difficulty finding partners, but the university had a computer, one of those huge affairs with the space requirements of an elephant, but the memory of a mouse. Yet it was a start, a huge leap from the abacus and the adding machine, neither of which would have been capable of matching up students for a ball.

'It seemed like a good idea,' says Patterson, a laconic character who looks and sounds like the actor John Hurt. He lights a slim cigar, answers a telephone call, and exhibits a shrewd gaze that becomes mischievous and conspiratorial during an outrageous conversation about his five-year-old son. It's a 'wind-up', a way of being that is peculiar to the highly successful who have made it early in their careers. Patterson is probably the most successful matchmaker of all time: more than a million men and women have passed through his computer. He gets 150,000 enquiries a year and at any one time there are 40,000 active members, or heading that way. His office, the Dateline headquarters in Kensington, is unpretentious, rather like a high-street hairdressing salon. Most of the custom is mail-order, but some call in personally. It was a hot day when I visited, the man sitting next to me in the waiting area was hopefully looking for a woman with a washing-machine.

It took a while for the idea to be taken seriously in Britain. Patterson, despite his relaxed manner, is deeply committed to what he does, and it still rankles that most of the media wouldn't take his advertisements for the first few years. 'In the eyes of many editors, computer dating was like escort agencies, i.e. prostitution. *The Times* and *Private Eye* were the first to take ads. *The Times* because they have an intelligent way of seeing things, and *Private Eye* because they couldn't care less – and you can quote me.'

Dateline got going through leaflets distributed to all the universities and throughout the streets of London. 'In the sixties people treated it as a joke, a bit of fun, but deep down they were thinking "I just wonder if one of the people I am going to meet might turn out to be the right one?" Now it is much clearer, 96 per cent are looking for permanent relationships. Socio-economically they are ABC1, people who have succeeded in their jobs, but found themselves in a social vacuum. We know of thousands a year who have married, but a lot don't tell us. Most are aged between 25 and 40, but the range is 16 to 70. All we do is introduce them to people they would not have met in their normal social environment.'

It costs over £100 to join Dateline, and you have to fill in a questionnaire called 'You too can find love'. Pictured on the front cover are good-looking but homely couples – Leslie and Eve, Rachel and Mark, Terry and Marion. There are 198 questions covering smoking, politics, moods, whether you'd rather go to the cinema than for a walk, read a serious Sunday newspaper or a popular daily, prefer team activities to individual sports. You're matched up with people who score 500 points or more against your requirements; over 700 and it's as good as made in heaven.

Patterson says his favourite 'matches' are those where divorced couples, without either knowing, have joined and, quite naturally, been matched by the computer. It's happened quite often, and couples have got back together.

New members usually receive six introductions from the first computer run, and most go for a total of three runs. To prove the point, and possibly to check me out, Patterson keys in 'Chapman'. He seems surprised there isn't a Jennifer. I tell him I couldn't afford to change partners, I have too many children.

Apparently, we are all less promiscuous these days compared with the early years of Dateline. 'It has a certain amount to do with AIDS, but it's a moral thing, too, and something the government is actively trying to promote for a stable society.' Cheaper too, he points out: stable societies have lower crime rates, the burden on the taxpayer goes down, and the pressure on housing is eased. 'Generally, stable marital arrangements benefit society.' Yet Dateline has neither asked for nor received any sort of grant for its good work.

Jane, whose story began in Chapter Ten and who also appeared in Chapter Twelve, joined Dateline in the mid-1980s. Actually, it was the second time she'd been a member; back in 1971 she, like most of the young people who tried it in the early years, saw it as no more than a bit of a lark. 'I was sharing a house with two other people, one was a bloke who was a bit desperate, and he did Dateline. It was really quite something in those days, and if you joined, a friend could join too, for no fee. The other girl in the house and I did a composite personality, then when the dates started arriving we'd look out of the window and watch them parking. "You", "me", we'd say. Sometimes we didn't answer the door.

'We met some extremely interesting people – I went out with a brain surgeon. In the end we had a party and invited them all. One or two were cross because they didn't want other men to know, but it was OK in the end – we'd made a huge spaghetti bolognese, laced liberally with hash.'

One person not invited to the party was Jane's boyfriend at the time, Lawrence, who she married and divorced in Chapter Twelve. 'Wouldn't you just know it, his name was top of the list of dates from Dateline. I was furious.

'The second time I joined it seemed like common sense. I was separated, stuck at home with the children, not working, not meeting anybody, and it had been such fun the first time. But it was hard. I was 41, and the men this time were quite different, more serious. I only got two from the first computer run. I'm short, and all my life I've been plagued by small men, so I requested men 5 feet 10 inches to six feet tall. Dateline sent me a note suggesting I should widen the height range, and I got two RAF pilots over six feet and Roger, who is 6 feet 3 inches.

'There were others too, and I used the babysitter excuse to

get away from the non-starters. Some were very attractive, some not at all. None of them expected sex on the first date, not like they had a decade earlier.

'I liked Roger straight away. He wasn't on the defensive about doing Dateline, but he was ten years younger than me, and he went on a bit too much about his wife who he was divorcing. I thought, if he goes on about her the next time we meet I won't see him again, but he didn't. I was sexually attracted to him, and he was funny, he made me laugh (viz. great SOH – the most popular TLA (three-letter acronym) in the personal advertisements that appear in Dateline's magazine). He came and stayed overnight and I knew then that I didn't want to see anyone else.' As I write this, Jane has been with Roger for seven years, and they plan to marry when Jane's children have left school. An anomaly of the Church school Jane's children attend is the awarding of free places to the offspring of lone parents, thus encouraging cohabitation rather than marriage. It's a moral dilemma that seems to run through the British Establishment.

Roger too, had met other potential partners through Dateline, but as Jane says, 'You can meet a hundred people and like them, but unless there's that little click: the magic, the chemistry . . . , Dateline just enables you to meet people in a respectable way.'

An arranged marriage, by computer or parent, might have worked better for Dr B., a senior member of the Muslim community in Britain, and a rash romantic who flouted the Islamic system in which he grew up, and married for love. On the desk there's an ornate wooden plaque bearing the word 'smile', understandable when you know that the doctor is a dentist, but the man himself has nothing much to smile about these days. He's lost the wife he loved for more than twenty years, and perhaps he wishes he'd remained in Egypt, the country of his birth and a place where wayward wives don't end up with half their husbands' property.

The doctor is an eminent man in his field as well as in his religion; I first met him when I was writing a book about the ordination of women and I wanted an Islamic view on the debate. What he told me made all the bickering going on in the Anglican Church seem rather silly; in Islam, men and women were equal, and the differentiation in their roles was purely practical rather than based on any sort of theological prejudice. The doctor argues a convincing case, even in the face of self-evident inequality.

When I went to see him about this book, hoping he would tell me about Muslim marriage in Britain, maybe introduce me to an anonymous couple who would be prepared to talk about their attitudes and experience, I didn't expect the great man to talk about his own marriage – surely this would be like asking the Relate gurus to discuss the intimate details of their own conjugality. At the time of this second meeting I didn't even know if the doctor had one wife, two, three or four.

'The idea that a Muslim has more than one wife is absurb and not typical. It's quite rare in Egypt, in fact it's not that common anywhere in the Muslim world, especially among the wealthy and educated. It began to decline centuries ago when the number of women compared with the number of men began to decrease, when there were no longer so many men being killed in wars. People in Britain think polygamy is about lust, but it was based on care, looking after women when there were not enough men to go round.'

The doctor's own, monogamous marriage took place in Egypt in the late sixties when he was 21: 'It was a love marriage, which wasn't as common as the traditional arranged marriage. Usually, when a man decides he wants to marry he asks his family and friends to introduce some eligible young ladies; this is because Muslim marriage is also between families, not just the couple concerned. When he has chosen somebody the man has to take some time to study her suitability, and she usually appoints her father to be her agent to study the man and to discuss the marriage contract. All this can take years, but it can happen in just a week.' For the doctor, his marriage, although triggered by love, was to take years to become a reality.

In normal circumstances his parents would have been involved in the early stages of negotiation, the meeting of families, the picking over of character and personality, the couple's potential for compatibility, but the doctor's mother and father were trapped in Israeli-occupied Gaza, and, besides, the doctor had fallen in love and already asked the girl to marry him. She was a year younger and studying at the same college, with three years to go before she qualified. Her father, safeguarding his daughter's good name, insisted on the marriage taking place as soon as possible but with the proviso that it would not be consummated until her studies were completed. 'Education is very important for women in Islam.'

Officially married, unofficially celibate, it was the full three years before the Doctor slept with his wife – there had never been any thought of sex before the marriage: 'There is a woman you sleep with and a woman you marry.' (Who marries the women who have already been slept with, I wonder?) 'Sleeping with your wife before marriage is not on the menu at all. She would not be respected by her husband, apart from anyone else.'

As soon as the marriage became real, the doctor and his wife moved to Britain, the doctor to begin a career that would take him to the top of his profession, while his wife, equally qualified, failed to make any further progress. Their marriage contract had given the doctor a dowry 'equal to a year's salary', and his wife a sum of '29 months' salary' in the event of divorce. Inflation was unknown at the time, but the doctor says the second sum was understood to be index-linked, not that either of them gave much thought to what they assumed to be hypothetical – after all, they were in love.

This, according to the doctor, is where they came unstuck. An arranged marriage, rather like a property 'search', would have guaranteed, prior to exchange of contracts, that there were none of the incompatibilities destined to dog his own union; but, before he gets to this bit, he tells me the ground rules: 'In Islam a wife is not expected to contribute to the finances – whatever she earns she keeps. It is shameful for a husband to live on his wife's earnings, shameful if he is not able to support her. All that a wife is expected to contribute is comfort for her husband, comfort, tranquillity and peace – she is not even expected to cook for him or to wash his dishes. Marriage is between two equals and this principle of equality is paramount. The Qur'an mocks the idea that man could be superior to woman.' Yet without even a 'but', the doctor continues: 'If there is a disagreement the husband has the final say and it is the duty of the woman to obey her husband. It is important psychologically, a woman who obeys her husband is making a love gesture, making him feel secure. It is a principle not meant to subdue a woman, but to safeguard marriage from the rocks of divorce.

'Now my wife was always disobedient. She was always rebellious. Everything I wanted, she didn't, even to the matter of food – I love fish and therefore she never cooked it. She felt that if she did what I wanted then she would be my servant. I didn't let it affect me – when I wanted fish I cooked it myself.'

The doctor went on cooking his own fish for twenty years. His wife, perhaps thwarted, became depressed. She didn't want to sleep with him any more and suggested he take a second wife. He laughed and suggested she open a marriage bureau for Muslims, to cheer herself up and to fulfil a need in this country: dislocated from their families, many Muslim men find it difficult to arrange a marriage. But the plan backfired on the doctor, and his wife soon found other fish not to fry. She arranged her own divorce and second marriage to a man fifteen years her junior. The doctor believes the man was 'planted' on his wife by his enemies, that it is all part of a long-running plot to undermine his influence in Islamic matters in Britain. His wife demanded the divorce. He resisted, fought her through the courts, lost the marriage but succeeded in winning custody of the three children by proving something unpleasant about his wife's new husband. He is bitter that it has cost him £40,000 in legal fees while his wife was granted legal aid. He is even more bitter about the British divorce law that could have robbed him of everything if he hadn't had the money to fight. In Egypt it would have been different.

In an open letter to God, published in the *New Statesman*'s 1991 Christmas supplement, he wrote: 'The ethos of your system is that a husband and a wife are two equal distinct individuals, with distinct personalities, separate economic, social, and political identities, with all that follows in matters of property and so forth. In the man-made system, they make, or pretend to make, the two identities fuse together – in favour of the man, of course. When I first came to this country, 21 years ago, I could not understand why there was a space on my tax return called wife's income. What was that to do with me? I wondered. I did not know then that a wife was considered a property of her husband. It was not so long ago that it was illegal here for a woman to carry tenpence in her purse. Her income was, and still is, treated as a property of her husband's. But when it comes to divorce, look what can happen. The laws here discriminate so wickedly against men. Divorce laws are, simply, unjust.

'In divorce, a man here usually loses almost everything, particularly the children. My heart bleeds for the oppressed male divorcees who cannot even get their voices heard because it is not currently fashionable to speak of men's rights, only of women's.

'Muhammad Ali, the greatest boxer-entertainer of all time, said once: "It cost me two dollars to get married and two million to get divorced." Why, I wondered, should his wife get half his fortune, when she never threw a punch for him? No divorced wife of his, thankfully, ever had to take a share of his Parkinsonism. Why should a divorced wife take half the assets of her husband when she did not make them? What is even worse is that the wife takes half the assets, but as for the liabilities, they are all his. Is that fair?

'Please God, help them to see that this is not good for anyone, especially women. Divorce has become a big industry in which many people have vested interests. Not many people think of, and provide for, the possibility of divorce when they get married. That is why divorce is often war. You say, "Live together in goodness or separate in goodness." I do not know many people who do.

'It will not be long before the discerning male will do whatever he can to escape the "marriage trap" out of fear of divorce. Would that then be good for women? Would that then be good for men?'

The doctor says he is about to launch a campaign for divorce reform in Britain and the introduction of marriage contracts which include the divorce settlement. The British way of marriage, he says, could be improved by being more like the Egyptian way. I began to argue with him about the fairness of our law compared with a system which sees ownership as an exclusively male preserve, a system which places the children of divorced couples with the mother until they reach the age of nine, then wrenches them from her and gives them to the father. 'But a divorced woman without children has a better chance of finding another husband,' he says. I disagree, but tell him that if there is any logic in this, then the same applies to a divorced man.

I am being naive, of course. I gaze over the 'smile' plaque to a coffee mug with 'Free Kuwait' printed behind the glaze. Kuwait is free, but real freedom in that country and most of its neighbours is still enjoyed only by the men. The doctor, a man I like and respect, and would even entrust with my teeth, inhabits a different country of thought despite his twenty years in Britain and his adopted British nationality. Is it surprising that his wife adopted British ways more wholeheartedly? 'My marriage would not have broken if I'd still been living in Egypt. There is too much permissiveness here. Divorce law in Britain is legitimate robbery. The man who took my wife could have kicked me out of my home and taken my children. In Islamic law your property is your property and you keep it.'

Elizabeth, a solicitor who has specialised in divorce and family law for nearly 40 years, sees the other side. Her clients are old ladies in their seventies who, after a lifetime of devotion to husband and family, find themselves dumped in favour of younger women. They don't have £40,000 to fight their corner, and because legal aid is rarely, if ever, granted to fight against a divorce petition, they have to settle for a lonely and impecunious existence for their remaining years.

The 1984 Matrimonial and Family Proceedings Act already discussed in Chapter Nine put a much greater burden on wives to adjust to the changed circumstances of their life following divorce, but, as Elizabeth says, in some cases this is just about impossible. If the wife is past retirement age and has never worked, how does she set about providing for herself?

Perhaps the doctor's ideas for further reform in this country would benefit Elizabeth's clients. Divorce settlements built into marriage contracts – with shares of pensions and inheritances as well as more obvious marital monies sorted out from the start – could be a comfort all round; but the more likely direction of future reform will take divorce further away from the process of law. Mediation is the key, encouraging disputing couples to reach their own agreement about children, property and finance rather than subjecting them to court-imposed settlements. Mediators have tended to be people already trained as social workers, but their role is developing at such a pace that the job is becoming a generic profession. Before long, the errant spouse might be chastised with 'I'm going to consult *our* mediator' instead of '*my* solicitor', although the lawyers are likely to retain a role for as long as marriage remains established in Britain.

David Barkla of Relate says this would be the really big change, if marriage were to be disestablished, no longer recognised in law. The idea of marriage would probably survive, but as a private arrangement with no official recognition. As far as the State would be concerned, we'd be registered only twice, at birth and death, with anything and everything in between entirely our own affair. As a lateral solution to scandalously high divorce-rates it would be an overnight winner.

Meanwhile, people like Elizabeth are working at finding better ways to divorce. They want civilised agreements that cause the least hurt all round and move yet further away from the dishonesty that is still forced on couples who want a quick parting, who have to make up stories about unreasonable behaviour in just the same way people used to sit in hotel bedrooms with total strangers in order to 'prove' non-existent adultery. The way forward, though seen by some as making divorce too easy and thus undermining marriage, will surely be 'no blame' divorce, no 'grounds', just the registering of parting with everything sorted out by the couple and rubber-stamped by the court. Two-year separation and mutual agreement to divorce is the most civilised option available to date, but it does not tie up all the loose ends of child custody and financial arrangements; and there are some couples who, for a variety of practical and emotional reasons, simply don't want to wait two years. But change in such matters moves more slowly than the divorce revolution of the past couple of decades would suggest, and funding for research and new ideas relies heavily on private benefaction topped up by car boot sales, wine-tastings and the like. Such is the British way, although I couldn't make the tasting Elizabeth invited me to – 6.30 p.m. is a bad time for wives with supper to cook.

Writing this book has made me realise that I'm more old-fashioned than I thought; actually, I didn't think I was old-fashioned at all before I began the research and found my own attitude creeping through the questions I asked. Perhaps we all have ideas about how marriage should be, while living a different pattern ourselves. I'm all for equality, while not fully allowing it myself, yet I'm not dissatisfied with my own marriage; I can't speak for my husband. Like most marriages, the problems we have are trivial, yet at times they can seem insurmountable. For instance, heating, or rather the lack of it as far as I'm concerned. We suffer constant arguments about having the fire on because I feel the cold and he doesn't, and the fact that women are less able to tolerate cold weather, due to lower body weight and greater skin surface, cuts no ice. The British climate, of course, doesn't help. And hearing, or not listening, as I see it. How many wives complain that their husbands don't listen to them? Again, the facts don't assuage the irritation, the knowledge that male hearing begins to decline at around 32, while women don't miss much until we're past 37. 'Give and take' is what the golden oldies and diamond wedding couples say when interviewed in the local press and asked what has kept them together. Perhaps more to the point, marriage has kept them alive – on average for five years longer than if they were alone. Most of us expect our own marriages to last the full stretch – 91 per cent – although our expectation of other people's is much lower. A high proportion of us, more than 70 per cent, according to a 1990s *Observer*/Harris poll, believe we have met the one and only Mr or Ms Right, but, disconcertingly, only 63 per cent believe this person to be their current partner.

Nobody can doubt that Phil and Jill are right for one another, and their marriage, if not made in heaven, started pretty close. In a sense it's never been more than a bit of paper, but scripted over the years into something near perfect, the ideal marriage, a model for the rest of us. At least, that's what I thought as I journeyed to Ambridge.

Jill, an orphan, her background so mysterious that even she doesn't know much about it, met Phil in 1956 at an agricultural show where she was demonstrating a household 'drudge', a new-fangled cleaning gadget of just conceivable interest to a recently widowed young farmer. But Phil was far more taken with the demonstrator than the demonstration: 'He kept on hanging around my stall – I suppose the pheromones were working.'

It was less than a year since the fire, since the night Phil's first wife, Grace, had died. Phil wasn't certain, but Grace was probably expecting their first child. 'My whole world fell apart. We hadn't even been married a year, but I was the type to either marry again immediately or not at all. I'd put everything into farming to overcome the grief, but meeting Jill, well, suddenly I was alive again, although there were still ghosts . . .'

'It was a whirlwind courtship then a very quiet wedding – after the death of Grace we couldn't make too much of it. We married in church, but I wasn't in white, just a neat two-piece, and there were no photos. I would have liked a big wedding, and I did feel, for years, that we were living with a ghost; I was very much aware of Grace, that I had moved into her house. We didn't talk about it, but Phil went into a 'blue study' every anniversary of her death. It seemed as if he just couldn't let go. The whole family was like it, and I did feel they were being a bit self-indulgent about her, that she warrantd a holy hush because she had come from a wealthy family.'

'It was difficult for Jill,' Phil murmurs.

'But we were desperately in love, and here was a family and a home, security and the feeling that my feet were at last on the ground. The family's attitude was "isn't it good for Phil", never whether it was good for me, but things were different in those days, the MCP thing was very strong and I was seen as Phil's little helpmate. I spent my entire time being an old-fashioned wife and mother, all my energy was devoted to making the family work. I was a cipher for many years, but I was determined to be better than the ghost.'

Phil says it was inevitable that he would compare his two wives, even though he knew, early on, that Jill was far more what he needed than Grace could ever have been; Grace, the glamorous, spoilt darling of a rich family.

Despite the ethereal presence of Grace, maybe because of it, the marriage seems to have worked well in most respects. Phil thinks so. 'We have never been a rowing couple, and there has never been a moment when we have wished to be married to anyone else,' he says. 'There have been one or two little wobbles, but never any real unfaithfulness – I never wanted to be pulled over the brink.' 'The bedroom department has always been rather splendid,' Jill says, 'although, of course, there was no sex before the marriage.' Shock waves would have run through the nation if there had been.

The twins, Kenton and Shula, arrived early on in the marriage, then David, and the youngest, Elizabeth, whose hole in the heart brought the first real trauma in Phil and Jill's life together. Shula became a worry later on when she displayed wayward tendencies, camping out with seventies hippies; but Elizabeth has caused the greatest upset in recent times – Phil and Jill were able to accept that their first grandchild was going to be illegitimate, but the subsequent abortion hurt them badly. They are people of strong religious faith, but more to the point, it seemed that Elizabeth had rejected their support.

The farm has been another recent cause for concern, the possibility of losing it after Phil's father, Dan, died and death duties hung over the family like a scriptwriter's axe.

As in many families, economic necessity has had a liberating effect on Jill; after all the years of acting the traditional farmer's wife – a role she was happy to accept, she has now come into her own with her new bed and breakfast business. Phil, true to MCP form, wasn't too sure about the project at first, and showed signs of resenting Jill's divided attention, even leaving the marital bed for several nights, decamping to David and his wife Ruth's nearby bungalow. Family, friends, neighbours and 8 million listeners could hardly believe what was happening – was nothing still sacred? Even the discovery, several years ago, that the Queen slept alone was less of a shock.

Phil came home, and he and Jill now brush the episode aside as if it were merely a brief practical solution to something that was nothing more than a practical problem. Yet, at the time, it was very worrying, because if Phil and Jill could do such a thing, what hope was there for the rest of us? 'A happy marriage is a fairly rare commodity,' says Phil. 'A lot of marriages just tick over, but what we have is rare and special. We never allow anyone to say a word against the other or say anything ourselves that is hurtful. The way to get it right is not to say more than is necessary – there are certain understood things, pauses that speak more than words.'

The pauses, as well as the words, have been written and rehearsed for Phil and Jill, giving them an advantage the rest of us don't have, but it's clever the way they have emerged as more than just a scripted married couple. There is that intangible something that does make their marriage good, regardless of events and old, ghostly influences. They seem like people who are stronger and more substantial than most, who can be nice to the rest of the world because they are so nice to one another. It's a marriage that is heard, but never seen, as cosy as bedsocks, more reliable than anything real; after all, how many married couples communicate to such an extent and only fail to do so when it is deliberate and designed not to hurt? Ah, I wish I lived in Ambridge.

14 Don't put your daughter on the altar

WHY DO PEOPLE marry in Britain in the 1990s? There's no need to, none of the old imperatives apply, and morality hardly seems to come into it. Even the clergy have been heard to say it's better to live together in sincerity and truth, albeit 'sin', than to get married for the sake of having 'a wedding', where photographers and milliners are more likely to enjoy lasting benefit than are the bride and groom.

The cost of many a 1990s wedding is three times what I paid for my first house in 1972. The figure bandied about on *Woman's Hour* during a wedding special broadcast at Easter 1992 was £9,000! It may seem mean, too money-minded, penny-pinching, spoil-sportish – call it what you like – but if you are the parent of *four* daughters, the thought of spending £36,000 'giving them away' is enough to make a dishonest woman of you.

'You don't want to do all that "sacrificial offering" bit, do you?' I wheedle, hoping to sound more like a feminist than a stingy parent. But of course they do. They want the white dress, the vintage car, the canapés and cake, me to dress up properly and not be embarrassing in the preferred Oxfam chic. And they want it in church, with a male vicar, bellringers and choir, the latter two costing extra.

Nine thousand pounds and going up by the daughter. There are 400,000 weddings a year in Britain, and the majority of couples choose church and all the trimmings. 'It starts with the engagement ring, how the stone is cut, will it flatter the finger?' say the women with 'Beryl' voices who make it their business to talk about such things on the radio. Ordering the car seems to come a close second. 'You get the girl 'phoning up all excited because she's just been proposed to: "Hello. Do you do weddings? Have you got a white Rolls-Royce, open top?" With the better class of weddings the bride's mother rings.' Ben Hogan has driven more than 100 brides to church over the last two or three years. Old cars are his hobby, a 1912 Renault, blue and brass, a '56 Daimler Hooper Empress 'like the Queen and Lady Docker had', and a 1934 black and beige Rolls six-light limo: ' "six-light" means it's got lots of windows so the bride can be seen'.

Ben, whose day job involves jetting around the world in the business of electronics, loves his cars; they came first, the weddings following on, like the cart before the horse. ' "Are you getting married in white?" I ask the girls who want a white Rolls. "Of course. There's nothing wrong with me!" "It won't work against a white car for the photos," I tell them, "and if it's open you'll turn up at the church looking like the Wreck of the Hesperus." The car should be in the classic colours of the time, and with, at least, a hood.' It costs about £200, including Ben in his livery – the one he wore for *Miss Marple* on the telly. Ben gets around.

'Being in uniform makes me seem official, and I end up having to organise everybody. In the end, everyone else has gone off and you are left there with the bride and her father. One time I had to go down the street knocking on neighbours' doors to try to borrow a size 17 collar shirt for the bride's father. Her brother had taken the wrong one.

'. . . then there were the bodybuilders, both of them, the groom and the bride. They chose the Daimler. She had the most magnificent dress – most tasteless, too, duck feathers all over it. Father had the grey Burton suit and the Hush Puppies, always a give-away, I find, Hush Puppies. Now these two, the bride and groom, they didn't look happy, didn't say a word when we set off for the reception, not until she suddenly says, "You know that bit where the priest says about having this man for your lawful wedded? Well, I hadn't made up my mind, you know." After that they had the most enormous row, until the groom said "Driver, stop the car, I want to get out." Well, we were in the middle of nowhere, so I suggested he waited until we got to the reception so that he could 'phone for a taxi.

'I've never had a not-turning-up at the church, although

the groom was terribly late one time. He was coming with the coach party and the driver missed the turn off the motorway. The bride said she'd take me on the honeymoon if the groom didn't show up. Pity about that.

'I've had my mishaps. We've limped and spitted to the church once or twice; but the worst time was when the bumper got caught in the chain link fencing put up round the garden of the bride's home specially for the wedding. I'd pulled out 32 posts and was towing the whole lot down the road before I realised. The bride's father was a university professor, not very good with his hands, but his main contribution had been erecting this fence. He wanted to put it all back before we carried on to the church.

'You get a buzz in the house when everything is all right, when it's going to be a happy wedding. The bride is usually quite nervous and tense. I ask if she'd like to stop off and do a bit of shopping at Tesco's on the way. It is a strain, this great occasion. The bride and her father are very subdued on the way there, but it's different on the way back, with the bride and groom; I had one couple who nearly made love in the back of the car.

'The photos take longer than the ceremony, at least three-quarters of an hour, and increasingly people want videos as well. The amount of money spent is colossal, and a year later they're getting divorced.

'Still, people really like the old cars – getting married is the one day in your life when you want to be different. They say you go in a limousine twice in your life. Do you know who owns the most Rolls-Royces in this country? The Co-op.

'As regards payment, the etiquette is that the mother of the bride chooses the vehicle and the groom pays. The upper classes take longer to settle the account. The big fear is breaking down, although it's never happened so far. The only thing to do would be to stop a passing car, obviously you'd choose a reasonably good-looking one. I heard of a police car stopping to pick up a stranded bride – so she did end up in a white car. By the way, green cars are unlucky.' And by the way, Ben's own daughter has told him she'd rather have the cash.

David Barkla of Relate says people prefer church for their weddings because there is the capacity for more of a show, although he has heard it said that the reception is what really matters these days. The Revd Patrick Bright, a rural dean in Hertfordshire who inhabits one of the most beautifully showy parishes in the county, views modern church weddings with less cynicism. His experience of today's would-be newlyweds is that they take it all much more seriously than a decade or two ago. 'I hope they mean what they say in church. The majority are not churchgoers, but I find most intend to try to keep their vows of lifetime commitment.

'I talk to them about fidelity and the Christian view of sex as sacramental, something spiritually set up as well as the physical relationship in bed; but the days of wife-swapping have gone, and there's been a reaction against that sixties permissiveness. The girls are still quite romantic, and it's surprising the number that want to obey, about a quarter. I ask them if it's going to be worth the paper it's written on. Hopefully, "obey" doesn't enter into it, and it was never meant to be abject submission, although I do detect a few blokes who think it should be, and there are a few girls who are far too submissive.'

More often these days, the couples Patrick marries are 'regularising existing situations', as he puts it. 'They shouldn't wear white, most of the brides, and I notice some wear cream. I would personally prefer it if they hadn't lived together beforehand, and there was a time when they might have been a bit "iffy" about the vicar knowing; but nowadays they are totally unashamed. I've only had one couple in the past year who were not already living together.'

And what of the failure rate? 'I know couples I am happy about and couples I am not. It's when the solicitor rings up for the marriage lines that I think, yes, that one's gone for a burton.' Wouldn't it be an idea to have a proper contract along with the ceremony, and some sort of divorce contingency? Absolutely not. It would be a logical contradiction, I am told, in Christian marriage, and Patrick will not marry divorced people. One suspects this is because he holds an unalterable belief that divorce is wrong, although he says it is because he is not prepared to judge people, to decide who is a guilty party and who innocent. I suppose to be even-handed he would have to assume each to be guilty as it would be less likely that both could be innocent, and as the Church will not marry guilty parties the whole question rapidly accelerates towards a Catch 22.

But I had another question, something much more fundamental, in an area where the Church could further its newly acquired image in the field of equal opportunities, and without compromising its principles. I've already bumped on about 'sacrificial offerings' in the shape of brides in white dresses being given away by one man to another. Why shouldn't the Church rewrite the marriage ceremony – they've done it before – and make it a set of vows between two equal adults? Patrick looks bemused. It's an idea, although he'd never thought about the 'sacrificial offering' aspect, but there again, he probably wouldn't, being a man. David Barkla says he sees the 'giving away' bit as 'rather Father Christmas-ish – in other words, the bride's father has lost control over her years ago'.

The big white dress element, the bit that somehow offends the feminist eye perhaps more than it should, is not as medieval as its symbolism. It was invented by the Victorian upper classes and not copied throughout society until after the Second World War. Echoing the dress is the cake, similar in shape and colour and consumability. You can't have your virgin and eat it. Cakes these days can cost as much as £700, and everyone has to have a bit, although tradition still saves the top tier for the first christening.

Tradition, of course, is what it is all about, but some might balk at what lies behind elements of the ritual. I didn't know, until a colleague genned up on what was expected of him, that the best man had to marry the bride if he fails to get the groom to church on time. 'I was terrified,' my colleague, Ian, said. 'I couldn't believe it anyway, that my friend was getting married. He was the first of my really good friends to go.'

Ian took his task seriously. 'There were several important jobs to do before the wedding: the last ceremonial fish-and-chip supper before marriage and nagging about waistlines, and the stag night – I wanted to give my friend a good send-off, although I didn't want to embarrass him terribly. He's a bit strait-laced and would have found a stripagram or anything like that very embarrassing. I was also worried that if I arranged anything in that line the wedding might be called off, so we went to an Italian restaurant and my friend wore a kamikaze headband throughout the meal.' The groom's father had hired a transit van for the obligatory pub-crawl that followed. Ian's friend, a normally sober civil servant, made himself extremely ill, and didn't see much of the videos hired for the rest of the night. 'It took him a day and half to recover, but it was better than tying him up naked and driving him to Liverpool. It was a meeting of old mates, one last good time together.

'I was really dreading the speech I'd have to make at the reception. I spent ages writing the thing and had little prompt cards, and it went all right. Afterwards, this old lady came up and said she'd have me on television in two weeks.

'The bride promised to obey, and I would insist that my wife obeyed me, although I haven't discussed it with my girlfriend – she would think a wedding was on the cards. She keeps asking me to marry her – it is a leap year, I suppose, but the problem is she wants children and I'm not sure. I would not insist that she gave up her job, but I won't marry her until I can afford to look after her.'

Ian is a Cambridge classicist, and says that having studied traditional things all his life he appreciates that the old ways are often the best. 'I would never want to marry in a registry office. Getting married is so special that you should do it properly, whether you're religious or not. I will do it the traditional way, but we will definitely live together first. It would be suicide not to, at least for a year, in the same house.'

This is the course Ian's friend took, and everyone thought it right and proper, perhaps even a codicil to tradition, although it was quite common during the eighteenth century and earlier, when the practice of betrothal was very similar to modern cohabitation.

Some would say that Ian has been jolly lucky to have a girlfriend who not only wants to live with him, but to marry him as well. A new phenomenon has developed in our society that seems to be leaving men on the shelf rather than the other way around. 'I have all the trappings of happiness in the 1990s. I drive a very nice car, I shop at Giorgio Armani in Knightsbridge and I eat in the best restaurants, but when I open my front door at night, there is nobody there waiting for me,' moaned a male lonely-heart in the columns of *The Sunday Times* in April 1992. 'More and more marriageable high-status women are dropping out as potential partners because they don't want to get married,' the report continued. Indeed, report after report, from Susan Faludi's *Backlash*, a 592-page tome subtitled *The undeclared war against women*, to *Woman's Hour* presenter Jenni Murray's tirade against the married state in the July 1992 issue of *Options* magazine, insists that the happiest people are single women and married men.

'We can find independence in or out of a relationship, if we eschew that ever-tightening band of gold,' says Jenni, and at its extreme, what she says really hits home when you talk to women whose husbands have battered them into dependence, crushing their will and sense of self-worth, through sheer brute force.

Beth is a big woman, but the husband who gave her a savage beating when she was nine months pregnant is a lot bigger, six feet four inches, sixteen stone, and with a misogyny so deep-rooted that he is incapable of loving even his own daughter. When I met Beth she was about to go to court to fight for custody of her three-year-old son; but the baby girl was not in question, her father didn't want her, only the boy.

That Beth's former husband should have thought he had a chance of gaining custody of either child is testimony to the peculiar attitude of such men to their own behaviour. Some shut it out, disbelieving that they could ever have inflicted such harm; others, like Beth's husband, think wife-beating is par for the marriage course.

Beth is among thousands of women in Britain today who have sought refuge with Women's Aid. She lives in a house with a deliberately anonymous facade, a secret address in a town hundreds of miles from her home. She shares it with 40 other women and their children, all of them victims of violence and a society which still allows men who murder their wives to go free, while imprisoning the women who kill vicious husbands. When Beth was pregnant with her daughter, and her husband had beaten her to the point of haemorrhage; when the police had been called and still he continued, smashing a plate over her head, ripping her clothes, the officers' response was 'they do wind you up, don't they?' Anyone who exhibited such lack of control in driving a car would lose their licence, perhaps the same should happen with the licence to marry.

But why do women marry such men, and why do they take so much before they leave? Beth's first husband had left her and their two sons when she met John. She'd married at eighteen, to the boyfriend she'd known since she was fourteen, and they had, quite simply, grown out of one another. 'We were like brother and sister, still are. We're the best of friends.' When she met John she was grateful to him for being interested in a woman with two small children. She didn't know that the marriage he'd just left had ended because of his violence. He took her and the boys out a lot, gave them a good time, was always nice to them. 'The first inkling I had about him was in the solicitor's office when we were buying a house with my money. He wanted everything in his name, but I still had a backbone then, and when we got home I ripped the papers up.'

After that the relationship quickly deteriorated, along with Beth's backbone. She found that the money she earned and the maintenance payments she was receiving for the boys all got poured down John's throat. She dug her heels in one night and refused to go to work if he was going to drink all her earnings: 'That's when I got my first smacking, a black eye. He was very sorry afterwards, said he'd never do anything like it again, and I believed him. You believe anything if you want to, and I thought I must be doing something wrong, that it had to be me. I really thought I needed him and that he was there to look after us, the boys and me.'

The house they bought together was away from Beth's old home and close to John's family, and it was then that the trouble really started, the regular 'smacking', as Beth calls it, subconsciously using a term more associated with the chastisement of naughty children. She lost all her confidence, says she 'went to being a cabbage', misery-eating from a size 12 to clothes that had to accommodate an extra three stone. She began to get terrible headaches as soon as John arrived home from work, and she was pregnant.

'He promised everything would be better if we married, but after the wedding it got really bad. He was constantly drunk.' Worse still, with the birth of his own son, John turned against

Beth's little boys from her first marriage; they were terrified of him, hiding under their beds to avoid his bruising fists and the plates of food he hurled at them. By this time their father had applied for custody and within weeks Beth had lost them, but willingly, knowing the increasing danger they faced, while she was pregnant again.

Beth's fourth baby was five days overdue when John planned a camping weekend in Blackpool. The first morning Beth woke to the aroma of campfire bacon, the breakfast John was cooking for himself, but not for her, or their little boy. When he had finished eating he began to load everything into the car, pulling the tent down around Beth in her nightie and her pregnancy and her child. It was a rough, inexplicably angry dismantling; frightening too, because Beth knew John like this. Keep quiet. Don't ask why. Don't say a word and it might not go too far, over the edge into punching and kicking. Be invisible, if you can with so much extra weight, the very vulnerability of its mass fuelling the rage.

Invisible maybe she was. John drove off and left her and the little boy, sitting in the field, wet and whimpering, bewildered. The rain had started, but still not the baby; she stayed inside, even after the punching and kicking that came that night back home. Hours they'd waited in that field, and when John had come back for them they'd been glad.

A few days later, when the baby came and the midwives said 'you've got your little girl', Beth felt no joy, only fear: what might John do to a girl child? When they went home there was nobody there, none of the wonderment that a new baby produces in a household. It was cold in the house, but there was no fire lit, no trace of a welcome or pleasure in the new life. 'Fat bastard' John said when he came in from the pub. The baby, mercifully, he ignored.

'After my daughter was born I knew I couldn't let her have this sort of life.' Yet Beth stayed another seven months, suffered a prolapse from further beatings, and watched John put his hand over the crying baby's face and threaten to kill the child if her mother couldn't shut her up.

'The last beating made me bleed internally and he kicked me so hard in the face I thought I was going to die, but it was the baby I was really frightened for, I thought he was going to damage her. After that beating I broke into the car when he wasn't there, the neighbours helped me to do it, and I piled it up and drove off with the two babies and £5.50 in my purse.' At the end of that day Beth had found refuge with Women's Aid, and spent the next three sitting in their 'crying chair'. Then she phoned John and begged him to forgive her and allow her to come home. 'I had to prove to myself one last time that he was a bastard.' It took only ten days. Beth and her two babies had been back at the refuge three months when I met her. She had got a divorce, found a job and was waiting to be rehoused. Her little boy, John's son, had stopped wetting the bed, stopped calling his mother 'fat bastard'. 'John wanted me fat and unattractive so nobody else would want me. He called me "the big fat bastard" when he was talking to other people. I wish I could tell you why I married him and why I still love him. He made me feel everything that happened was my fault. Some women want it, the violence, they provoke it, but I did everything I could to avoid it. John thought my first husband was a wimp because he didn't beat me.'

Beth says most of the people she knew when she lived with John had bad marriages, peppered with violence, attempted suicides and mental brutality. The seed of John's violence was sown in childhood as he watched his father beat his mother. It's an inheritance that is no respecter of class or intellect; among the women who have fled to Women's Aid are the wives of lawyers and social workers and policemen. They are women whose confidence has been beaten into the ground, who have believed the illogical propaganda pummelled into them that it is all their fault. As the police officer said to John, 'they do provoke you, don't they?', and, increasingly, the 'provoked' are middle class, the white-collar unemployed whose homes have been repossessed and whose self-regard sacrificed to the god of market forces. This was not the case with John, which makes him the more pitiable, and it is the men, not their wives, who are really without hope. Beth seems OK now, but the sheen of life has left her, and she's only 30. The one really hopeless thing she said about her marriage to John was that the sex life was fantastic. She enjoyed the meal even if the food poisoned her.

Twenty-five per cent of all violent crime in Britain is wife assault. 'The home is still the most dangerous place for many women to be,' says Gloria Steinem, but she, like other leading feminists from the seventies, seems to be advocating a softer approach for the nineties and beyond. The battle for equality may not be won – as Jenni Murray points out, 'When you marry you are still declared "man and wife", but somehow the sexes have to live together, and domestic terrorism, by either partner, takes too much energy from the rest of life from which the equality, ultimately, comes.'

Again, the question is why do we marry at all now that we don't need to in order to survive, to have children, to be cared for and protected? I suppose the answer lies partly in the rejection of our mortality and the need for a sense of permanence. Everything about marrying, the rings, the photos, the videos, the memorable occasion, is a grasping on to permanence, a stab at immortality through the joining of souls and the expectation of unbroken bloodlines for generations to come. It is argued that much the same can be achieved without marriage, but it is not official, is it, not carved in stone, cake-icing and videotape?

Just as I was about to finish this book I read the most terrible, chilling story about a 15-month-old boy who'd been missing for a year. He'd disappeared while his family were staying on a Greek island, and there was much fuss and concern over the way the case had been·handled. The family said the local police had not done all that they could, and the police, making all sorts of excuses and counter-accusations, finally commented: 'The mother did not need a baby because they were not a real family. They were not even married.' Perhaps this horrible story points to the most basic reason for marrying, that somehow it makes things count.

Another theory to explain why we marry and why we expect such a lot from the relationship these days is again to do with having reached a level beyond basic survival, but within a society that has too few interesting jobs available. As a result, we look to marriage to make up the difference. Yet perhaps it is too cynical to look at it this way round. In a recent Euro-wide survey, 88 per cent of the men and women questioned put family life at the top of their list of priorities, while only 49 per cent said work was what really counted.

Made in Heaven

In Britain, it won't be work that dictates our way of marriage in the 21st century, it will be child care. Demography has it that we shall all be working into our dotage once the relatively short-term effects of recession have passed. Child care provision in this country will have to be revved up to enable everyone to work, such will be the shortage of labour. This will lead to greater equality of opportunity for women and consequently greater equality within marriage. It's not such a puzzle that Britain currently has one of the highest divorce rates in Europe and also one of the lowest levels of child care provision.

This adds to my conclusion that the British way of marriage is changed by what women do, and bogged down by what men don't do. It may still be tradition that men 'pop the question', although this is often heavily prompted – viz. a scribbled reminder to herself a temp in our office left on her desk 'ask Paul to get engaged': thereafter, women take over and we do with marriage what we can. Women's place is still in the home, because when the phrase was formed home meant marriage, and it is as true today as ever that marriage is women's territory. It is our actions that have brought about the changes and will continue to do so, because the truth is men are not that interested. In a recent national survey carried out by the *Observer* less than 50 per cent of the men questioned rated family relationships as most enhancing to the quality of life; a far greater proportion put their faith in a booming economy.

So why do we bother? Surely it is not just because the day offers one of the few opportunities left to most of us to dress up like spring flower-beds, to delight in toast racks, to shed a pretty tear and sing a hymn. David Barkla of Relate has already said that the reception (i.e. an excuse for a party) appears to be why some of us marry. He sees cohabitation becoming 'stiffer' and marriage less so, the boundary getting ever more blurred in the eyes of society and the law. He predicts a decrease in both first and second marriages, but I predict an increase in third. I have friends marrying for the third time, although a high proportion of the women I know say they would not marry at all if they had their time over again, even if they might choose the same partner. I say the same myself – the only thing is, I'm not sure I believe it. As my husband says, some of us (actually, most of us) are just the marrying kind. We want that 'closed' relationship peculiar to marriage. We want the 'specialness' of it. The balance of power is quite something else.